.NET Performance Testing and Optimization

By Paul Glavich and Chris Farrell

First published by Simple Talk Publishing 2010

Technical Review by Alex Davies, Jeff McWherter, and Corneliu Tusnea
Cover Image by Paul Vlaar
Edited by Chris Massey
Typeset & Designed by Matthew Tye & Gower Associates

Table of Contents

About the authors

Paul Glavich

Paul has been an ASP.NET MVP for the last six years, and works as a solution architect for Datacom. Past roles have included technical architect for EDS Australia, and senior consultant for Readify. He has accumulated 20 years of industry experience ranging all the way from from PICK, C, C++, Delphi, and Visual Basic 3/4/5/6 to his current speciality in .NET with ASP.NET.

Paul has been developing in .NET technologies since .NET was first in Beta. He was technical architect for one of the world's first Internet Banking solutions using .NET technology.

He can be found on various .NET-related newsgroups, and has presented at the Sydney .NET user group (WWW.SDNUG.ORG) and TechEd Australia on numerous occasions. He is also a member of ASPInsiders (WWW.ASPINSIDERS.COM) with direct lines of communication to the ASP.NET team. He has co-authored two books on ASP.NET Ajax, has written technical articles which can be seen on community sites such as ASPAlliance.com (WWW.ASPALLIANCE.COM), and also has his own blog at HTTP://WEBLOGS.ASP.NET/PGLAVICH. On top of all this, he also runs the Sydney Architecture User group (HTTP://THESAUG.COM).

Paul's current interests in technology revolve around anything in ASP.NET, but he also has a strong interest in Windows Communication Foundation, on which he is a Microsoft Certified Technical Specialist. Naturally, performance testing and optimisation have both been a major focus throughout this entire period.

On a more personal note, he is married, with three children and two grandkids, and he holds a 5th Degree black belt in a form of martial arts known as Budo-Jitsu, a free-style eclectic method of close quarter combat.

Acknowledgements

We are living in an age where information has never been so accessible, nor the available content so huge in scope. Much of what we do and say is the result of influences from a wide variety of factors, be they technical, social, or emotional, and this book is no exception. One cannot go through life without the help and assistance of others, and it is such a small thing to acknowledge these factors, though they exert such a huge influence on a person's ability to succeed. To that end, it would have been impossible to write this book without the support and love of my family. My wife Michele shows never-ending tolerance to my late nights writing, researching, and technical tinkering (and sometimes gaming). My children Kristy, Marc, and Elizabeth are a constant blessing to me, and also put up with many late nights, and with me just being a geek. My two lovely grandchildren infuse me with some of their boundless energy, which I desperately need sometimes. My parents bought me my first computer, a Vic 20, so long ago, and watched as I spent hours in front of a seemingly uninteresting screen, and it all began from there. Without all this, I would not have even started down the technical path, and I am constantly amazed at how lucky I am.

Having been in the computing industry for approximately 20 years tends to bring about a real appreciation for where the industry is at today. Developing complex applications was exponentially harder even 5 to 10 years ago, let alone 20 years ago. Distributed, transactional, high-performing applications are easier than ever to develop. To make this process even easier, abstractions on complex technologies are developed, and services, frameworks, components, libraries, and runtimes are all mingled together to create the applications of today. Measuring the performance of these applications is still somewhat of a "black art." It is, without question, easier than ever, but if you have ever tried writing your own performance test tools, or using early versions of performance test tools, you will understand how tedious and time consuming it can be. Even with a wealth of information available to us, it is still quite difficult and complex to research the proper steps to setting up a performance rig, what metrics to analyze, how to record, execute, and analyze performance tests, and what to do when problems arise.

During my career I have performed a number of performance testing engagements. Without exception, this involved bringing together substantial amounts of information from various sources such as blogs, articles, books, product documentation, fellow colleagues, and anything else I could find. There was no single cohesive source for the information I needed, and that is how the idea to create this single gospel of performance testing and optimisation information was born. As a result, if you're doing .NET performance testing, you can save yourself countless hours of effort by using this book

A good friend of mine, Wallace B. McClure (also a book author), started me on the path to book writing, and I am indebted to him for providing me with that initial opportunity. It was from that experience that I was able to form a plan for this book and present it to Red Gate. Red Gate has been a great company in terms of technology, and produces an excellent set of both SQL and profiling tools. They wasted no time in moving the idea forward, for which I am deeply thankful. It would be remiss of me not to mention my editor, Chris Massey, who has been extremely helpful and responsive throughout the entire book's progress. In addition, my co-author, Chris Farrell, has made this book what it is by not only contributing quality content, but by taking on additional content above and beyond any initial agreements, and allowing this book to be delivered in a timely manner.

Finally, my thanks go out to you, the reader, for taking the time to read this book. I believe it will prove extremely valuable to you, and I look forward to using more high performing applications in the years to come.

Chris Farrell

Chris Farrell has over 18 years of development experience, and has spent the last seven as a .NET consultant and trainer. For the last three years, his focus has shifted to application performance assurance, and the use of tools to identify performance problems in complex .NET applications. Working with many of the world's largest corporations, he has helped development teams find and fix performance, stability and scalability problems with an emphasis on training developers to find problems independently in the future.

In 2009, after working at Compuware as a consultant for two years, Chris joined the independent consultancy CodeAssure UK (WWW.CODEASSURE.CO.UK) as their lead performance consultant.

When not analyzing underperforming websites, Chris loves to spend time with his wife and young son swimming, bike riding, and playing tennis. His dream is to encourage his son to play tennis to a standard good enough to reach a Wimbledon final, although a semi would also be fine.

Acknowledgements

I would like to thank Paul Glavich for his brilliant focus, and editor, Chris Massey, for his help and support. Thanks, also, to my wife and son, Gail and Daniel, the sources of my happiness and inspiration.

About the Technical Reviewers

Alex Davies

Alex Davies is a software engineer, and works on the .NET tools from Red Gate software. He got his degree in Computer Science from Cambridge University, and now blogs on Simple-Talk (www.simple-talk.com) on topics such as .NET performance, debugging, and design patterns.

Jeff McWherter

Jeff McWherter is the Co-Founder of Gravity Works Design and Development, a design/development firm based in East Lansing, Michigan. He is also an ASP.NET MVP, ASP Insider and author, as well as Program Director and a founding member of the Greater Lansing Users for .NET (www.glug.net).

His lifelong interest in programming began with a Home Computing Magazine in 1983, which included an article about writing a game called "Boa Alley" in BASIC. Jeff currently lives in a farming community near Lansing, MI, and when he is not in front of the computer, he enjoys rock- and ice-climbing, snowboarding, and road trips with his wife and two dogs.

Corneliu Tusnea

Corneliu I. Tusnea is an Australian consultant specializing in developing high-performance systems, and a Microsoft MVP in Development Security. He has more than 12 years' experience in designing and developing performance-critical trading systems for various trading exchanges around the world, as well as developing and optimizing high-traffic websites for some of the most popular online destinations in Australia. He keeps a blog at www.acorns.com.au and can be reached at corneliu@acorns.com.au with questions about performance or security in .NET.

Foreword

As we develop the applications to meet current and future needs, it is only natural to use current best practices and techniques for our designs and implementations. In the quest to improve how we develop, we can access a true wealth of information which is available on design patterns, object-oriented analysis, low-level code techniques and language features.

The technology community is full of articles, blog posts, books, and videos describing things such as generics, how to implement the observer pattern, LINQ to SQL techniques, CSS tricks, and a host of other topics. These points are often easily described in a single post or article, wherein a thorough dissemination of the technique can be presented, and readers and viewers can quickly gain a much better understanding of the technique or point in question.

Indeed, when broken down into individual and easily digestible components, almost anything complex becomes much easier to grasp. From the point of view of sophisticated developing, it is a constant battle to understand how all these components work together, and what the net effect of that synergy will be. From a functional perspective, we can simply "connect the technology dots" and ensure that an application performs its intended functions but, from a *performance* perspective, this is not so easy. Due to the high levels of abstraction offered by today's many frameworks, the amount of moving parts to consider is huge.

Yet that vast store of knowledge isn't all good news, because the knowledge of how to effectively test and optimize your fledgling application's performance is also distributed across an distressingly wide virtual area, making it difficult to pull all that expertise together on demand. With this book, I've strived to bring those expertise together for you, and to provide a distillation of the knowledge you'll need to make sure everything you develop using .NET runs blisteringly fast. I hope you find it useful.

– Paul

Chapter 1: Introduction – The What and the Why

Performance in web applications is clearly very important. The web potentially allows millions of users to access your application simultaneously. How is your application going to cope with such a load? How much hardware do you need to ensure it can handle the required number of users? What happens to your application when its peak capacity is exceeded? These are questions that really need to be answered.

As a business, I want to know that the applications supporting my commercial endeavors can cope with the size and usage patterns of my customer base. I also want to make accurate estimations around the amount of infrastructure required to support my current customer base, and what infrastructure is going to be required to support my *future* customers, based on a projected growth factor. All this can apply to both intranet and broader Internet applications.

As solution developers, we try to write software that is fast, responsive and scalable; but until we can measure and quantify these factors, we can really only make guesses based on the technology and techniques used, and the environment that the application must operate in.

Effective performance, load, and stress testing can be used to answer all these questions. It removes the vague assumptions around an application's performance, and provides a level of confidence about what the application can do in a given scenario. But what do we mean by performance testing, load testing, and stress testing? Often, these terms will be used interchangeably, but they actually refer to slightly different aspects of an overall process.

Performance testing

This involves testing the application at increasing levels of concurrent users, and measuring how the system reacts under the increasing load (not to be confused with load testing, which I'll come to in a moment). The concept of "concurrent usage levels" is one which gets thrown around a lot in testing and profiling, and it refers to the number of users that are accessing your web application at the same time.

Typically, a performance test may start out by simulating a low level of concurrent users, say ten, and then increase the number of concurrent users on the system at defined intervals, and measure the effects.

This type of testing is used to examine response times and system usage patterns such as CPU usage, memory usage, request execution time, and a host of other factors which will be discussed in detail later in this book. These attributes are used to characterize the system at various points, and to define patterns in the application's behavior when operating at various levels of concurrent users.

Performance testing is used, not only to determine patterns or characteristics of an application at various levels of concurrent users, but also to determine bottlenecks and operational capacity. This all contributes to the overall capability of an application.

Load testing

Load testing involves executing tests against the system at a consistently high load level or, typically, a high number of concurrent users. The number of concurrent users is naturally relative to each application, but is high enough to present a large load to the system being tested. While load testing is technically a separate, but related, aspect of performance, it can be combined with general performance testing. The primary reason to keep them separate is that you don't really know what a high load is for your application until you begin actually testing it and analyzing the metrics

This type of testing is often referred to as "volume testing," as the application is tested against high volumes of load for extended periods of time to determine its reliability, robustness, and availability characteristics. In other words, how does your application perform when it needs to handle nearly its maximum capacity for hours or even days at a time?

Stress testing

Stress testing is very similar to load testing, except that the focus is on continuous stress being applied to the system being tested. The goal is to examine the system as it is being overwhelmed with applied load. As you can imagine, this can cause the tested system to operate at levels beyond what it's capable of, and the net result is usually some form of failure, ranging from requests being rejected to complete system failure. The primary question behind stress testing is, "What is the recoverability of the application being tested?" which also contributes towards the overall availability of the application.

This may seem somewhat unrealistic, but you are trying to determine how the application functions when placed under extreme conditions. Does the application refuse requests and then recover gracefully after a short period, or does the application never recover at all?

This information can be used to confidently answer questions of the "What if..." variety. To take an obvious example, a project stakeholder may ask, "What happens if the system gets overloaded with requests? Will it stop functioning?" Stress testing allows you to answer these kinds of questions with confidence and a good degree of accuracy.

Profiling

Performance, load, and stress testing all represent a broad, general approach to determining the performance characteristics of your application. In order to improve application performance, you need to determine what specific aspects of the application need improving. You also need to be able to quantify the performance of isolated parts of the application, so that you can accurately determine when you have improved them.

This is what profiling is all about – getting a performance profile of your application or, more specifically, quantifying the performance characteristics of a "slice" of it.

Whereas the broad-based performance testing will identify slow pages or how the application copes with a high load, profiling will highlight, at a granular level, what methods take a long time to execute, what objects are utilizing excessive amounts of memory, and so on.

With that in mind, there are generally two types of profiling when it comes to .NET applications: performance-based and memory-based. Performance profiling measures how long a method or function may take to run, and memory profiling measures how much memory certain aspects of the application (or even individual objects) use.

Profiling is a crucial part of the overall performance testing process. Performance testing can provide the broad metrics and characteristics required to determine where changes need to be made, and profiling can pinpoint the exact areas that need those changes.

Cost benefits of performance and load testing

Performance testing is a comprehensive and expensive operation. It takes a lot of time to design tests, execute them, and then gather, manage, and analyze the data. Once you have the results and have drawn some conclusions, you often need to make some changes to improve the overall performance of your application. This typically involves changing and refactoring it to improve upon the areas that are performing badly.

In addition, the hardware and infrastructure costs can also be prohibitive, depending on how hard you would like to push your performance tests. If you want to simulate a large number of users, you are going to need an isolated network and enough machines to simulate that load.

This whole process can take a significant amount of time, and means that resources are diverted away from enhancing the functional aspects of the application. It's easy to see why many organizations shy away from performance testing, or only partially address the situation.

This is exactly why it is so important to do it properly. Making sure that your tests are effective and require minimal effort to execute is important to the success of your performance-testing regime. Automation of tests is crucial in this regard, and the collection of results should be as painless as possible. You want to be able to get the results of your tests easily, analyze them quickly, know exactly where to make changes, and demonstrate the benefits to the business.

There are really two major beneficiaries of performance testing. The first is the business. The business, which is typically sponsoring your application, not only has a vested interest in having it perform well; it also needs the metrics you provide through performance testing to ensure infrastructure, budgets, and projected growth requirements are all taken into account.

The second set of beneficiaries of performance testing are the application developers themselves. The metrics can be used to ensure that the development process is not itself generating performance issues. You can ensure that developers are not writing inefficient code, and that the architecture of the application is not an impediment to performance. Regular or periodic testing can ensure that development always stays on track from a performance perspective which, in turn, will cause less stress all round.

So far we have discussed the individual aspects of performance testing and what they mean. This does not mean that we should necessarily execute them in isolation. Given the related nature of performance, load and stress testing, you can run all these types of tests together, provided you carefully manage their execution and the subsequent collection of metric data.

The following chapters in this book will demonstrate how to do exactly that: to provide the most value, for as little effort as possible.

Example scenarios

What value does performance testing really offer to the business? I can most easily describe this by providing two comparative scenarios. One, where performance testing was not done, and one, where it was. Consider the following two scenes.

Scenario 1

Business Stakeholder
"We currently have a user base of approximately 15,000 users. We expect about 5,000 of these users on the system at any one time. Can the system handle that?"

Solution Architect
"Well, I cannot be exactly sure, but we have used best practices for the system architecture and coding techniques, so it should be able to handle a reasonable number of users."

Business Stakeholder
"What exactly does this mean? I have a budget for three web servers, maybe four, but I am unsure how many we need. How many users can a single web server sustain?"

Solution Architect
"Again, I cannot give you an accurate estimate, but I think three web servers should be enough. I think that one web server may be able to handle around 2,000 concurrent users, so three should be sufficient. If you have the budget for four servers, then that's probably a wise decision to go with, just in case."

Business Stakeholder
"What about our usage peaks, as well as our projected growth? During certain peak usage times, we could experience up to 10,000 concurrent users. We also expect to grow our customer base by approximately 1,000 users per year. At what point should we be purchasing extra infrastructure?"

Solution Architect
"Hmm, I'm not really sure right now. I'll need to perform some investigations and get back to you."

Scenario 2

Business Stakeholder
"We currently have a user base of approximately 15,000 users. We expect about 5,000 of these users on the system at any one time. Can the system handle that?"

Solution Architect
"We have measured the application on a single web server of a slightly lower specification than what is in production. On this machine, we could achieve approximately 2,000 concurrent users with a response time of less than five seconds. A system of three web servers could handle this required load with good response times."

Business Stakeholder

"What exactly does this mean? I have a budget for three web servers, maybe four, but I am unsure how many we need. How many users can a single web server sustain?"

Solution Architect

"As I mentioned, one web server, of lower specification than production, can handle approximately 2,000 concurrent users at any one time. A higher specification machine, such as the one in production could handle a little more, perhaps up to 2,100. Three web servers in a load-balanced scenario will easily cope with the desired load. I would recommend that the fourth web server be utilized to ensure adequate breathing space and allow for some growth."

Business Stakeholder

"What about our usage peaks, as well as our projected growth? During certain peak usage times, we could experience up to 10,000 concurrent users. We also expect to grow our customer base by approximately 1,000 users per year. At what point should we be purchasing extra infrastructure?"

Solution Architect

"Our current test metrics show that, while the system could sustain that load, response times may degrade to approximately 10–15 seconds per page. If this is acceptable by the business, then the four web servers you've mentioned will be sufficient. If you want to maintain the 'five seconds or less' response time, I would recommend having two extra web servers on hand to share the load at expected peak times or, if budget permits, to be online constantly. At your projected growth rate, the system will easily cope for approximately two years, so I would suggest you look at provisioning a new server every eighteen months. You would be wise to assess the customer growth every year to ensure that it has not massively exceeded expectation. If that occurs, the system may become unacceptably slow, and cause the load to exceed acceptable operational capacity."

In these two scenes, it is obvious that the second is the situation that a business stakeholder wants to be in – provided with the answers to all their questions, and armed with enough information to be able to make accurate estimations for budget and infrastructure. Ultimately, being able to properly service the current and future customer base is a very attractive end result for any business. Performance testing provides known quantities for characteristics of your application that, *without* performance testing, are unknown and, at best, rough guesswork.

Sometimes, what seems right can be wrong.

As solution architects, we are presented with numerous theories on best practices, a constantly changing technology landscape, and widely varying opinions from highly rated industry experts. This, on top of a host of other variables, makes definitive statements about the performance capability of our applications very difficult.

There are many good practices to utilize when it comes to flexible, easy-to-test solutions, including inversion of control (IoC), design patterns, and tiered architecture, not to mention using the latest and greatest technology. Yet, quite often, the most flexible and loosely coupled architecture comes at the expense of performance, and the allure of utilizing the latest technology can actually be a big performance risk.

Many development-related technologies are aimed at making developers' lives easier and more productive, meaning that a runtime or technology stack does a lot of the work for the developers. But how is this implemented in the runtime? It might be easy to implement, and have taken an incredibly short time to develop, but has it cost the application a lot in terms of performance?

Without testing, we can never really be sure. Technologies such as LINQ (.NET Language Integrated Query) enable fantastic productivity gains, but the danger is that they can make complex things too easy. Later in this book, we will have a look at some of these technologies that make developers' lives easier, but which can come at the cost of performance if not used with caution.

Conclusion

As the title implied, this chapter has just been an introduction to what performance testing really means, and what the different aspects of performance testing are. Performance testing, stress testing, load testing and profiling are all singular measures of an application's performance, which contribute to the overall understanding of its usability experience. Quite often, these measures are intangible until your application is deployed and being used by thousands of users, by which time it's really too late to be worrying about how it's going to cope.

The wonderful functionality or fantastic user interface features of your applications will all count for nothing if the application takes over 20 seconds to load a single page.

Clearly, it is extremely important to be able to quantify the performance aspects of your application, not just for the business (although this is one of the most crucial reasons) but also to validate the architectural and technological decisions made about the application itself.

Currently, there is a vast amount of vague, high-level information describing how someone might go about achieving the goals I've mentioned. In the chapters that follow, you will find detailed instructions on how you can achieve these goals, and effectively demonstrate the performance characteristics of your applications.

No longer will performance testing be a mystical "black art," dominated by the all-knowing few but, rather, a regular part of your application life cycle, integrated into the development and deployment plan, and producing tangible value.

Chapter 2: Understanding Performance Targets

Identifying performance targets

Naturally, in order to achieve a goal, you first need to understand what that goal *is*. So, before you can determine whether your application performs well, you need to understand what that means in terms of the metrics your application needs to produce.

Whether or not your application performs well is a relative target; not all applications are the same, so it stands to reason that the measure by which an application's performance is tracked changes, based on its requirements. This is where the business side of things comes in.

It is easy to say that a given business has a customer base of 5,000 concurrent users, but what does that really mean? It means you need to ask yourself questions like those below.

- If your application is being used by the entire customer base, what is the typical usage pattern?

- What percentage of users are performing searches?

- What percentage of the users are buying goods?

- What percentage of users are simply browsing around?

Having an accurate determination of user behavior is absolutely critical to determining whether your application can meet the performance needs of your customer base, and this is what the business needs to decide. This task is made a lot easier if there is existing behavior that can be used as an example. If there is no existing data on "typical" user behavior, then an educated guess obviously needs to be made. Also, given that technical staff usually have a biased view of the application usage, it is probably best if the business can provide some metrics around what users are doing on the site (by that, I mean what percentages of users are performing what actions on the site).

Structuring test breakdowns

An application can have many functional paths, and the amount that a functional path is exercised is based upon typical business scenarios and user behaviors. These assessments are made far more accurate if based on statistical evidence, such as evidence based on past activity or, perhaps, analytical statistics gathered from companies specifically engaged to measure usage patterns of the site. This kind of data will provide a perfect template from which to draw test breakdowns. If no such analytical evidence is available, then the business must provide as accurate an estimation as possible around usage patterns and functional paths to the site.

Quite often, a site map will be produced as part of the functional or technical specification of a web application, and this can be used as the basis from which to ascribe weighted percentages to customer use (although they can often contain too much detail). An example of a usage diagram might look something like Figure 2.1.

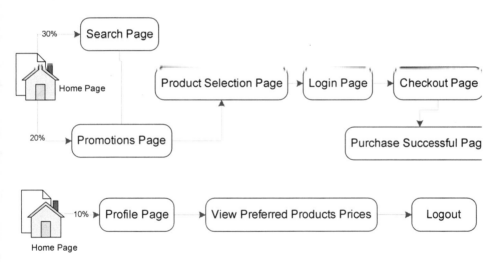

Figure 2.1: Example usage patterns.

While this example is somewhat simplistic, it is indicative of the type of diagram or "breakdown" required when structuring your performance tests. It is important to ensure that you exercise any aspects of the application which are deemed "heavy" in terms of performance (i.e. performing a lot of work) to gain metrics on just how much of an impact they are having. However, it is also important to note that performance tests are not like unit or integration tests, as it is not vitally important to cover every functional path and achieve high code coverage when running performance tests.

For example, consider the fact that different functional paths and usage scenarios quite often exercise similar code paths. In the same way, from a performance perspective, the same, or very similar, performance can also be achieved from different usage patterns. Obviously, it is necessary to model the different usage patterns that the business has identified, but trying to exercise every single aspect in fine detail will often end up causing a lot more work than is necessary, while achieving comparatively little extra value from a performance-measurement perspective. Generally speaking, performance testing is a broader approach than unit, integration, and functional testing.

Determining what load to target

By this point, we have a good understanding of what tests we need to run, and how these tests are going to be distributed across a performance run to accurately simulate the target application's performance requirements.

What we still need to determine is how many concurrent users the application needs to be able to handle at various times. This is not a simple static number, though, as a typical application needs to be able to deal with concurrent user load in a number of ways. Specifically, it needs to be able to:

- remain responsive during a normal day's use, with a "typical" amount of customer or client concurrent usage

- remain responsive during the high peak times, where almost the entire user base might be using the application concurrently

- be resilient enough to sustain extreme loads without complete failure, and return to normal operation when stress or load levels return to normal.

There are a few points here which are open to interpretation. For example, when the application needs to "remain responsive," exactly what does this mean? Unfortunately, this is something that can only be answered by the business in consultation with technical staff. Quite often, if you ask the business how responsive each page in the application should be, they respond with "sub-second" as a default answer for all pages. While this *might* be achievable, there may often be some aspects of the web application that require serious computation, and are thus very hard to deliver in sub-second time-frames.

It is also important to allow for some variance in these response figures at different load levels. The response times during normal daily use may differ quite significantly compared with times when the server is under extreme loads. In an ideal world, it would be preferable to have a consistent response time across all load levels, but this can be costly and sometimes extremely difficult to achieve. If it is achievable (as with the ideal sub-second response time), it might require significant additional computational power, and this cost will need to be quantified and justified to the business. Indeed, the business needs to be involved more or less throughout this entire stage of the profiling process, as you will need to be able to make several informed judgments before you can proceed with the actual testing.

> *Note*
>
> *It is important to specify a frame of reference regarding what are acceptable response times for your pages. This is also why it is important to involve technical staff in your consultations, so that the mechanics behind each page and function can be given due consideration when determining how they should perform.*

So, what are the metrics we actually need to identify in terms of concurrent users? There are no hard-and-fast rules here, as this is often dictated by the application and what is important to the business. Generally speaking, you will almost certainly be looking at:

- The number of typical concurrent users that represents average usage.

  - This might be expressed by number of page views per hour, or number of total users visiting the site per day (assuming an even number of page views per user). As long as a metric-over-time is provided by the business, the average typical concurrent user rate can be calculated from this.

- The number of concurrent users during peak times.

  - This figure represents the peak usage times of the application, and is an estimation of what the absolute peak number of concurrent users is. It is obviously important that the application can handle these peaks, as well as the normal day's usage.

- The project growth of the user-base over time.

  - This is important for the application to accommodate future growth and not need sudden provisioning of extra resources soon after implementation.

In addition to specifying the accepted response times during these various concurrent use cases, it is also worth considering differences in these times across the different pages on the site. In most applications, there is a small subset of pages which have exceptionally high traffic (such as login pages, home pages, etc.) and these pages should often be considered individually for testing purposes. In any case, different pages will frequently have different computational costs, so it may be acceptable to have longer response times on some pages.

This may not be the case for most of the pages so, where certain pages involve more resources or computational cost, special consideration must be given to achieving the desired response times. At the very least, the cost of achieving the response time target should be known, so the business can properly make a value decision.

There does not need to be a formal document listing these considerations, but some common location for reference and comparison purposes is a good idea. This might be a wiki page, a Word or Excel document, or some other listing of the agreed and expected targets and response times. A simple example of this is shown in Table 2.1.

Scenario	Concurrent users	Accepted response times	Pages applicable to	Projected growth in concurrent users	
				Next year	Next 2 years
Typical usage	1,000	< 5 seconds	reporting.aspx	1,500	2,500
Typical usage	1,000	1–3 seconds	all (except reporting.aspx)	1,500	2,500
Peak	2,500–3,000	< 8 seconds	reporting.aspx	1,500	2,500
Peak	2,500–3,000	3–5 seconds	all (except reporting.aspx)	3,500–4,000	4,000–5,000

Table 2.1: Example of response time expectations.

This table show a very simplistic example of what may be produced by discussions between the business and technical staff around expected response times and concurrent user load. The goal of this is to produce explicit guidelines of what is acceptable by the business at various points of the application's usage, within the context of the current user base. Without explicit guidelines in these areas, all the relevant test conclusions are subjective and open to interpretation. Bearing that in mind, it is once again up to the business, in conjunction with consultation from appropriate technical staff, to come up with realistic and achievable goals that meet business needs.

Now that we have clear expectations around application performance, you would think we have set our targets to achieve when doing performance testing, right? Not quite.

Contingency in your estimations

As part of a general rule, when the table of estimations has been produced around concurrency expectations and response times, it is important to emphasize that these are just estimations. They have plenty of potential to be incorrect. In fact they probably *are* incorrect but, because we have used whatever metric data we can, as well as knowledge of usage patterns and systems, they should be reasonably close to reality. As a result of all this, even using these estimations as our limits for performance testing is not going to be accurate, either. I generally recommend that you double the concurrent load targets for any given scenario.

Why should you double your estimates, you ask? This can be thought of as our contingency component. In many estimation processes, such as when you judge the time and effort taken to complete a project, some level of contingency is usually introduced to cater for errors or unknowns in the estimation process itself. If we double our performance targets, it is reasonable to assume that, if we can hit them, then even if our initial estimations were incorrect by a small margin, those errors are accounted for. We can then be confident, not only that the application does meet the required business goals, but also that it can handle more load than anticipated, and performs well within our set bounds.

The performance targets in Table 2.1 may seem excessive once doubled, but remember that part of the purpose of performance testing is to give the business a relatively accurate determination of hardware and infrastructure requirements for current and future use of the application. Using doubled performance targets clearly ensures that we cover current requirements, future requirements, and also any contingency that either the business or technical estimations may have failed to address. It provides a safeguard in the sometimes tenuous game of estimation.

As a bonus, this will obviously also guarantee responsiveness under normal circumstances; If the system maintains acceptable responsiveness under double the expected load, then it will be even more responsive under the originally estimated load.

The previously shown table, and its double, are by no means the only way to express estimated loads, current needs, projected growth, and performance targets. These are provided simply as examples, and you can use them as they are, or find different ways, that suit your individual needs, to express your targets. The main point here is that it is absolutely essential to ascertain these targets before any testing is performed. If you don't, then there will only be a vague understanding of what needs to be achieved in the performance testing process. As I said, performance testing is an expensive process, and the need to gain valuable results, as opposed to ambiguous results which do not allow proper conclusions, is of paramount importance.

One final thing to consider is the percentage of new users accessing the site, compared to returning users. This will have implications in terms of browser caching efficiency, and will affect how many requests are issued against the server. The more returning users visit the site, the more data will be cached by the clients' browsers, and so fewer requests are likely to be issued against the server for resources within a particular page.

This will also be dependent on the type of application; this metric is quite important for public-facing web applications, but intranet-based applications may place less significance on it. Often, to present a worst case scenario, the amount of new users will be assumed to be 100%.

This means that each test will consistently request all resources for a page, whereas all common web browsers do cache resources.

Estimate the mix of browsers for your web application

Finally, in a web application, it is also important to be able to estimate the percentage of different browsers that will be used to access the website. Different browsers from different vendors naturally all have different performance characteristics, and therefore impose different performance factors on the site.

If the website is public-facing, generally the percentage of different browsers can be gleaned by the respective market share of each browser. Quite often, the business will dictate which browsers should be used, and even which version will be supported.

If the website is intranet based, or has its visibility limited to within certain units of the organization, then the organization in question will often have set standards about what browsers are permitted as part of the standard operating environment.

The final outcome of all these estimations is that you will be able to record tests that exercise accurate, or at least realistic, usage patterns of the site. Once these are recorded, you can then weight the results by applying percentages according to how often each test is executed as part of the entire load test, which will be essential in establishing which result-sets are the most relevant for your purposes. In addition, you can also specify how much each browser is simulated within the overall load test. Within Visual Studio Team Test, you can end up with a load test, specifying a test and browser mix, looking something like Figure 2.2.

We will discuss in detail how to set up the test percentage and browser mix in a later chapter.

What data do we measure?

We have now identified our performance targets across a number of scenarios, and we have also identified the response times required across them by the business. Now we need to establish what metrics we use to compare against our targets.

A huge variety of metrics are measured and analyzed as part of performance and load testing. For comparative purposes against the targets that were identified earlier, we are primarily concerned with a few key metrics which will give us an immediate idea of the application's performance. These are **Time to First Byte** and **total page response time**.

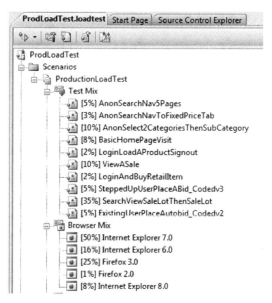

Figure 2.2: Sample test and browser distribution.

Time to First Byte

Time to First Byte (TTFB) represents the time it takes a server to issue the first byte of information, typically in response to a request from a web browser. This time covers the socket connection time, the time taken to send the HTTP request, and the time taken to get the first byte of the page. It is a good indicator of the responsiveness of the web application, as the server must receive the request, interpret it, execute the ASP.NET pipeline to process the request, and produce a response.

This is one of the primary metrics to use when determining how responsive a site or web application is. A large TTFB value means that a typical user will see no activity in their browser (apart from whatever "waiting" indicator the browser uses) for a long time, until that first byte of information is received from the server and the browser can start parsing.

This is also typically a good indicator of how fast the web application can process the requests made against it, as no response will be issued until the web server/ASP.NET has finished processing a given request. There are caveats to this, but I'll cover them alongside analysis in later chapters.

Total page response time

The total page response time is often referred to as simply "response time." This metric includes, not only the TTFB time described previously, but also all the dependent requests required to completely load and display all aspects of a web page. This can include items such as images, JavaScript files, and Cascading Style Sheet (CSS) files.

In contrast to the TTFB measurement, the total page response time measures the time it takes for a page to completely finish loading all resources required to present the page to the user. This may include non-functional aspects as well, such as tracking images hosted on external sites. It is important to quantify the effect that external tracking mechanisms can impose upon the site. Once this is done, it is valuable to remove this component during performance testing, to get a more accurate view of the site's performance. External tracking mechanisms are normally beyond the control of the application and cannot, therefore, be modified or improved.

To further illustrate these points, the following diagrams show some TTFB and total page response time breakdowns. The first diagram represents a personal, hobby site, HTTP://WWW.THEGLAVS.COM and the second site represents the Microsoft main site at HTTP://WWW.MICROSOFT.COM.

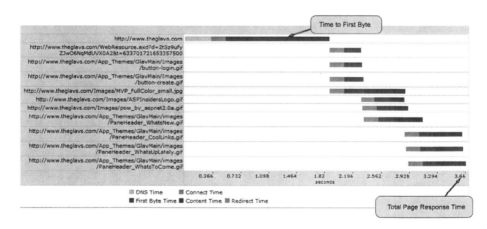

Figure 2.3: www.theglavs.com response times.

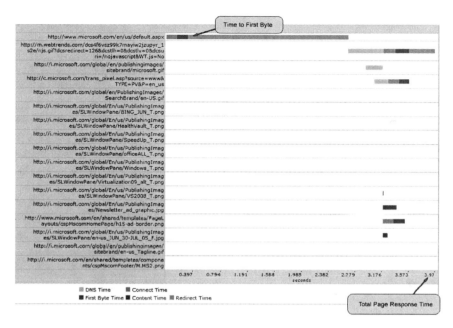

Figure 2.4: www.microsoft.com response times.

From the previous two diagrams, it is evident that the Time to First Byte and the total page response times can vary quite considerably. This will be dependent upon the number of other resources and artifacts that are present on the particular page being measured. It is important to be able to quantify these differences, as your web application may respond very fast on its own, but the dependent requests and resources in the page may be degrading the performance considerably.

What about average response time?

The average response time for a web application is often a misleading metric, as there is ambiguity around what the average time actually means.

*   Does it refer to the average TTFB?

*   Does it refer to the average total page response time?

*   Does it include static resources such as CSS and image files?

*   Does it include the low end figures at low levels of load or at other different times?

It is worth bearing in mind that serving static files will be much faster than processing a request through the full request execution pipeline so, if static files are included in this metric, then average response times will appear faster than they really are. The result is obviously more ambiguity, and the metric will provide no real correlation to page responsiveness and overall application performance.

There is also the question of the point at which the metric samples are taken to determine the average. A common practice is to use percentile brackets to determine the average response time. For example, if a 90th percentile was used to determine the average response time, this would mean that, out of 100 requests, ordered from best to worst times, the requests in the last 10% of requests (that is, the ten worst-performing requests) are used to find the average.

Because of this ambiguity, the average response time is generally best used to compare against previous averages for the same time period, but only for the purposes of determining if the latest performance run has shown improvement or degradation compared to the last run (in other words, it's used as a relative measure).

This can be a useful metric, though I always recommend that this percentile bracket should be used in conjunction with examining the more specific TTFB and total page response times discussed previously. Equally, you don't necessarily have to use the 90th percentile – the 85th percentile could just as easily be chosen to determine averages. That being said, I recommend that you use the 85th, 90th, and 95th percentile brackets, as these provide a valuable insight into the worst case scenario of response times for whatever is being tested, in terms of both Time to First Byte and total page response time.

Sweet spots and operational ceilings

We've seen that the performance targets which have been identified by the business represent acceptable response times under various load conditions. Irrespective of the current system load, these response times are often referred to as the "sweet spot," and are the response times and usable states that best serve the users of the application.

The sweet spot may initially be nowhere near what the business requires from the application. The response times expected of the application may initially be at concurrent user levels far below what is deemed necessary to serve the customer base. It is crucial to identify the sweet spot, and how far from that target the application currently is, as you'll need to make those two states match before business requirements can be met.

However, the sweet spot is just one aspect of the application. It is also important to know what the limit of the application is, and whether it is resilient enough to cope with extremely large user loads.

This is the stress-testing aspect of performance testing and analysis, and requires you to ask the questions below.

•   How long can the application cope with relatively high concurrent user loads before it becomes totally unresponsive?

•   In addition, what characteristics does the application exhibit at these high concurrent user loads?

These are important questions in determining the operational characteristics of the application. The number of concurrent users (or "load") that the application can withstand before becoming totally unresponsive is referred to as its "operational ceiling." That is, the ceiling or limit at which the application can operate before failure. This limit will typically involve excessive response times that make the website practically unusable, but this metric still serves as a good comparative indicator against previous performance tests. It also provides valuable evidence as to what will happen when the application experiences a larger load than it can handle.

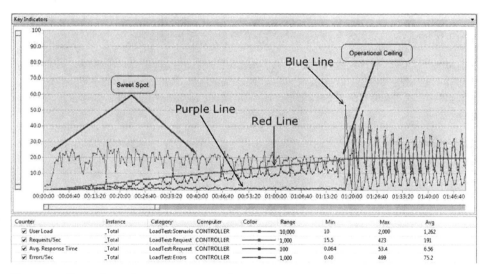

Figure 2.5: Example performance run graph.

Figure 2.5 shows an example performance run. The red line represents concurrent user load, the blue line represents response time, the purple line represents errors per second, and the X-axis represents the time component of the performance test. It is clearly apparent where the operational ceiling is, as errors per second and response time make a sharp change at approximately one hour and twenty minutes into the run.

In addition, we can discern that the sweet spot for this application (in this case, a Time to First Byte response time of less than five seconds) is between the start of the performance run and approximately forty minutes into the test.

Using Visual Studio Team Test we can drill into these results to determine the concurrent user load at the sweet spot as well as the operational ceiling. This process will be described later in the book.

Conclusion

The objective of this chapter is to provide an understanding and a framework around determining what targets need to be identified for a web application to be classified as a well-performing application. This is a relative term that needs to factor in the user base and the business which the application serves. There are no "right" answers, but the more experience a developer gains, the more honed their instincts will become.

Having these targets identified means that the relatively expensive exercise of performance testing has a well-defined set of goals which can be measured and tested against. In addition, the business has a clear set of measurements from which to determine whether the application meets its requirements. These measurements provide a degree of confidence in a technical procedure that is typically unfamiliar territory for businesses.

The sweet spot and the operational ceiling aspects of the application provide valuable evidence into how the application performs at various load levels. With this evidence, as solution architects, we can provide informed conclusions around the application capabilities, and also how estimate much time and effort is needed to achieve the goals of the business.

The following chapters will take you through the technical steps required to ensure that the business and technical staff alike can ensure that the application performs as required.

Chapter 3: Performance and Load Test Metrics

What metrics do we need?

The purpose of running performance, load, and stress testing is to gather metrics about a system so that you can determine which parts of it are performing well, and which are not.

This sounds simple enough, but the myriad combination of data-types to record can make choosing which to use difficult. For example, if the wrong set of metrics were recorded for a performance test run, the system might appear to be able to cope with a given load relatively easily. However, in reality the system may have been experiencing severe problems in areas that simply weren't measured.

Equally, one of the most frustrating things is to have just enough data to show that a problem exists, and vaguely where it is, but not enough to provide accurate information as to why.

The short answer as to what metrics to record would be that recording everything possible is ideal. Indeed, if at all possible, then this is a fail-safe approach to ensuring you have all the data necessary for analysis. However, as you can imagine, this is often just not practical for any one of a variety of reasons. When discussing performance and load test metrics, the data gathered is quite different from data gathered during application profiling. This chapter will deal primarily with the former. I'll discuss profiling data in the context of profiling itself (and the associated toolset) in Chapter 6.

To start with, we'll deal with the most basic metrics that will provide the quickest indications of application performance in most typical scenarios, before moving on to more specialized metrics for given scenarios.

Basic metrics

So what is required to meet the most diverse set of needs? There are some basic metrics which are important at all levels of testing, regardless of whether data is being collected from a database server, application server, web server or even a workstation running a web browser to access a web application. Most of the data is gathered via the performance counters that will be discussed in Chapter 5.

These are typically accessed using the PerfMon tool (**perfmon.exe**) or via Visual Studio Team Test. Visual Studio Team Test also collects additional metric data specific to web applications.

The most common (and mandatory) counters required at any level of testing are CPU utilization and memory usage. Both are early indicators of problems in an application.

High CPU utilization can indicate that an application is performing tasks very inefficiently, or is perhaps running computationally intensive tasks in unexpected ways; as a benchmark, an application that constantly maintains more than 90% processor utilization would be considered to have high CPU utilization. Although today's high-level languages and frameworks provide constructs that are easy to implement, it is often not apparent what processing is required to achieve the desired functionality.

High memory utilization can indicate that an application is not using memory efficiently, or is perhaps not releasing resources appropriately. There are obviously instances where using a lot of memory is required, but not releasing that memory as soon as possible is a serious issue, and this is how memory leaks can manifest. As an application is used over time, a memory leak causes memory usage to increase steadily until the available resources are exhausted and, since running low on memory obviously has a big impact on system performance, it is imperative that memory be managed correctly. It is a common misconception that because of the .NET garbage collector silently operating in the background, cleaning up memory, memory leaks cannot occur. This is far from the truth. Items such as static objects, event handlers referencing shared data and many other things are ways in which the .NET garbage collector can interpret an object as in use, when in fact it is not. This can build up over time and cause memory issues. Later in this book, we will look at the common mistakes with respect to memory and performance issues, what to watch out for and how to overcome them.

CPU and memory usage are also applicable at all levels of an application, regardless of physical topology. Even a user's system, accessing an application via a web browser, is a good candidate to record CPU and memory usage. High indicators in this situation could indicate inefficient JavaScript being executed in the browser on that machine, for example.

CPU utilization and memory usage are basic indicators that should form part of every metric set recorded, regardless of system role. System performance problems will almost always manifest via one of these broad metric counters, indicating the need to investigate further. PerfMon can be used to gather this data and, in fact, defaults to capturing processor utilization (amongst other counters).

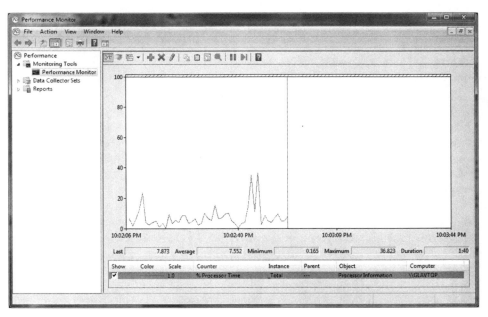

Figure 3.1: Default PerfMon counters – Windows 7 / Server 2008.

For the basic performance counters, **% Processor Time** in the processor category and **% Committed bytes in use** (for a high-level view), **Committed bytes**, or **Available Mbytes** in the memory category are sufficient for initial analysis.

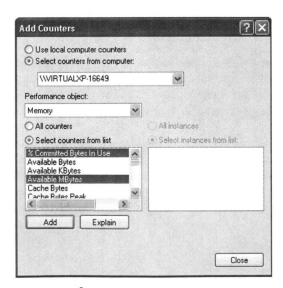

Figure 3.2: PerfMon memory performance counters.

Much like PerfMon, Visual Studio Team Test will capture CPU utilization and memory usage in every performance test run by default. However, remember that this relies on remote WMI (Windows Management Instrumentation) communication, and sometimes this cannot work. Also, performance metrics may need to be analyzed by teams or individuals who do not have Visual Studio Team Test or access to the results of the performance tests; hence the need for separate PerfMon-recorded data.

Web application basic metrics

In addition to the basic CPU and memory counters, web applications are often broadly measured by two other characteristics: response time and requests per second. Response time refers to how quickly the server can provide a response to the browser, and requests per second indicates the throughput of the server, and shows how many requests it can handle every second. Both metrics provide an indication of how efficient an application and server are at processing requests and providing responses. Low CPU utilization and low memory usage will not mean much if a web page takes a long time to load.

Quite often when designing web applications, a business will specify that a particular page is considered to be performing well if the response time is less than a certain amount, usually measured in seconds. For example, the business can specify that the home page of the web application must load in less than five seconds.

At this point, it is important to note that "response time" is a broad term that can be interpreted in a few ways. Since part of the purpose of performance testing is to remove ambiguity about an application's performance and the business's expectations, it is necessary to clarify exactly what response time means.

A web page is typically made of many assets, including such things as the HTML itself, images, Cascading Style Sheets (CSS), JavaScript, and many others. A web browser will not load all these assets as one sequential block and subsequently display them on screen, but will rather load the page in parts. The HTML is downloaded first, and then any referenced assets are requested. These secondary assets are often referred to as "dependent requests," and are usually accessing static resources such as CSS files, image files, and so on.

Static resources are typically delivered much faster than the HTML markup itself, since no real processing is required to serve them to the browser; they are simply loaded from disk as requested. In addition, Internet Information Server has extensive support for caching these requests, making accessing them even quicker.

By contrast, the application is typically required to perform some processing before sending the resulting HTML to the browser. In ASP.NET webforms applications, the application will go through the full page event life cycle (in simplified terms, consisting of 18 individual steps) before finally rendering some content. Just as an example of just how much is involved in this, when an ASP.NET webforms page is requested, the following (albeit simplified) page life cycle is executed:

- `ProcessRequest`

  - `DeterminePostBackMode`

  - `PerformPreInit` and `OnPreInit`

  - `InitialiseThemes` and `ApplyMasterPage`

  - `ApplyControlSkin`

  - `OnInit`

  - `TrackViewState`

  - `LoadControlState` and `LoadViewState`

  - `OnPreLoad`

  - `OnLoad`

  - `RaiseChangedEvents` and `RaisePostbackEvent`

  - `OnLoadComplete`

  - `EnsureChildControls` and `CreateChildControls`

  - `OnPreRender`

  - `SaveControlState` and `SaveViewState`

  - `RenderControl`

  - `BeginRender` and `Render`

- `EndRender`

Clearly, a lot of processing occurs before the actual rendering of any content to the browser, so the efficiency of the application code executing during this life cycle is what will determine the overall response time of the page.

While the life cycle of an ASP.NET MVC request is not as substantial as a webforms request, there are still significant processing steps required to generate the HTML response.

Once the browser receives the first byte of HTML, the client can be assured that the server processing is complete and the results of processing are being sent to the browser. This time is referred to as Time to First Byte (TTFB) and is one of the primary measures of response time in web applications.

Given the amount of processing required for ASP.NET to send a response to the browser, it is easy to see how static resource requests can be much quicker than any page. This is important to note as, when response times are averaged across a performance run, only page response times should be factored into the calculation. Including static resource requests will cause the average figures to look much better than they really are!

Static resources will be addressed later in this book when dealing with Content Delivery Networks (CDNs) and other mechanisms to help static resource load times.

To illustrate the point, this effect is highlighted in the following graph of a website response time report, issued by a service called "Gomez," a paid-for service for measuring response times, provided by Telstra. Many companies provide similar services and associated reports for monitoring websites.

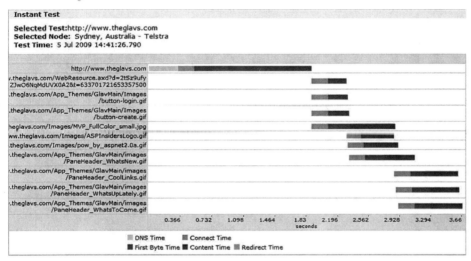

Figure 3.3: Response time report.

The end of the purple bars indicate the TTFB response time, and you can see that the initial request to HTTP://WWW.THEGLAVS.COM takes considerably longer than the dependent requests that comprise the rest of the page.

This is why it is important to only factor in the main request TTFB time. The dependent request response times should not be ignored, as they contribute to overall page load time. Some dependent requests may actually be the cause of long overall page load times but, to improve the performance of the application, only the page itself should be considered. Later chapters in this book will deal with the issue of dependent requests and how to improve load times for these artifacts.

Visual Studio Team Test provides a convenient way to analyze these key metrics. When a performance run is executed and the test run data loaded into Visual Studio, the results are displayed in a series of graphs for easy analysis, as you can see below.

48

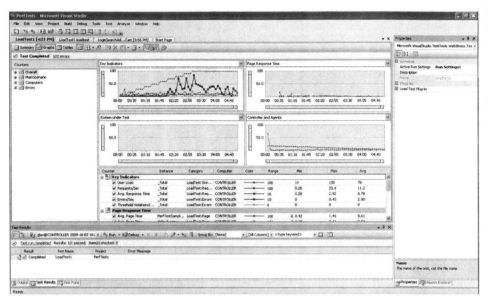

Figure 3.4: Performance run initial result display.

The areas of concern for this example are the **Key Indicators** and **Page Response Time** graphs, which can be easily focused on using the **2 Horizontal Panels** option from the **View Graph** button.

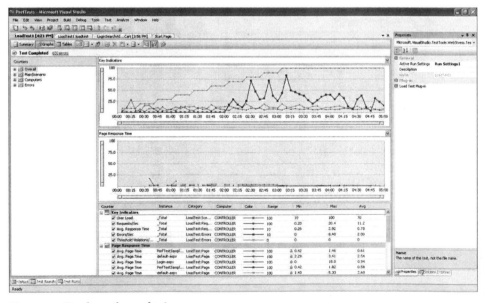

Figure 3.5: Dual graph result view.

The available data summaries will automatically adjust to only display results from whichever graphs you happen to be focusing on at any given time.

What to look for

The basic metrics that have been discussed can provide a good indicator of an application's performance at a quick glance. There are other metrics to factor in, which will be discussed later in this chapter, but these key metrics are a good start for determining if an application will meet its performance criteria. In combination, they are the best way to quickly assess if an application performs acceptably, without going through the time-consuming task of analyzing all the possible metric data in detail.

CPU utilization

Naturally, the CPU utilization should ideally be as low as possible. If the CPU is being measured on a database server, then the usage should remain low at all times; an average of 20–30% is generally acceptable. Anything over this could indicate that the database server will begin to be overloaded and exhibit slower than usual performance.

An average CPU utilization of 20–30% on a web or application server is excellent, and 50–70% is a well utilized system. An average CPU utilization above 75% indicates that a system is reaching its computational capacity; however, there's usually no need to panic if you have an average of 90–95%, as you may be able to horizontally scale out by adding an additional server.

Obviously, in this last scenario, adding extra load may mean the system consistently achieves 100% CPU utilization. For a web or application server, this is actually not that uncommon, and the ideal is to have a stateless system which can be horizontally scaled as required. As a matter of fact, if a web server is averaging 100% CPU utilization, but the database server's load is only 30% CPU utilization, this is actually a good scenario to be in. This means that the database server has capacity to serve more load, and that the web server is being well utilized. Simply adding an extra web server into the farm at this point would be an easy, relatively predictable way to address the web tier's capacity to handle extra load.

Some tasks, such as cryptographic functions, are computationally intensive and will cause CPU "spikes" even at a relatively low load. In these instances, it is important to design the system in such a way that it can be easily scaled out appropriately, and not be tied to a single server (which is known as having Server Affinity.)

Memory utilization

A system with no available memory will not be able to cope with any more work to do, and will potentially be unstable, so it's important to ensure available memory is monitored, and remains at acceptable levels.

As I mentioned in passing earlier, it is important to ensure that memory consumption does not steadily increase over long periods of time until there is none available, as this usually indicates a memory leak.

Memory utilization is obviously relative to the amount of memory on the system in question and, as long as the available memory remains above approximately 25%, then the system should have enough "head room" to operate efficiently. Again, this is not an exact figure and a system can operate with less than that, but this can indicate that memory thresholds are being reached and any spike in activity or load could cause unexpected (and often undesirable) results. At best, paging will occur, wherein memory will be read and written from disk, causing the system to operate very slowly. At worst, further load or requests will be unable to be serviced, connections will be refused, memory exceptions will occur, and the system's reliability will be compromised.

In .NET, memory usage should ideally follow a predictable "saw-tooth" pattern. This is because memory is allocated during normal program execution and then, at certain points determined by the .NET garbage collector, the memory is reclaimed. When objects are no longer in use, or are out of scope, they are removed from memory, and the memory is returned to the system for use. The following screen shot shows a typical graph of memory usage for an application, made using a tool called CLRProfiler, a memory profiling tool freely available from Microsoft at HTTP://TINYURL.COM/CLRPROFILER, which will be discussed in Chapter 6.

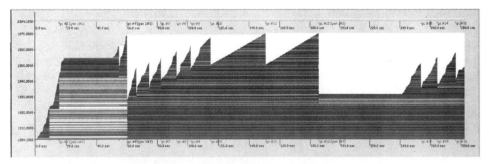

Figure 3.6: "Saw-tooth" memory usage pattern.

The saw-tooth pattern represents memory being allocated, peaking, and then being reclaimed by the garbage collector. Memory usage then climbs again as objects are allocated, the garbage collector initiates another collection, and the cycle continues.

What we *don't* want to see is a saw-tooth pattern that is ever increasing, as below.

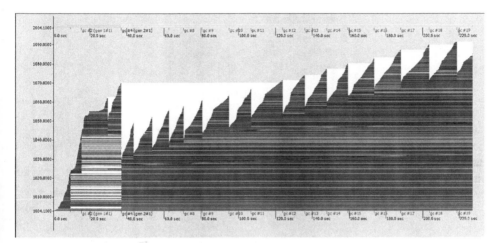

Figure 3.7: "Saw-tooth" memory usage pattern – potential memory leak

Figure 3.7 shows a classic indication of a memory leak in an application, but this can occur in both web applications and desktop or service applications.

Both of the previous graphs present a low-level, detailed view of memory usage. If memory usage was viewed at a higher level using a tool such as PerfMon or even Visual Studio Team Test, the saw-tooth pattern would not be as evident, but the general pattern would remain the same – a relatively flat horizontal line for good and predictable memory usage by an application, and a line trending upwards for a memory leak-type situation.

A database server should typically remain at a relatively constant level of memory usage without too much variation. Again, this is dependent on other system activities such as scheduled tasks, but memory usage should, in general, remain even. The average amount of memory used will naturally depend on how much work the database has to do, and the nature of the queries themselves. Memory will occasionally dip and spike but should always return to the normal operating level.

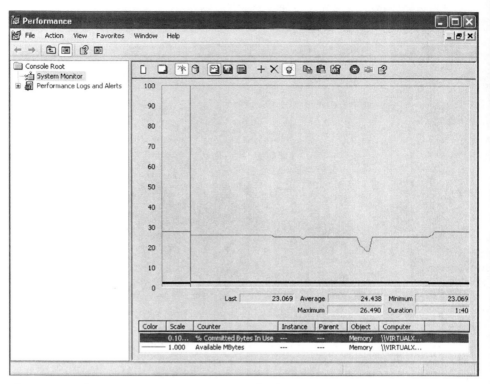

Figure 3.8: PerfMon – even memory usage on a database server.

Response time

Response time (as measured in TTFB) is relatively easy to assess. Generally, any response time over 3–4 seconds is perceived as slow, although this obviously varies for each individual case.

When developing business applications, it is best to let the business decide what is an appropriate response time, although this metric must be determined in conjunction with the development team. It would be potentially unrealistic if a business were to stipulate that every page must respond in less than one second (although this is possible, and some businesses manage it!). Latency and the operations a page performs play a huge part in these decisions. If a page needed to produce a complex and computationally heavy report, then this response goal would be very hard to achieve without some high-end servers and computational equipment. Business value and realistic response times in these types of scenario are clearly matters for negotiation.

Creating a baseline

Before performance tests can be properly analyzed, it is essential to establish a good way of comparing performance data to determine if improvements have been made from one test run to another.

The first step is to establish a "baseline" performance run against the application. A baseline performance run is a performance test run executed against the application for the very first time, without specific performance modifications (aside from normal development). In short, the application as it currently stands.

Always keep track of your baseline run data, as this will allow future performance runs to be compared to it to determine if performance has altered anywhere. The performance run can be named as a baseline within Visual Studio Team Test; alternatively, a separate list or spreadsheet can be used to catalog performance runs against their purpose or context.

Utilizing a spreadsheet, with each run, its date/time, and any details such as performance modifications made, is an extremely valuable way to collate and manage performance test run data. It then becomes easy to quickly glance over the list and view what changes were made to achieve the performance aspects of a particular test run.

However, without a baseline run, each subsequent performance test has nothing to compare against. Modifications made at some point in the development process could have seriously hampered performance, rather than increasing it, and this would not be apparent without a baseline run.

Using Visual Studio to analyze the results

Visual Studio Team Test provides excellent tools to interactively analyze performance test results and investigate the large amount of metric data in tabular or visual form.

Firstly, we need to load in the results of a performance test run. If a test run has just been executed, then the results will be loaded immediately afterwards. However, if we need to load in a previous set of results we can do so using the following two main methods.

Using the Test Results management window

- Select the **Test > Windows > Test Results** menu option to activate the **Test Runs** window.

- Open the **Connect** drop-down and select a controller.

- Completed performance runs will be listed and can be selected to load in the performance test results.

Using the Open and Manage Test Results dialog

To use this option, a performance test solution needs to be open, and a load test must be loaded into the Visual Studio Editor.

- Click on the **Open and Manage Test Results** button to open the dialog window.

- Select a Controller to use, and then select a load test whose results you wish to load. A list of performance test results will be shown. Select a performance test result and click the **Open** button.

Note

*Occasionally, for whatever reason, Visual Studio may fail to list the results in the **Test Runs** window. This rarely happens, but it can sometimes be caused by the correlating result metadata files not being present or being corrupt. This means you cannot load the performance test results via the **Test Runs** window as they will not be shown. Using the **Open and Manage Test Results** dialog will allow you to get around this issue.*

Now that we have some performance test results to analyze, let's start off by looking at response times. Initially, Visual Studio presents four graphs of key results. **Key Indicators** is one of these graphs, and has an average response time metric listed in the table of results shown below the graph in Figure 3.9.

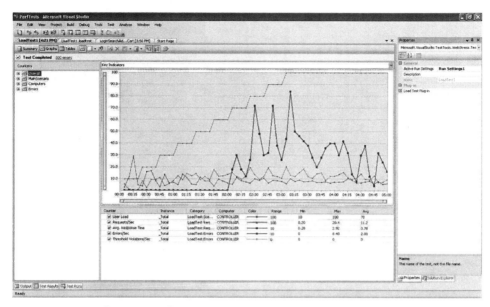

Figure 3.9: Key Indicators graph.

The average response time metric is only a general indication. Dependent requests can factor into this figure, in addition to the response time for low concurrent users, which skews the result to look more favorable than it should.

Filtering performance test result selection

In order to get a better average response time figure for a particular number of concurrent users (or, in fact, any metric data) we can use the dynamic filtering and selection feature of Visual Studio Team Test.

By using the timeline grab handles, it is possible to constrain the result set to a specified time window. For example, we may wish to see the average response time when the concurrent user count is between 50 and 80 concurrent users, To do this, drag the start and end timeline grab handles until the **Min User Load** column equals 50, and the **Max User Load** column equals 80. The grab handles are circled in Figure 3.10.

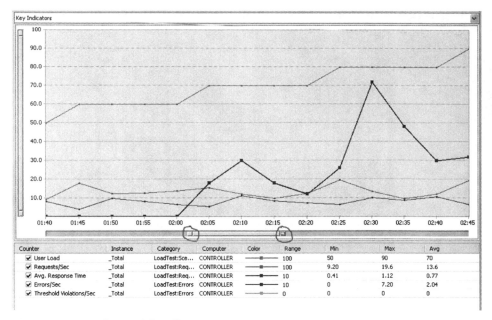

Figure 3.10: Timeline grab handles.

Note that the timeline grab handles can also be moved using the keyboard for finer adjustment, although the handle must be selected with the mouse first. There are also grab handles on the vertical axis to change the scale upon which the graph is shown, and these operate in exactly the same way as the timeline grab handles.

An alternative way of selecting a portion of the results is by selecting an area on the graph itself, although this is a little less accurate, and fine-grained control is not as easy. Click and drag the mouse to select an area. Once the area is selected, only that set of metrics will be displayed on the graph and in the tabular results below the graph.

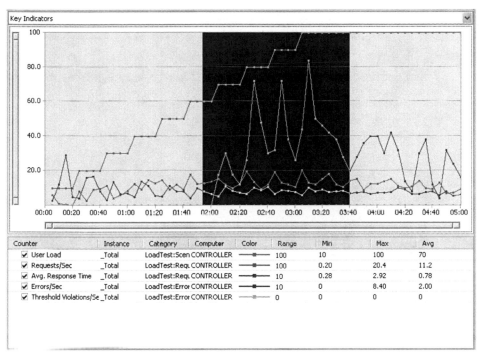

Figure 3.11: Selecting or filtering results via mouse selection on the graph.

This concept can be taken a little further. One of the first items to analyze in a performance test run is the response time at a certain concurrent user level. For example, let's say we would like to look at the response times when there are between 80 and 100 concurrent users. We need to ensure that the test run's user load is set to **Step Up** at periodic levels of the performance test run, which can be set in the properties for the load test scenario. The pattern must be set to either **Step Up** or **Goal Based** with user load increment values and time periods for the increments set to your desired values.

With a graph selection on and the key indicators graph selected, adjust the timeline grab handles so that the **User Load** has a minimum value of 80 and a maximum value of 100. Now select the drop-down box where **Key Indicators** is shown and select **Page Response Time** as shown in Figure 3.12.

The page response times will be shown, but will be constrained to the same time period and concurrent load that was selected while the **Key Indicators** graph was selected (see Figure 3.13).

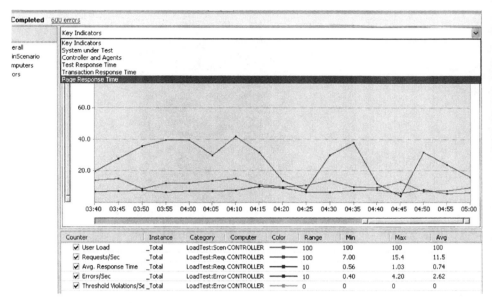

Figure 3.12: Selecting the Page Response Time graph.

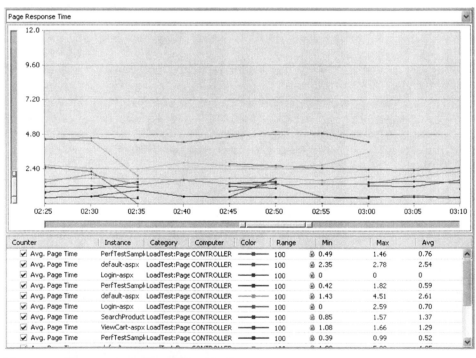

Figure 3.13: Page response times filtered by 80–100 concurrent users.

This is an extremely easy way to visualize each page's response time at a particular concurrent user level. If we take a step back and examine part of the business objectives of performance testing that were mentioned earlier, we can see that the goal was to validate that particular pages can respond in a set time (TTFB) at a particular concurrent user load.

Using this technique, it is easy to examine any page response time at any particular point in time or concurrent user level. If the response time for a page exceeds the agreed business requirements, then some performance modifications need to be made. However, even if the pages meet the required response times, it is still important to gauge what happens beyond the required concurrent user load.

Sweet spots and operational ceilings

Using the techniques discussed previously, it is easy to plot the response time characteristic of the application as concurrent user load is increased. In web applications, there is a typical pattern of response time progression as the concurrent user load is increased. This means that during the low concurrent user-load stages of the performance test run, response time is excellent.

There comes a point where response time is still good and within acceptable bounds, but beyond this point response times start to increase sharply and keep increasing until timeouts begin to occur. The period before the sharp increase is what is referred to as the "optimal operating period" or "sweet spot." These terms refer to the time where the application can service the largest possible number of users without incurring a large or unacceptable response time. This is best shown in an example (see Figure 3.14).

Figure 3.14 shows a typical performance run. The optimal operating period, or sweet spot, was achieved relatively early in the run. The concurrent user load was relatively low at 200–300 concurrent users, with page response times of 3 seconds or less. This is the time when the application is performing at its most efficient and maintaining good response times. After this, the application still services requests, but sharp spikes in response time start to appear (represented by the blue line in the graph). Beyond this period, the response time continues to increase until erratic measurements occur. This is the operational ceiling, where the application begins to refuse requests and return **Service Unavailable**-type errors.

It is important to note that, while the business objectives have been exceeded before the application hits its operational ceiling, the behavior of the application can still be observed. This is important, as it shows the resilience of the application and what could potentially happen if a sharp spike in load occurs that exceeds estimates.

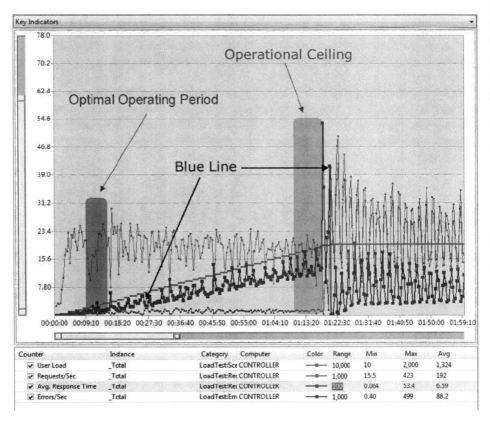

Figure 3.14: Sweet spot and operational ceiling.

In addition, during times of high stress, the functional aspects of the application will be exercised at maximum capacity and it will be easier to see what components of the application are performing more work than others. This will be relatively easy to see through the use of detailed performance metrics which are discussed later in the book.

While performance graphs and PerfMon metrics are extremely valuable in determining the sweet spot of an application, there is nothing quite like practical usage. In order to truly verify that the application is responsive and functional at the estimated sweet spot, it is best to actually perform a performance test run and simulate the number of concurrent users that is being applied at the estimated sweet spot. During this time, enlist the business users or stakeholders to use the application and report on its responsiveness. It will become quickly apparent whether the application is indeed responsive during the given load and, thus, whether the optimal operating period is the one that has been estimated.

Detailed performance metrics

With an indication of system performance in hand (using the key metric values), as well as the ability to filter and isolate portions of a performance test run, it is now important to examine performance metrics in detail.

In particular, it is important to understand what the various metrics that are available mean in the context of a performance run. Whilst the key metrics discussed previously usually show whether there is a potential performance issue or not, they do not provide much insight into what the problem is.

This is where a detailed investigation and analysis needs to be performed on all available performance metric data to ascertain the nature of the performance issue. It is also important to understand what areas of the application can be generally improved. The immediate performance issue is an obvious choice, but many other areas may exist that could also be improved and contribute to an overall performance gain.

We'll start by first looking at the general performance metrics which can be relevant to almost all applications, whether on a server or desktop machine, and then the web application specific metrics will be discussed. It is important to note that not every single performance counter will be listed here as there are a huge number of them, details of which can be found in the Microsoft reference documentation. Here, we will be concentrating on the performance counters that aid in the detailed analysis of a test run – in other words, the counters that deliver real value in analyzing performance test run data.

Almost all metrics and counters are normally available within the PerfMon tool. The web specific metrics, such as response time, are only available via the Visual Studio Team Test tool and will be listed as such. It may seem obvious, but note that ASP.NET performance counters are typically only available on machines with the .NET runtime installed, such as web or application servers. Database servers would not typically have the runtime installed. Finally, rather than simply provide the detailed set of counters and their definitions, I'll also provide a discussion on typical analysis paths using these counters. Having the counters and their definition is not usually enough, as it is equally important to determine what counters are worth examining in certain situations, and what indicators to look for. This is where many people can become confused as, after determining that there is a problem, it is hard to choose what metrics and indicators to use in the various categories of further investigation.

Performance metrics

For the following counter sets, it is generally recommended to monitor only the specific process in question. For web applications, this is typically the worker process (**aspnet_wp** in Windows XP and **W3WP** in Windows Server) that IIS uses to host them. For desktop and other applications, such as services, it will be necessary to monitor the specific application or host process. This is to minimize the performance counter variance that other, unrelated processes may introduce into the measurements.

General

Category: Processor

- **% Processor Time**
  The main counter is the **% Processor Time**, which shows the total percentage of processor utilization across all processes. This provides a good general indication of system utilization and is the best starting point when looking at system performance. Visual Studio Team Test has predefined threshold levels for CPU utilization and will provide visual warnings when this counter goes beyond them.

Category: Process

- **% Processor Time**
  The **% Processor Time** counter is exactly the same as the previously discussed processor category counter, but the processor utilization can be measured specific to a single process. For example, the **W3WP.exe** process (the web server host process) can be specifically measured for processor utilization in order to exclude any other process activity. This allows a good segregation of data and makes it possible to potentially pinpoint CPU intensive processes outside of the application itself.

- **Working Set**
  The **Working Set** counter shows the amount of memory pages in use by all threads within the process, and is listed in bytes. This is a good way to examine the memory usage of a specific process.

Category: Memory

- **Available Mbytes**
  This represents the amount of available physical memory in the system. Ongoing monitoring of this counter can show if an application has a memory leak. This condition can actually be mitigated somewhat in a web application using IIS health monitoring. This is where IIS will recycle or restart an application pool (and thus the processes running within it) when a memory limit has been reached. While this can alleviate the consumption of all available memory by the process, it is a defensive measure only, and the root cause of the memory leak should be investigated.

- **Pages/Sec**
  This counter effectively represents the number of hard faults per second. A hard fault is when pages of memory are read from, or written to, disk; since disk operations are relatively slow compared to memory operations, hard faults are quite expensive in terms of system performance. The larger this counter, the worse the overall system performance will be. This counter should ideally be zero, or at least very low. If it's high, this can indicate serious memory issues and that physical memory is either near limits or not used effectively.

- **Page Faults/Sec**
  This counter should be used in conjunction with the previously mentioned **Pages/Sec** counter, and represents the number of hard and soft faults per second. A soft fault is where a page of memory was elsewhere in physical memory, and needed to be swapped into the process address space. Since memory operations are very fast, having a high number of soft faults is generally OK, as most systems can cope with this. Monitoring this counter can help provide the tipping point where hard faults begin to occur and where soft faults become excessive.

Category: .NET CLR Memory

- **Gen 0 heap size, Gen 1 heap size, Gen 2 heap size**

- **#Gen 0 Collections, #Gen 1 Collections, #Gen 2 Collections**
  Both the heap size set of counters and the collection counters should show similar patterns of behavior. The .NET CLR garbage collector is a "mark and sweep" collection mechanism that partitions objects into different generations, Generation 0 (Gen0) being the shortest lived, most often collected and least expensive to collect. Generation 2 contains the longest-living objects, is collected the least often, and is the most expensive in terms of performance to collect. The #Gen 0, #Gen 1, and #Gen 2 collection counters represent the number of times each generation had a garbage collection performed, whereas the Gen 0 heap size, Gen 1 heap size, and Gen 2 heap size represent the memory heap size of each respective generation. While not an unbreakable rule, both sets of

counters should show approximately a 1:10 ratio between each generation. That is, the #Gen 0, #Gen 1, and #Gen 2 collections should follow a 100:10:1 pattern, and the heap size counters should show approximately a 1:10:100 pattern. This ratio of garbage collection statistics shows a healthy and normal memory usage by the application. Metrics that are largely different from this ratio can indicate erratic and inefficient memory usage or use of the garbage collector itself. Note that, for web applications, measuring only the **W3WP** process is preferable to looking at the total memory pattern and, for a desktop application, monitoring the application itself is preferable. For those of you uncomfortable with firm assertions, these ratios are supported by Microsoft performance documentation, mentioned by Rico Mariani (a Microsoft performance specialist), and are something I've often encountered myself. Whilst deviation from these ratios does not prove that there is an issue, it can often provide a strong indication.

Category: .NET CLR Exceptions

*   **# of Exceps Thrown / sec**
    This counter represents the number of exceptions being thrown per second by the application, and should be very low. Throwing exceptions is a relatively expensive operation and should be performed only in exceptional circumstances (i.e. actual, legitimate exceptions) not for control flow. Again, in web applications it is best to monitor only the **W3WP** process specific to IIS web hosting process. The exception to this rule is if a web application utilizes a lot of Response.Redirect calls because they generate a thread aborted exception. If this figure is high and there are a lot of Response.Redirect calls in the web application, then the figure may be representative of this, and it may be worthwhile trying to replace the calls with ones to the overload of Response.Redirect, which also takes a bool as the second parameter, and set that bool to false. This causes the request to not immediately terminate processing of the current page, (which is what causes the thread aborted exception).

Category: .NET CLR Jit

*   **% Time in Jit**
    This counter shows the percentage of elapsed time the CLR spent in a Just in Time (JIT) compilation phase. This figure should be relatively low, ideally below 20%. Figures above this level can indicate that perhaps some code is being emitted and dynamically compiled by the application. Once a code path is JIT compiled, it should not need to be compiled again. Using the NGEN command-line tool against your application assemblies to create a native, pre-JIT compiled image for the target platform can reduce this figure. Too much time spent in JIT compilation can cause CPU spikes and seriously hamper the overall system performance. Visual Studio Team Test provides a threshold warning when this counter has gone beyond a predefined acceptance level, which is 20% by default.

Category: .NET CLR Security

- **% Time in RT Checks**
  This counter represents the percentage of time spent performing Code Access Security (CAS) checks. CAS checks are expensive from a performance perspective and cause the runtime to traverse the current stack to compare security context and code identity for evaluation purposes. Ideally, this should be very low, preferably zero. An excessive figure here (by that, I mean a figure exceeding 20%) can hamper system performance and cause excessive CPU utilization. This can often be caused by accessing resources across a network share or SAN where network credentials and security contexts need to be evaluated to gain access to the resource.

Category: .NET CLR Locks and Threads

- **Total # of Contentions**

- **Contention Rate/Sec**
  These counters represent the number of unsuccessful managed-lock acquisitions, the **Total # of Contentions** being the total number of unsuccessful lock acquisition attempts by threads managed by the CLR. The **Contention Rate/Sec** represents the same metric but expressed as a rate per second. Locks can be acquired in the CLR by using such constructs as the `lock` statement, `System.Monitor.Enter` statement, and the `MethodImplOptions.Synchronized` attribute. When a lock acquisition is attempted, this causes contention between the threads attempting to acquire the same lock, and blocks the thread until the lock is released. Unsuccessful locks can cause serious performance issues when the rate is high, as the threads are not only synchronized but ultimately unsuccessful, potentially throwing exceptions and waiting excessively. This rate should be very low, ideally zero.

Web/ASP.NET specific

Category: ASP.NET

- **Application Restarts**
  This counter represents the number of times that the ASP.NET worker process has been restarted. Ideally, this should be zero. IIS has features to detect problems and restart worker processes, but this is a defensive measure for problem applications. Enabling these features for performance testing will detract from the value of collecting ongoing performance metrics for a test run. Ideally, the application should coexist with the infrastructure well enough to not require restarts.

The restarts of the worker process usually indicate that IIS has detected a memory condition, CPU condition, or unresponsive worker process, and forced the process to restart. The memory and CPU thresholds before IIS restarts a worker process can be configured within the IIS management tool. In addition, the amount of time to wait before a health check request is returned from the worker process can also be defined in the IIS management tool, although this is usually performed within the specific application pool that the application belongs to within IIS. The options for application pool health monitoring are shown in Figure 3.15.

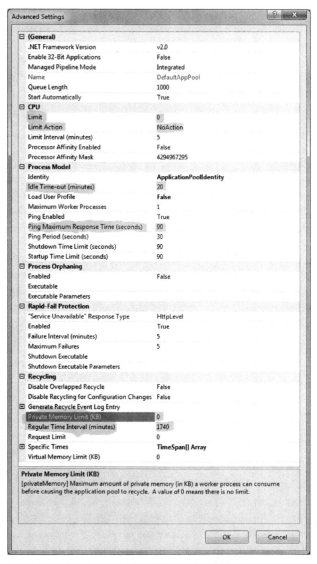

Figure 3.15: Options for application pool health monitoring.

Category: ASP.NET Applications

- **Pipeline Instance Count**
  This counter represents the number of concurrent or active requests currently in the ASP.NET pipeline. Ideally (in case of very fast requests) there should be a very low number of concurrent requests, but this is not always possible. After reaching ASP.NET concurrency limits, requests begin to be queued. If requests are not executed quickly enough, more and more requests will be added to the queue, until it becomes full and no more requests can be serviced. While this counter in itself does not indicate poorly performing requests in the pipeline, it can show a pattern in behavior at various load levels. In conjunction with the **Requests in Application Queue** counter (covered next), this can indicate at what point the system experiences too much load to efficiently handle all requests.

- **Requests in Application Queue**
  This counter represents the number of requests waiting to be added to the pipeline for processing. This counter should remain at 0 most of the time, otherwise the web server is not capable of processing requests as fast as possible. Occasional spikes are acceptable, but ongoing system usage with requests being added to the queue will eventually exhaust the web server's ability to process requests in a timely fashion. Long response times will result, eventually resulting in timeouts or **Service Unavailable** type errors.

- **Request Execution Time**
  This represents the number of milliseconds it took to execute the most recent request. The lower this figure, the faster ASP.NET is processing requests. This figure should be compared against a baseline figure when attempting to improve the performance of the application.

- **Requests/Second**
  This is the number of requests executing concurrently per second, and is effectively the throughput of the application. This counter is closely tied with the **Request Execution Time** and **Pipeline Instance Count** counters. The higher this figure, the better, as it indicates that more requests can be serviced by the application. Visual Studio Team Test provides the requests-per-second figure in the metrics in the Key Indicators graph.

Database

It should be noted that, in a very general sense, if CPU utilization and memory utilization are within acceptable bounds, then a database server is able to perform optimally.

CPU utilization should ideally be as low as possible and not exceed 50–60%. An average of 15–20% is a good optimum operating value.

Memory utilization should also remain as low as possible, ideally averaging below 50%. An average of 30% is a good figure. Memory is key for a database server's fast performance, since a database engine will generally use as much memory as possible for caching execution plans and similar items to achieve high throughput.

While the above figures are gross generalizations, many performance issues will manifest on the database server as high CPU or Memory utilization. Obviously, this does not include more subtle problems such as deadlocks, transactions, and disk I/O, which are covered later.

Remember, these counters are just good indicators. Further analysis using tracing and profiling tools may be required, and is covered in later chapters in this book, along with typical scenarios in which performance issues can arise.

Category: Physical Disk

- **Avg. Disk Queue Length**
  The physical disk subsystem on a database server is extremely important due to the I/O intensive operations that a database server performs. This counter represents the average number of read and write requests that have been queued and are yet to be fulfilled. As the number of simultaneous requests for data from the disk increases, the disk subsystem can become overloaded and unable to fulfill the requests as fast as required. The requests then become queued until the system can service the request. If the queue continues to grow, then the database server may be experiencing performance issues. Fewer requests, more efficient requests, and a faster disk subsystem can alleviate this issue.

Category: SQL Server: SQL Statistics

- **Batch Requests/Sec**
  This is the amount of effective work the database server must perform, and can roughly equate to CPU utilization. This figure is dependent on the hardware specifications of the database server. However, 1,000+ requests per second can indicate potential issues and that the server may soon begin to experience stress.

Category: SQL Server: Databases

- **Transactions/Sec**
  This counter simply represents the number of transactions the server is processing
  per second, and can be thought of as a submeasurement of the previously discussed
  Batch Requests/Sec. While not an accurate measure of the total work the server has to
  perform, this counter can provide an indication of how much relative transactional work
  is being performed when compared to the **Batch Requests/Sec** counter. Transactions are
  expensive from a performance perspective, and a high relative value may indicate a need
  to re-evaluate the isolation level and transaction policy of the application.

What do I do with all this information?

Performance testing is a very complex process, with the analysis and investigation of metric
data extremely dependent on your application's specifics and the surrounding environment.

The large variances that can occur are the reason why specific guidelines around what
to do in a given situation are very difficult to provide. In addition, it could be regarded as
irresponsible or misleading to provide specific guidance and problem resolution to a general
performance issue. This is not the aim here; my goal is to help you know where to start the
process, which can sometimes be the catalyst to finding answers. This section will therefore
attempt to provide some general guidance or clues to kick-start the analysis of performance
issues when dealing with common problems. Once experience is gained in this process,
individuals develop a general feel for the analysis process, and can begin the investigative
process with great efficiency.

- **Slow response times (TTFB) for a web application**

  - Examine the request execution time. If the request execution time is long, with
    high CPU utilization, then look at optimizing the code itself. Profiling can provide
    insight here, and is discussed in the next few chapters.

  - If request execution time is long, but CPU utilization is low, look at external
    systems such as database servers and/or web service calls. The system can be
    executing a database request or a web service and spending its time waiting for
    a response.

  - Examine the HTTP modules and handlers loaded for each request. Sometimes
    unnecessary handlers and/or modules can be configured for all requests, and will
    perform unnecessary processing as part of their default pipeline.

- **High CPU utilization**

  - This can occur for a large number of reasons and sometimes at very low load on the system. Areas to begin looking at can be:
    - CLR exceptions thrown/sec: lots of exceptions thrown can seriously hamper system performance and place extra load on the CPU.
    - % time in Jit: the Jit compilation phase can be computationally expensive. If the application is emitting any code or utilizing XML serialization assemblies, then this may be an issue. Optionally, test the code with all possible assemblies having native images generated via NGEN. Note that this counter may simply be a byproduct of the application and environment and, as such, cannot be alleviated. If attempts at alleviating this figure prove unsuccessful early in the process, then it is generally best to concentrate on other aspects.

  - Consider utilizing caching where possible, regardless of the issue. Caching is one of the single most important performance optimizations for all applications. The most efficient database query is the one that doesn't occur or use the database at all. Techniques such as Output Caching for web applications, and caching within the application itself can help CPU utilization, response time, and database performance.

    Granted, there are situations where it may not be p[ossible to use it (such as highly dynamic data) but that does not detract from its positive performance effects. Here, caching refers to either browser based, proxy caching, output caching, application level caching, or even SQL caching. This is the reason that Microsoft can support millions of users through ASP.NET site with relatively little hardware, and also the reason communities like Facebook can accommodate 350 million users. It is also the reason why systems such as memcached and Project Velocity by MSFT are so high on the priority list. (More or less as an aside, Rico Mariani and Microsoft's official best practices also support this kind of behavior.)

- **Aborted requests**

  - In a web application, this can manifest as HTTP 500 errors, and as exceptions in a desktop or service application. This can be for any number of reasons but things to look at can be:
    - SQL transactions and deadlocks: a deadlock can cause the victim query to be rejected and the request which instigated it to throw an error.
    - Downstream systems unable to handle the load: it is essential to have a good exception management policy in the application that will record external system activity and log all errors. Looking at request execution time and pipeline instance count metrics for web applications, and thread counts for service or desktop applications, can provide clues here. High values here can point to problems in this area.

- CLR Locks / Contention Rate/sec: this can indicate excessive locking in application code as threads of execution fight for resources, and often threads may abort after not acquiring those locks. At the very least, performance and throughput will be reduced.

- Exceptions in general: these should be caught and reported by the application; however, the exceptions/sec counter can provide clues if the figure is very high.

While this section has provided some clues as to what to begin investigating when performance issues are identified, there is simply nothing like deep knowledge of the application and infrastructure.

Often, developers or application architects will have a reasonable idea as to what might be causing the performance issues. Backing this up with metrics from various performance tests will enable quick and efficient identification of potential issues and, ultimately, resolution.

Conclusion

This chapter has looked at a wide range of counter and metric data related to application performance and performance tests. Initially, a set of basic metrics and indicators were examined to provide quick and immediate insight into the performance of an application, These were:

- CPU utilization

- Memory utilization

- Response time / Time to First Byte (for web applications).

Web application and database specific counters were also addressed to cover more detailed, but also indicative, counters that will provide relatively quick insights into performance issues on both web and database servers.

While far from comprehensive, these counters can provide the "at-a-glance" view of your application's performance. Once a general idea of application performance is established, the process of investigating and analyzing performance results can occur, as shown using the excellent tools available within Visual Studio.

Using Visual Studio, it is possible to discern how an application performs over time, at various load levels, utilizing a broad set of performance metrics.

The detailed look at performance counters and metrics does not cover every performance counter and metric available, and yet shows the vast possibilities and variances that can affect an application's performance. This huge number of variables is what can take an enormous amount of time in the investigation and analysis of performance issues. The detailed view, trigger points, and potential courses of action that have been discussed in this chapter should significantly reduce that investigative time.

Now that we know what we're looking for, we can get a detailed view of performance testing and metric collection. After that (Chapter 6 onwards), we'll look at more isolated forms of performance testing, such as profiling.

Following on from that will be practical advice on typical performance traps in applications, and how to overcome them. Integrating this process into the development process of software will complete the entire performance testing and analysis picture.

Chapter 4: Implementing Your Test Rig

Creating the performance test rig

So far, we have discussed the "why" and the "what" of performance testing. That is, why we do performance testing, and what metrics we can use to determine the performance of an application. This chapter will focus on the "how." Specifically, how is a performance test environment constructed so that we can record and perform performance tests?

Here, the architecture and construction of the performance rig will be discussed in detail, ranging from the test controller and test agents to the ideal network configuration to best support high volume performance testing. We will also cover performance metrics setup, collection, and automation to ensure that the metric data will be collected reliably and automatically, with the minimum of effort. This data is the most valuable output of performance testing as, without it, we cannot make any assertions and must instead resort to guesswork. Finally, we will discuss ideal environments for application profiling, and the implications that must be considered when using load balancing, i.e. whether to test first in a load-balanced environment, or to begin performance testing in a single server scenario.

It is important to note that, while profiling is an important part of determining the performance capability of an application, it is typically executed on a single workstation – more often than not, the developer's. Profiling will be discussed in greater detail later in this book but, for the most part, setting up for profiling is as simple as installing the necessary profiling tools on the workstation itself. However, the majority of this chapter will discuss the specifics of setting up a performance test rig.

Architecture and structure of a performance test rig

Being able to run high volume, effective performance tests requires more than a single workstation connected to a web server, simply executing multiple requests concurrently. When dealing with high loads, one workstation exercising a server is pretty soon going to run out of resources, whether memory, processor power, or network throughput. In addition, how are the user loads defined, what distribution of tests are run, how do we achieve high concurrent user loads for a sustained time, and how do we ensure that the network connection itself does not limit the amount of load generated against the server?

To help achieve these goals, a distributed performance test rig architecture is required. To that end, Visual Studio Team Test enables a remote workstation to connect to a dedicated controller machine. The controller manages test runs and coordinates the activities of one or more agents. The agents are actually responsible for running the tests and generating load against the desired server or servers, and they also collect data and communicate the test results back to the controller for storage and management.

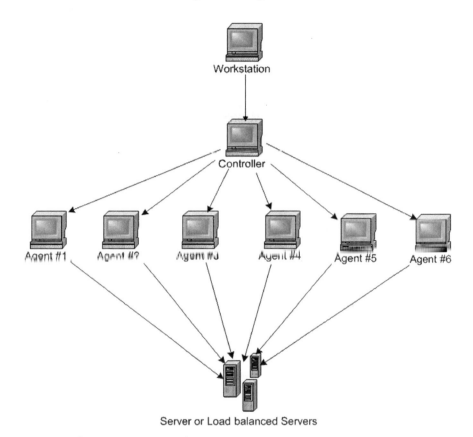

Figure 4.1: Performance test rig architecture.

Role breakdown

For now, I'll just give you a brief description of the role that each component plays in this architecture. A detailed discussion of installing, configuration, and management of each role within the system will follow later in this chapter.

Workstation

The workstation machine can be any machine with Visual Studio Team Test installed on it. Using Visual Studio Team Test, you can access a local or remote controller via the **Test** menu option, as shown in Figure 4.2.

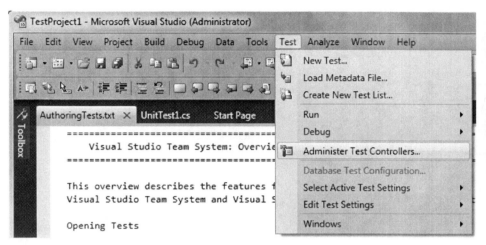

Figure 4.2: VSTS Test menu option.

Controller

The controller's role in the test rig is to coordinate the execution of the tests across multiple test agent machines, and manage the collection of results from all the test agents.

For larger-scale systems, a workstation with Visual Studio Team Test can be used to connect to a separate machine which acts as the controller; however, the workstation can also act as the controller itself. Setting up the controller involves a simple software install which will be discussed later in this chapter.

Whichever machine acts as the controller, it must have access to a SQL database. By default, SQL Express is used to store and manage test results, but a traditional SQL Server database can also be used. SQL Express has a size limit of only 4 GB so, if you anticipate going over this limit, it is obviously best to use a full-sized SQL Server.

The physical specifications of the controller machine should include a minimum of a 1.4 GHz processor and 1 GB of memory. A 2 GHz or greater processor, and 2 GB or greater of memory is relatively standard for today's workstations and is a recommended specification.

Test agent

Each test agent machine is responsible for executing the performance tests against the server, collecting the metric data for those tests, and then reporting those results back to the controller for storage and management.

When tests are scheduled for execution, the controller compiles them into assemblies and distributes these to the agents for execution. The controller manages the executing tests, ensuring that the appropriate number of concurrent users are simulated, as well as other factors and distribution details. Each agent, like the controller, requires a simple software installation, and the physical specifications of an agent machine should include a minimum of a 2 GHz processor and 1 GB of memory. Much like the controller, a 2 GHz or greater processor and 2 GB or greater of memory is relatively standard for today's workstations and is a recommended specification, although it's worth bearing in mind that memory is used heavily in agent machines, so the more the better.

Profiling system

As already mentioned, profiling an application is also an important part of assessing an application's performance and involves investigating said application at a finer-grained level than the broad approach of load testing. Because of this, profiling is the logical next step to load testing. However, it can be an intrusive operation, significantly affecting the performance of the application while it is being profiled. It can also, amongst other things, restart Internet Information Services in order to attach to profiling events to gain measurement data at a very low level.

Profiling can also be very memory- and processor-intensive, so the more memory and the better the processor, the better the profiling experience. Specific minimum requirements will depend on the profiling tool being used. For these various reasons, profiling is typically performed on a developer's workstation, as these are generally high-specification machines.

Setting up and configuration

Port setup and firewall considerations

In order to correctly install the controller and agent software on machines, certain criteria should be observed. It is important to remember that the controller and the agent are not normal user machines, and so should not contain all the security restrictions that regular organizational workstations may have. Imposing such restrictions typically restricts the type of operations that can be performed, as well as such things as what ports are open for communication. This can seriously impact the ability of the controller and agent software to install or operate correctly.

This is not to say that the coexistence of the test rig and any security restrictions cannot be achieved, but rather that it simply requires more work. That being said, sometimes diagnosing errors in this coexisting system is not trivial, and impedes the ability to even start *running* tests, let alone reliably execute them and receive results.

For these reasons, I recommend disabling firewall software on the controller and agent machines to ease setup and operational issues. Having no firewall restrictions means no possible port blockages at all, but it does also mean that these machines have no protection. This may not be an issue if they are on a separate network that is well isolated from any public networks, public access or other potential security risks, but this is not always possible. Should you decide to keep a firewall active on these machines, and selectively enable the ports required to allow communication between workstations, controllers and agents, the following list shows the default ports and protocols that need to be allowed to ensure correct setup and operation.

- **Workstation used to connect to controller**

    - File and printer sharing protocol

    - Port: 6901 (for test coordination)

- **Controller**

    - Port: 6901 (for test result collection)

- **Test agent**

    - Port: 6910 (for test distribution)

    - Ports: 137, 138, 139 (for performance counter collection).

Note

In case you're wondering, these details come from digging deep into blog posts by Ed Glass (a VSTS team member who has great, detailed content) and then verifying them experimentally.

Network segmentation/isolation

To get meaningful results from performance tests, it is important to make the metrics that you record as clear and unambiguous as possible. In order to ensure metrics are valid and unskewed, all unknown quantities and variables need to be removed from the tests.

It is often hard to determine what traffic is traversing a network, and this can affect test results. While a network may seem responsive enough to perform load testing on, when someone decides to download gigabytes-worth of data across this network, congestion can occur. Because of this, an important factor when setting up a performance rig is ensuring a clean and direct path between the agents (which execute the tests) and the server (or servers) which are the target of the performance tests.

In order to conserve hardware costs, it's often tempting to provide a single machine with a lot of memory as a controller-cum-agent machine, and to connect to the server (or servers) being tested through the regular public network, or even the corporate intranet. The problems with this approach are outlined below.

- Network throughput of a single machine could be a limiting factor when generating extremely large loads. The number of users being simulated might be 1,000 (for example), but the network interface may be saturated at the 500-user point, meaning that a true load is not being applied to the server.

- Latency, other traffic, and multiple network hops on the network path from the agent to the server may impede the speed at which data can be delivered to the server. Again, this may mean that the intended simulated load is not what is actually being delivered to the server. This may also mean that errors are generated in the tests which are not a direct effect of the load, and thus the results are colored. Latency and general traffic are a major impediment to the accurate application of load when you're attempting to generate it over a public Internet.

Note

Some organizations do offer performance testing services utilizing the general Internet and simulated browsers. They offer high load with attempts to mitigate the latency effect of the public Internet. The effectiveness of the tests themselves can only really be measured at a server level, and although the required load may simulated, this kind of testing is not as easily controlled, and a sustained high load cannot be easily guaranteed, as the amount of "interference" on the Internet may vary. This does not mean that this type of testing is ineffective, but just that repeatable and sustained testing can be difficult. Whatever your decision, the recording and analyzing of metric data recorded during these kinds of tests is the same, whichever method is employed.

The ideal scenario in which to execute tests is to have a completely separate and isolated network, as this means that there is no network interference from the corporate infrastructure or the general Internet. The amount of traffic can be strictly controlled, and the load simulated by the agents has a direct route to the servers, and, thus, a direct effect. In short, no factors outside your control can affect the simulated load and skew the results.

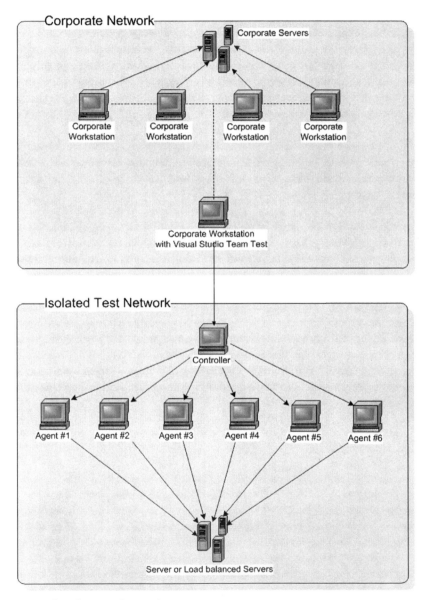

Figure 4.3: Isolated network test rig setup.

As shown in Figure 4.3, the workstation that exists in the corporate network has a direct connection to the controller machine, and so the controller is the only machine that has a path between the intranet/Internet/other network and the test network. The best way to achieve this is by using dual network interface cards (NIC); one with a direct route to the test network, and the other with a route to the intranet/Internet on which your workstation exists.

However, completely isolating a segment of your organization's network solely for performance testing is not always feasible, possible due to lack of time, money, or other resources. Remember that the goal is ultimately just to ensure a clean path from the test agents to your server or servers which are going to be tested, so that there can be no unknown elements introduced in load generation. Often, all the machines to be utilized as test agents are on the same network. Test agent machines are sometimes simply other users' workstations! To fit with this kind of infrastructure, it is common practice to install dual NICs in the machines that will act as test agents. Additionally, a simple network switch that supports the required number of ports for the test agents and server(s) can be used to create a separate network on which to run the performance tests. Figure 4.4 illustrates this.

In a dual NIC configuration, as has been described, the default configuration of agents may not work. I'll discuss this issue in detail in the Agent Setup section later in this chapter.

Test agents and controllers can be installed on almost any machine. Some of those machines can be fellow co-workers' workstations, rarely-used machines acting as file servers, etc., although these will most probably not be on an isolated network. Generating extremely high loads can require many agents, so any spare machines may be enlisted to assist. If this is your situation, then you simply need to work with what you have. The effects of a mixed test environment can be mitigated by recording results directly on the server and ensuring that the requisite load is being applied, or at least measuring the difference between simulated load at the agents and actual load at the server. I touched upon this towards the end of Chapter 3 – it simply requires a little more analysis work.

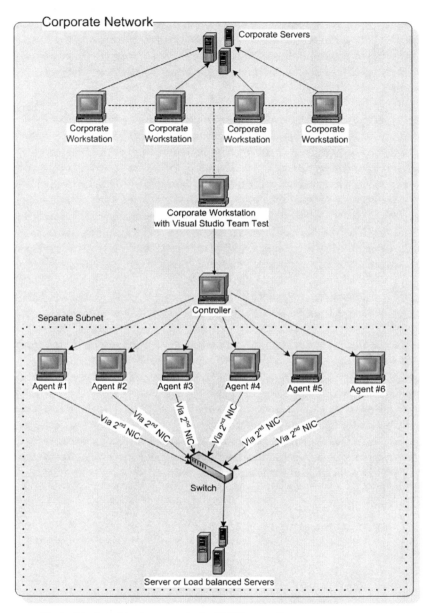

Figure 4.4: Typical isolated test segment, dual NIC setup for agents.

Controller setup

Both the controller and agent software are relatively easy to set up. It is important to install the controller software first, as the load agent software needs to be able to connect to the controller as part of the installation process.

Note

A trial version of the controller and load agent can be downloaded from the Microsoft website. The trial version can be used for 90 days from the installation date or for 25 test executions for the Load Agent.

Starting the controller installation process is a matter of executing the **setup.exe** application located on the install media. As is normal for Microsoft installations, you'll need to click **Next** through a series of screens, including a **User Experience Improvement Program** opt-in, the license agreement and specifying the destination folder for installation.

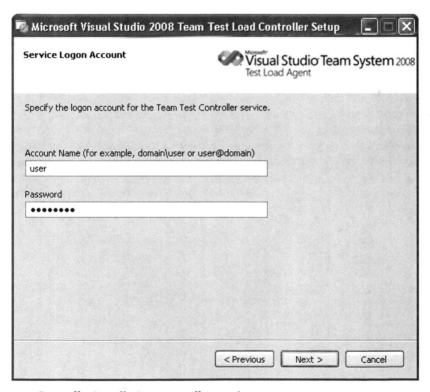

Figure 4.5: Controller installation, controller service user.

The final step prior to actually beginning the installation requires the specification of a user account which will be used to run the controller service. This can be a local user account or a domain account. It is best to ensure that this account does not have regular password expiration periods. While this is not best practice with respect to security, and most domain accounts would have this enabled, it does prevent having to re-enter the user's credentials each time the password expires.

This user must also have sufficient access privileges to be able to read performance counters from the computers under test – typically the server(s) being load tested – as that is the entire purpose of the controller.

A controller can also be running in workgroup mode, meaning that a non-domain-user is used for the controller and subsequent agents. If running in workgroup mode, there must be a local computer account on the controller which also exists on all the agents. When the agents are set up, this common user is specified as the agent service account, and so can connect to the controller successfully. However, for the security negotiation to occur successfully, the accounts must have the same username and password.

Once you've moved past all these dialogs, the actual installation should only take five to ten minutes.

Further notes on controller installation

In most typical client engagements I have been involved in, the workstation and the controller have been the same machine. This is generally due to the cost of an extra controller-specific machine and, most importantly, the extra effort it takes to connect to the controller from a workstation machine. The tangle of issues surrounding user access privileges, or matching up users on the controller and agents, means that making the controller and workstation the same machine is a common scenario. This setup is made more attractive by the fact that the controller only coordinates tests and does not need excessive resources to run.

Once the controller setup is complete, there are three new groups created on the controller machine. These are:

• TeamTestControllerAdmins

• TeamTestControllerUsers

• TeamTestAgentService.

If a workstation machine needs to connect to the controller, the user context being used must be a member of the TeamTestControllerUsers group.

Note

Any workstation, controller or agents that are participating in the test rig must all be on the same version of Visual Studio, right down to the Service Packs.

After the controller is installed, access to it is limited to the TeamTestControllerUsers and TeamTestControllerAdmins groups that were created during setup, and to the Administrators group. Add appropriate users and/or groups to one of these groups to allow them to access the controller. Members of the TeamTestControllerAdmins group or the Administrators group can administer the controller by clicking the **Test** menu in Visual Studio, and then choosing **Administer Test Controller**. Bear in mind that members of the TeamTestControllerAdmins group must also be power users or administrators on the controller computer.

In order for agents to connect to the controller, they must be members of the TeamTestControllerUsers group at the very least. Normally the user is added to this group during the agent installation process. However, there may be instances where you change users on the agent manually, thus you need to ensure this alternate user is also in the appropriate group on the controller.

Creating the load test database

When the controller is installed, a database is created to hold all the performance metrics and recorded results. Wherever this database is located, be it on another database server, or on some other instance other than the default, it *must* have the correct schema. To that end, when the controller software is installed, a SQL script file is also installed which can recreate the load test database with the correct schema and everything required to hold the performance test results. By default, this script is located at:
C:\Program Files (x86)\Microsoft Visual Studio 9.0 Team Test Load Agent\LoadTest\ loadtestresultsrepository.sql.

By executing this file against a database, typically using a tool such as SQL Management Studio, a new database called **LoadTest** is created and is ready to be used as the repository for performance test results.

Guest policy on Windows XP in workgroup mode

Finally, if the controller software has been installed on a Windows XP machine in a workgroup environment, then Windows XP will have the **ForceGuest** policy setting enabled by default. This means that any time a remote user wishes to connect to this machine, it will only be allowed to connect as the **Guest** user. So, no matter which user the agent is configured to use when connecting to this controller, it will be forced to connect as the **Guest** user, which has very minimal security privileges.

The fix for this is not entirely straightforward, but not very difficult either. To disable the **ForceGuest** policy in Windows XP:

* Run the **Registry Editor** (open the **Run** dialog, type *RegEdit* and press **Enter**).

* Navigate to the key: HKEY_LOCAL_MACHINE\SYSTEM\CurrentControlSet\Control\ Lsa.

* Double-click on the **ForceGuest** item and change the value in the presented dialog from 1 to 0.

* Click **OK**, and you're done.

Note

This process should be performed on the controller as well as all agents, otherwise you may find your agents listed in the controller agent list, but they remain disconnected or offline. Any error mentioning that the server rejected the client's credentials is indicative of this problem.

Agent setup

Starting the agent installation process is also just a matter of executing the **setup.exe** application located on the install media. You will be presented with the same screen as shown in the controller setup, albeit with some different text. As with the controller setup, you will just need to move through the various screens until you reach the point at which you need to specify a user account under which to run the **Test Agent Service** process.

This is where it is important to have defined an appropriate test agent user on the controller machine so that, when the installation process executes, the test agent machine can connect successfully with the controller.

The next step in the installation is different from the controller setup, in that the user is asked which controller to connect to. Completing this process adds the user to the appropriate groups on the controller (if required) as well as setting up the user on the local agent machine.

Once the controller is specified, the installation process proceeds in exactly the same fashion as the controller setup.

Workstation setup

The workstation that is used to connect to the controller can, in fact, be the controller machine itself. Having separate machines for the controller and the connecting workstation is preferable, so that when the controller is busy coordinating tests and collecting data, the responsiveness and performance of the workstation remains unaffected.

Whether the controller is on the same machine or a separate machine, to connect to it from within Visual Studio, simply select the **Test** menu option, and then the + menu option.

This will present the dialog in Figure 4.6.

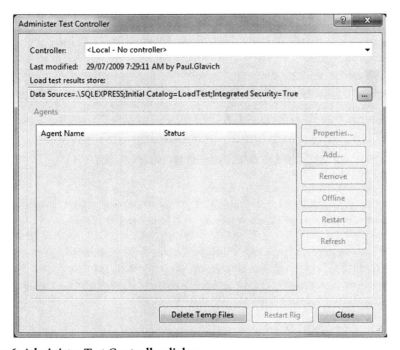

Figure 4.6: Administer Test Controller dialog.

As you can see in Figure 4.6, the default controller is listed as **<Local – No controller>**. The local machine is the default controller, but the controller software has not been installed. Entering the correct machine name or IP address in this text field will connect to the controller and list any test agents registered with that controller. The dialog should then update to list the number of agents installed and connected to the controller, and their current status.

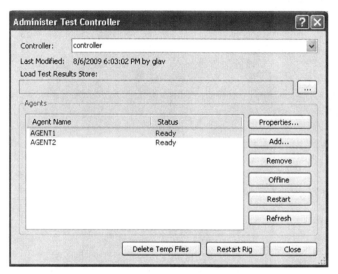

Figure 4.7: Administer Test Controller showing multiple agents connected.

Note that, if you have installed the controller software on your workstation, then invoking the dialog shown in Figure 4.7 will automatically connect to the local controller and display any agents already connected.

Troubleshooting the controller and agents

Getting all the components in a test rig to talk to each other nicely is often not an easy task, and things will sometimes not work for seemingly non-existent reasons.

When both the controller and agents are installed, there are certain settings within each configuration that can help in diagnosing issues. Since the issues can be numerous and very environment-specific it would be impossible to list them all; however, I can provide some knowledge on the techniques to find out what the issues are.

Both the controller and agents utilize settings from their respective configuration files, which reside in the same directory as the controller and load agent respectively.

By default, the **Load Test Agent** configuration file is located in a directory such as:

For VSTS 2005: **<Program Files>\Microsoft Visual Studio 2005 Team Test Load Agent\ LoadTest\QTAgentService.exe.config**

For VSTS 2008: **<Program Files>\Microsoft Visual Studio 9.0 Team Test Load Agent\ LoadTest\QTAgentService.exe.config**

The QTAgentService.exe.config file contains the configuration of the agent.

Similarly, for the controller, the default location of the configuration file is:

For VSTS 2005: **<Program Files>\Microsoft Visual Studio 2005 Team Test Load Agent\ LoadTest\QTController.exe.config**

For VSTS 2008: **<Program Files>\Microsoft Visual Studio 9.0 Team Test Load Agent\ LoadTest\QTController.exe.config**

And the QTController.exe.config file contains the configuration of the controller.

The controller and agent configuration files are almost identical in their settings. Both contain appSettings and system.diagnostics sections that define the specific settings, and on default installation look similar to this:

```
<system.diagnostics>
  <switches>
    <!-- You must use integral values for "value".
         Use 0 for off, 1 for error, 2 for warn, 3 for info,
and 4 for verbose. -->
    <add name="EqtTraceLevel" value="3" />
  </switches>
</system.diagnostics>  <appSettings>
    <add key="LogSizeLimitInMegs" value="20"/>
    <add key="AgentConnectionTimeoutInSeconds" value="120"/>
    <add key="AgentSyncTimeoutInSeconds" value="300"/>
    <add key="ControllerServicePort" value="6901"/>
    <add key="ControllerUsersGroup" value="TeamTestControllerUse
rs"/>
    <add key="ControllerAdminsGroup" value="TeamTestControllerAdm
ins"/>
    <add key="CreateTraceListener" value="no"/>
  </appSettings>
```

In order to enable trace logging for either the controller or the agent, change the following settings in the configuration file:

- In the `appSettings` section, set the **CreateTraceListener** value to **yes**.

- In the `system.diagnostics` section, set the **EqtTraceLevel** to **4**.

The respective services will need to be restarted before any changes will take effect. A log file will then be produced in the same directory as the configuration file, and will be named `VSTTAgent.log` for the test agent and `VSTTController.log` for the controller.

With logging enabled, exhaustive detail will be written to the log file, providing very fine-grained insight into what is happening and why a problem may be occurring. By default, the **LogSizeLimitInMegs** setting limits the log file size to 20 megabytes, which is sufficient for most purposes. If this limit is reached, a new log file will created and named in numerical sequence. Setting the **LogSizeLimitInMegs** value to 0 allows unbounded log file size, limited only by the available disk space.

Note

*A tool called **DebugView** can be used to show logged data without actually writing to a file, or having to monitor and refresh the log file's content. The tool is a free download from* HTTP://TINYURL.COM/MSDEBUGVIEW. *By simply setting the **EqtTraceLevel** to 4 in the* `appSettings` *section in the configuration file, log information will be captured by* **DebugView** *and displayed immediately in a separate window.*

As already discussed earlier, often either controllers or test agents will be set up in a dual NIC configuration (dual Network Interface cards). In this instance, the controller/agent needs to know which network card to use to communicate with the rest of the test rig. In order to specify this, you can add the `BindTo` configuration value to the configuration file, and specify the IP address of the network card to use. For example, adding the following line to the `appSettings` section of a configuration file will tell the controller/agent to communicate on the network interface card with the IP address, 192.168.1.10:

```
<add key="BindTo" value="192.168.1.10" />
```

If this value is omitted, then this could quickly result in problems with the agent connecting to the controller or vice versa.

When dealing with issues specific to the test agents, you can also use the provided command-line tool to configure various aspects of the agents. The command-line tool is named **AgentConfigUtil.exe**, and exists in the same directory as the agent executable and configuration file mentioned earlier. To use this tool, open a command prompt and navigate to the load agent installation directory (by default this is **C:\Program Files\Microsoft Visual Studio 9.0 Team Test Load Agent\LoadTest**) Type *AgentConfigUtil* and press **Enter**, and you will see a display of available commands.

```
C:\Program Files\Microsoft Visual Studio 9.0 Team Test Load
Agent\LoadTest>AgentConfigUtil.exe

Microsoft (R) Visual Studio Test Rig Command Line Tool Version
9.0.21022.8
Copyright (c) Microsoft Corporation. All rights reserved.
```

Usage:	AgentConfigUtil [options]
Description:	Used to perform test rig configuration operations.
Options:	
/help	Displays this usage message (short form: /? or /h).
/nologo	Do not display the startup banner and copyright message.
/nolog	Do not create setup log.
/unregister	Removes the agent's registration from the specified controller.
/controller:controllername[:port]	Displays the test controller name and port number [optional].
/controllerusername:[domain\]username	Domain and user name for connecting to the controller.
/controlleruserpassword:password	Password for connecting to the controller.
/agentserviceusername:[domain\]username	Domain and user name for the AgentServiceUser account.
/agentserviceuserpassword:password	Password for the AgentServiceUser account.

For example, using this tool, you can instruct the agent to re-register with the controller, specifying the controller machine name, port number, username, and password to use. Alternatively, you can unregister an agent from the controller. For example, to remove an agent from a controller called **TestController**, you would enter this command:

```
AgentConfigUtil /controller:TestController /unregister
```

Alternatively, to add an agent to a controller named **TestController** using port 6901, the command would be:

```
AgentConfigUtil /controller:TestController:6901
```

Setting up performance counter collection

When Visual Studio Team Test executes a load test, there are a number of metrics that are collected by default from test agents and the server(s) being tested. These are usually sufficient for most general purposes. What counters to record and their respective meaning was covered in Chapter 3. For now, we know that we can collect performance data from the agents and servers, and have those metrics recorded within the database that the controller is configured to use as a repository.

However, this only provides one location where data can be recorded. It is also important to record performance data directly onto the servers being tested where possible.

Before we discuss *how* to do this, let's discuss *why* we should. There are a few important reasons why you would also want to record performance metrics on each server being tested, even though this may seem somewhat redundant. The reasons include those below.

- In a few rare circumstances, performance data is not recorded to the controller's data store, possibly because of system problems on the controller, disk space, etc. While in some circumstances, the data is recoverable (this will be shown later), often it is not. Not being able to get the recorded data is the same as not running the test at all. As previously mentioned, performance testing is a relatively expensive operation, and having data recorded on each server ensures you have an alternative copy of this pricy data.

- If there are multiple servers being used in the load test, you can determine if certain servers are experiencing more stress than others. This could be for a variety of reasons, including load balancing configuration and system specification. Either way, ensuring that the load is evenly distributed is important. If one server has to handle substantially more load than others, then the ability of the entire system to handle the load will be determined by this particular server. Additionally, being able to measure the performance on individual servers means that tuning the configuration of a load balancer and observing the effects becomes a lot easier.

- Occasionally, a test agent may not send performance data to the controller for recording. When a test agent is under stress (due to lack of memory or processor capacity, for example), its data may not be able to be collected by the controller. This may appear as gaps in the visual graph that Visual Studio presents for visualizing the performance data. To be able to verify that load was still being generated during this period, or to validate other metrics not apparent in the Visual Studio visualization, the secondary performance data recorded on the servers can be used.

- Many individuals or teams may wish to analyze the performance data. This data may need to be sent to external parties for analysis. Other interested parties may not have access to the visualizations and analytical facilities provided by Visual Studio Team Test. Recording data at the server level, using commonly available tools ensures that performance data can be viewed and analyzed by anyone who requires it.

It is not strictly necessary to record performance data at the server in addition to using Visual Studio Team Test, but the cost of doing so is quite low. Given that performance testing is an expensive process, it is a worthwhile investment to be able to record the performance metrics on the server(s) as an alternative location for data storage.

One important component that needs to be looked at more closely in load testing is the database. Using PerfMon to record performance data on the database is extremely important, as the database plays such a crucial role in the majority of applications today. Having a set of recorded performance data on the database machine itself will allow individuals such as dedicated database administrators to examine said data and provide valuable insights into the performance of the database. Even if no other data is recorded via PerfMon on the web or application servers, then it is recommended that the database should have PerfMon recording SQL-specific performance metrics (along with standard counters such as CPU utilization).

You can set up recording performance metrics on the server(s) themselves using a tool called "Performance Monitor" which is available on all versions of Windows from XP to Server 2008. Performance Monitor will allow you to specify and record WMI counters, either to a file or to the database.

Note

Visual Studio uses a mechanism called WMI – Windows Management Instrumentation Counters to query and collect data.

To use this tool, select the **Start** menu, go to **Administrative Tools**, and select **Performance Monitor**. Alternatively, open the **Run** dialog and type *PerfMon*. The user interface looks a little different on Vista / Windows 7 / Server 2008 from how it does on older operating systems, but the functionality is very similar. You will be presented with a screen similar to that shown in Figure 4.8.

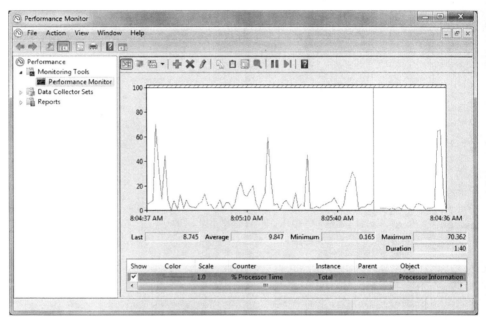

Figure 4.8: Performance Monitor on Vista / Windows 7 / Server 2008.

This initial view presents a real-time view of the currently selected performance metrics. By default, these metrics are **% of processor time**, **available memory** and **average disk queue length**. There are a huge number of performance counters that are available to monitor, and many products add extra counters (specific to their respective technology) to the list when they are installed. SQL Server or Windows Communication Foundation are examples of such products.

Adding counters to the monitoring instance is a simple process. Clicking the **Add** icon will display a dialog of counter categories and their associated counters that can be added from there.

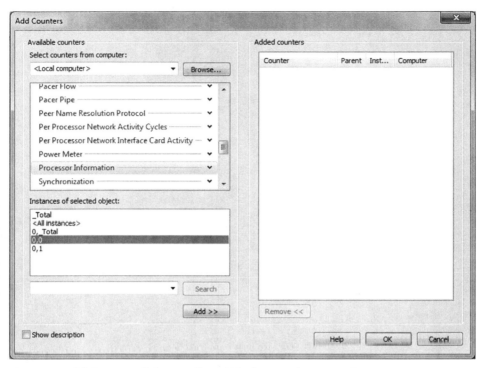

Figure 4.9: Add Counters dialog on Vista / Windows 7 / Server 2008.

Selecting a counter category will show the individual counters that can be selected and added. Multiple individual counters can be selected and added and, if you like, an entire category can be selected and added, with all the counters in that category added to the display.

You can obtain a brief description about each counter before adding it, by selecting the **Show Description** option (**Explain** in Windows XP/2000/2003). The dialog should look similar to the one in Figure 4.10.

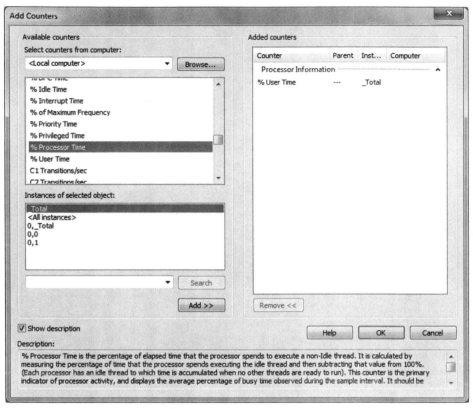

Figure 4.10: Add Counters dialog, "Show description" check box is selected in the lower left of the window.

The initial display of the performance monitor shows a real-time view of the system with the counters being measured shown in the display. Data can be recorded either to disk or to a database, and recorded performance data can be reloaded, viewed, and analyzed using this tool. This process, in addition to the range of counters and their meaning, was detailed in Chapter 3.

Conclusion

In this chapter, we looked at how to set up a performance testing rig. It is essential that this fundamental piece of infrastructure be set up correctly, otherwise we risk invalidating test results, and wasting considerable time and money in the process.

With a fully functional test rig, we are now able to record, execute, and analyze our performance tests. The test rig, once set up, can form an important facet of an organization's overall infrastructure. Setting up the rig is typically a one-time process that can be utilized for multiple projects, and which provides ongoing benefits.

The next chapter will focus on the recording, creation and automation of performance tests, as well as defining the load tests themselves. Later chapters will deal with the execution and analysis of the tests.

Now that we have built our new toy, it's time to play with it.

Chapter 5: Creating Performance Tests

Having a performance test rig is not very useful if you don't have any tests to execute with it. Creating tests is a relatively easy task, but it is important to have the functional path breakdown that was mentioned in Chapter 2. This way, there is a defined path to execute when recording the tests.

Basic solution structure

To start with, we need to create a separate project to house the performance tests. This can be added to the same solution that houses the main project and source code of your application, but it is best to place the performance test project in a project outside the main source code branch. This will prevent the main source code tree from being affected by the extra build time it takes to compile the performance test project, and will also keep the test outside the view of the main development team. It is a completely independent project that has no dependencies on the main project or solution being tested.

With this in mind, create a new test project in Visual Studio by opening the **File** menu, selecting the **New Project** menu option, then the **Test** project type, then selecting **Test Project** in the project template window. Name the project *PerfTests*, select a directory location and click **OK**.

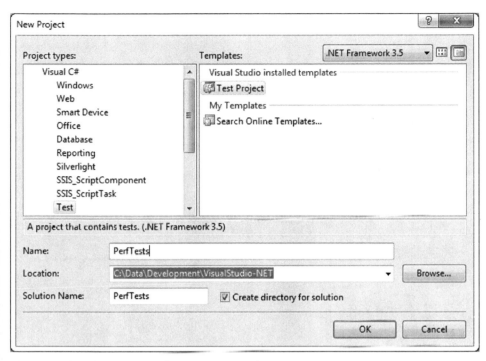

Figure 5.1: Creating a new performance test project.

Once you have performed this step, you should end up with a solution looking similar to Figure 5.2.

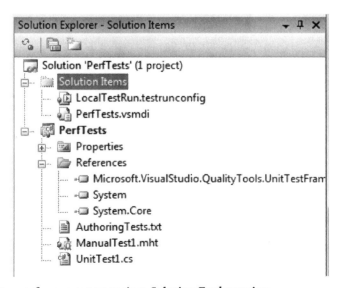

Figure 5.2: New performance test project, Solution Explorer view.

Note the presence of the **AuthoringTests.txt** and **ManualTest1.mht** files. The former provides general information around testing, and the latter provides a template for manual tests to be written. For the purposes of performance testing, these files can be safely deleted from the project. We can also remove the **UnitTest1.cs** file, as it does not apply to load tests.

In the solution items folder, the **LocalTestRun.testrunconfig** file holds general settings for the test run, such as which controller to use, test run naming schemes, deployment requirements and so on. These items can be edited by opening the **Test** menu, selecting the **Edit Test Run Configurations** option, and then selecting the test run configuration file.

There is currently only one configuration, but you can have several. Selecting this option displays a configuration dialog.

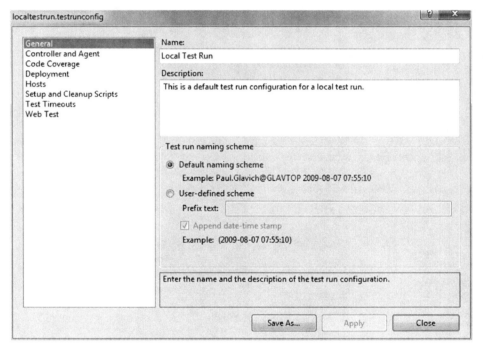

Figure 5.3: Test Run Configuration dialog.

For basic tests, these options can be left at defaults; but I'll cover these in more detail a little later.

Recording the web tests

The functional test breakdown and how it should be structured were discussed in previous chapters. When recording tests, the functional breakdown is used to determine what tests to record and what functions to exercise when recording them.

In order to be able to record a test, the machine used to do the recording must clearly be able to access the web application being tested. When a test is recorded, an instance of Internet Explorer is automatically launched by Visual Studio. While browsing using the newly launched instance of Internet Explorer, all web activity is recorded. This includes all browsing activity, not just those requests targeted at your application. This is why it is important to have a clear functional path, and only exercise singular aspects of the application at any given time. This way, the individual tests can be executed, recorded, and later attributed to the appropriate aspects of the application. When the tests are replayed, they are applied to the overall run according to what percentage of activity is set up within the test run (this will be detailed in later in this chapter). If you record too much activity in a single test, it becomes very hard to accurately allocate functional activity within the run. It then becomes very difficult to simulate the desired user behavior (and therefore the expected load) when spreading tests across a load test run.

To start recording a test, right-click the test project and select either the **Add > New Test** or the **Test > New Test** menu option (see Figure 5.4).

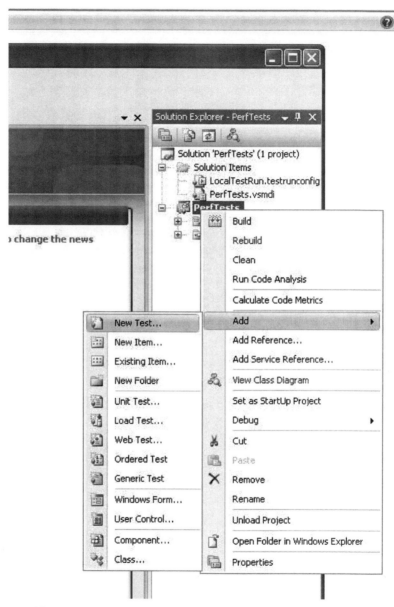

Figure 5.4: Add New Test option.

Bear in mind that Visual Studio Team Test is the minimum requirement installation in order for the Web Test option to be available. Once the **New Test** option is selected, a dialog allowing the user to select what type of test to add is presented. Selecting **Web Test** (Figure 5.5) will launch an instance of Internet Explorer and invite the user to begin navigating the site.

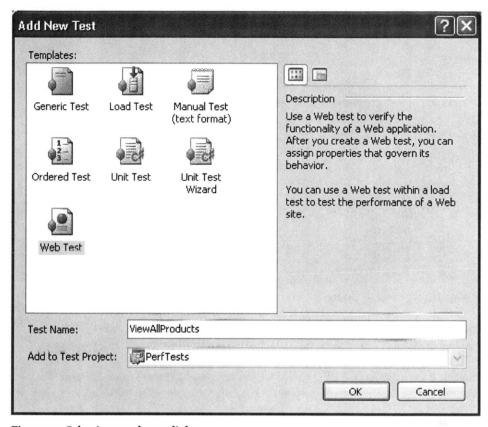

Figure 5.5: Selecting a web test dialog.

Once the test name is entered and you've clicked **OK**, the Internet Explorer instance is opened, and all actions are recorded as part of the web test. It is important to note that, if a particular home page is set, then accessing this home page will also be recorded, even if it has nothing to do with testing the application itself. It is best to set the Internet Explorer home page to a blank page so that no requests are recorded that do not pertain to the application being tested.

Once Internet Explorer is launched, start navigating the site in line with the functional area being tested. A web test of my own sample application can be seen in Figure 5.6.

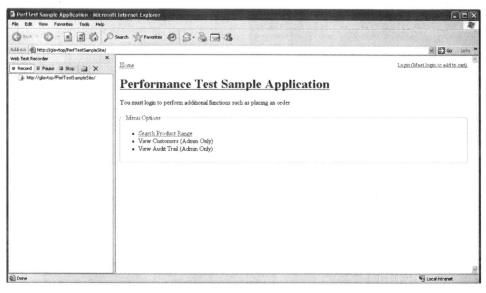

Figure 5.6: Recording a web test.

On the left side of the Internet Explorer window is a pane showing the currently recorded web test actions. As you navigate the site, each request or post will be listed in this pane.

Continue using the site according to the functional aspect being exercised and, once you have completed recording the necessary series of actions, close down the instance of Internet Explorer. Visual Studio will add the recorded **get** and **post** actions as part of the web test as shown in Figure 5.7.

Note

Be sure to name your tests appropriately. Good organization will make it easy to set up the appropriate weighting for the tests once recorded. Having tests named **Web test1**, **Web test2**, *etc., means you'll need to actually go into the test, and perhaps run it, to find out what aspect of functionality the test exercises. Instead, name your tests verbosely, such as* **LoginAndViewAllProducts**, *or* **LoginViewCartThenLogout**.

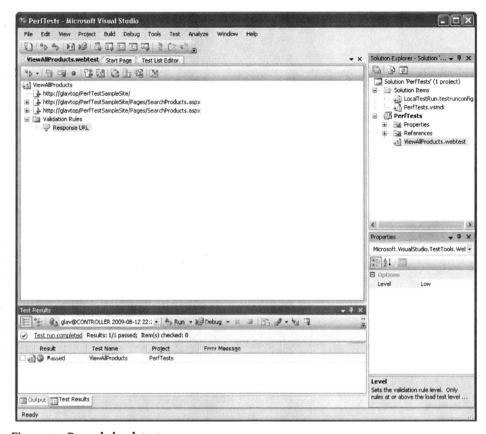

Figure 5.7: Recorded web test.

The web test actions are listed sequentially according to the URL accessed for that particular request. If a request has other elements to it, such as query string parameters, post parameters, or hidden fields, then these are associated with that request, and can be seen by expanding the request tree view. Clicking or selecting on the requests will display their properties in Visual Studio's properties windows.

106

Figure 5.8: Expanded web test request.

Figure 5.8 shows various form post parameters such as an **ASP.NET** viewstate and other parameter values forming part of the **POST** payload of the request, all of which are easily visible.

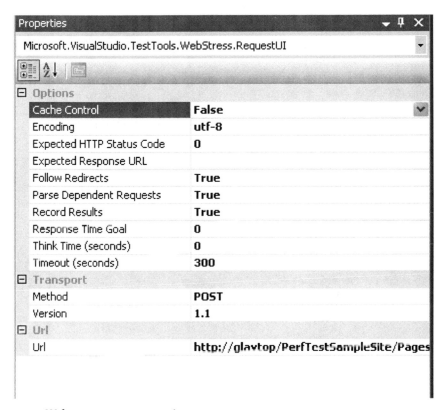

Figure 5.9: Web test request properties.

Figure 5.9 shows some common properties of all web test requests, together with values specific to this example request. Each request can have these properties modified to achieve different effects within the overall test, and potentially pass or fail a particular test.

- **Cache Control** and **Encoding** are relatively self-explanatory. Cache Control determines whether the request can be cached, and Encoding refers to the character encoding used for the request itself.

- **Method** and **Version** refer to the specific HTTP properties of the request.

On the other hand, the properties that affect the pass or fail status of a single request are:

- **Expected HTTP Status Code**
  Determines what the expected status code of a result of issuing this request should be. This is a standard HTTP status code, such as 404 for "Not Found." Leaving this value as 0 means default browsing behavior will be used which, in turn, means that any 200 or 300 level code indicates a successful request, but any 400 or 500 level code indicates a failure.

- **Expected Response URL**
  Indicates what the response or returned URL is after issuing this request. A blank value will not expect any particular URL but, if one is entered and a different URL is returned, this indicates a test failure.

- **Response Time Goal**
  Indicates the maximum time (in seconds) that this request should take to execute. If the request exceeds this time, then the test is deemed failed. No value for this indicates no expected or maximum response time.

- **Timeout (seconds)**
  Indicates the maximum amount of time (in seconds) that this request can take to execute.

Note

Test failures do not stop performance tests from running, but simply add to the metric or total data for failed tests.

The **Parse Dependent Requests** property is interesting, because it determines whether any further requests which would be typically required to satisfy this request in a real world scenario are made as a result of issuing the web test request. For example, stylesheets, images and script files are often requested by a browser after an initial request to the resource is made and the HTML has been parsed. Web tests will simulate this behavior by default as these are considered dependent requests.

However, in some cases you may want to disable the parsing of dependent requests to enable you to test only the processing efficiency of the web application, and not rely on possible latent connections for resources not directly affecting this performance. For example, if a page makes requests to external parties, such as Google, to request JavaScript files, or to a marketing company providing analytics for the site, then you may want to remove these requests from performance testing and only concentrate on your application. Obviously, these requests still affect the overall perceived performance of the request itself, but you may have little control over them, and not want to skew the measurements of your application's performance with these figures. If you're feeling really fine-grained, it may be useful to isolate each aspect of the request to further analyze what are the limiting factors.

Record Results indicates whether results for this request are recorded in the database. If this request is of no interest to you, then perhaps you may not wish to record any data about it, thus minimizing noise within the results.

Overall, the default settings for web test requests attempt to mimic the default browser behavior. Initially at least, it is best to leave these settings as is, though, during the course of performance test analysis, further investigation may require experimentation with them. This will be discussed later in the book when we look at performance load test metrics and iterative testing approaches.

Test replay

So now we have some tests. We can easily replay these by double-clicking them in the solution explorer to display them in the main window, and then selecting a **Run** option from the **Run** menu. The **Run/Play** menu is located in the top left of the main display window.

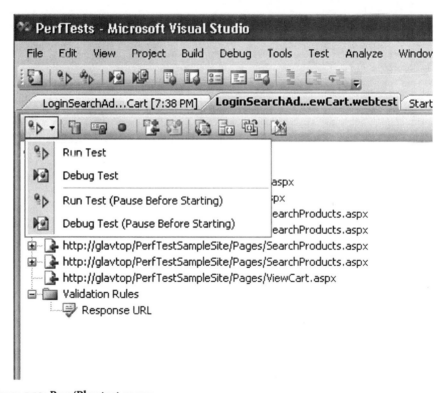

Figure 5.10: Run/Play test menu.

The menu shown in Figure 5.10, shows both the **Run** and **Debug** execution modes for replaying a test. **Debug** mode provides the ability to step through each request, examining the value of variables just as you would a normal .NET application. The options with **(Pause Before Starting)** against them will prepare to run the test, but will pause just before beginning execution, allowing you to step through each request using the **Step** menu option located to the right of the **Run** button. Also to the right, in order, are the **Pause** and **Stop** test options.

Once a test has been run, the status will be displayed in the **Test Result**s window, as well as in the top left window of the test results main window.

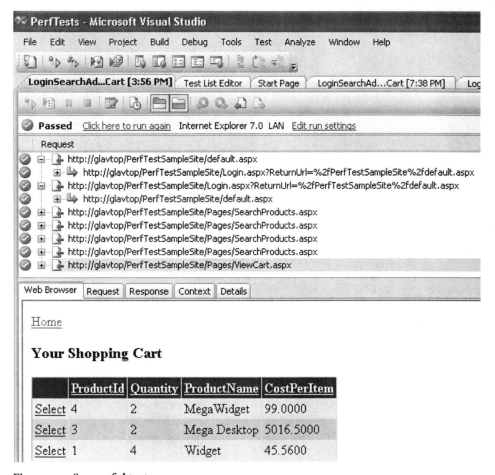

Figure 5.11: Successful test run.

Whether the test has run successfully or not, you can now examine each request in detail. Selecting a request will display its particular results in the **Web Browser** tab shown just below the test results in Figure 5.11. In addition, you can expand the main request to show any dependent requests, and selecting a dependent request also shows its results.

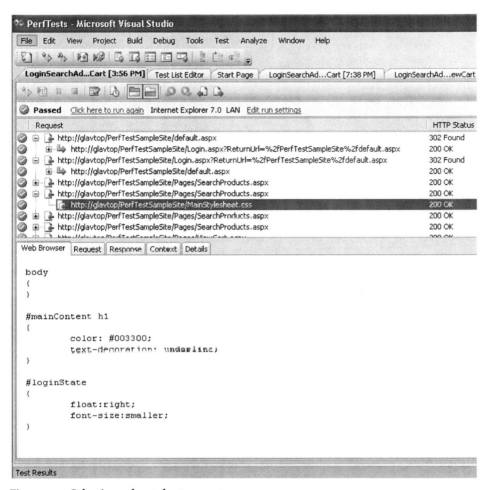

Figure 5.12: Selecting a dependent request.

In the example in Figure 5.12, we can see that the dependent request was a CSS file. To the right of the **Web Browser** tab are the **Request** and **Response** tabs.

Figure 5.13: Web test Request tab.

The **Request** tab (Figure 5.13) allows you to examine individual header elements in a formatted, table-like display, or you can view the raw request by selecting the **Show raw data** check box in the bottom left-hand corner.

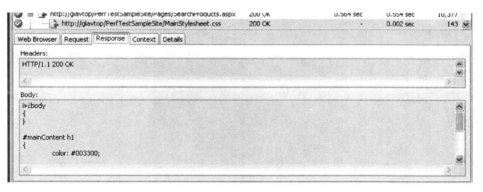

Figure 5.14: Web test Response tab.

The **Response** tab (Figure 5.14) shows the response to the selected request, with the information segregated to display the Headers and Body responses in separate fields.

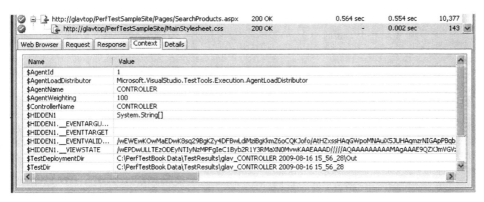

Figure 5.15: Web test Context tab.

The **Context** tab shows any contextual information related to the current request. This typically involves hidden fields in the request, test agent ID, environment variables such as test directory, deployment directory, and other elements depending on the request itself.

The **Details** tab lists any validation or extraction rules that have been applied to the test. Extraction rules are custom actions designed to extract data from a test response and assign it to a variable. Many of these are added by default to requests by the Visual Studio test engine when the test is recorded.

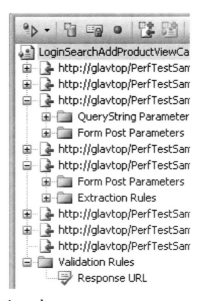

Figure 5.16: Web test validation rule.

Validation rules will cause a test to pass or fail based on an expected value within the test. By default, a **Response URL** validation rule is added to the last request of each test as shown in Figure 5.16.

Selecting the last request and then selecting the **Context** tab shows the result of the validation rule.

When a test is recorded, the explicit URL is recorded along with it. Sometimes, you may be recording the test against a development server, but wish to replay the test against a different server, perhaps a UAT (User Acceptance Test) server. It would be very time consuming to have to alter the URL of each request to reflect this. It would be nice to have a way of assigning a variable to the URL and have Visual Studio use this when replaying tests.

Fortunately, there is direct support for this via the **Parameterize Web Servers** option, which is found in the web test toolbar.

Figure 5.17: Parameterize Web Servers option.

Clicking this button will display a dialog allowing you to specify the variable name assigned to the web server address. By default, this is **WebServer1**.

Clicking the **Change** button will allow you to alter the name of the variable. If there were more than one server detected as part of the whole test, for example, if an HTTPS address were also used, and any other addresses as part of the test, they would be listed here.

Enter a name for the server you are targeting. This will then replace all the explicit URLs with a dynamic variable name according to what you have entered.

Once the explicit server address has been substituted with a context variable, changing the server address for all requests is then just a matter of altering the value of that context variable. Clicking on the same **Parameterize Web Servers** button will allow you to specify a different server.

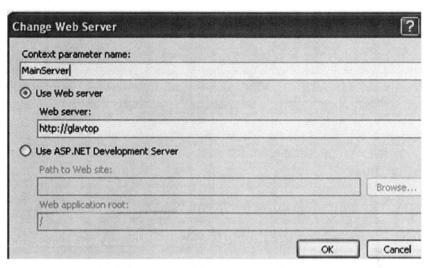

Figure 5.18: Assigning a web server a variable name in a web test.

Once you have assigned a name to the server address, all explicit references to that address will be replaced by a context variable with the name you have specified. The test will be altered accordingly,

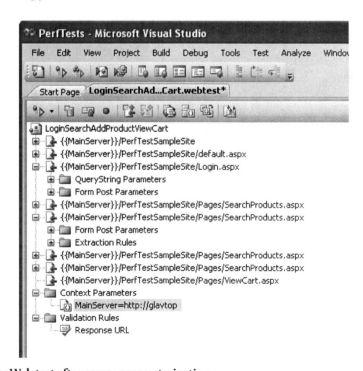

Figure 5.19: Web test after server parameterization.

116

Data binding web tests

Now that we have recorded our web tests, we would like to make them resilient enough to be played over and over again. In addition, we would like to introduce a random factor that ensures a different element is introduced for each web test, just like in real life.

A good example of this is a user login. We don't want one single user acting as the basis for all of the web tests. Ideally, a wide range of users is required to better simulate the expected user activity on a real site.

In order to do this, we first need a data source to be used as the source for our users within the test. Visual Studio supports a database, CSV file, or XML file as the basis for a data source. It expects a simplistic structure for the data source and simply extracts the data within either the database table, CSV file, or XML file as it is presented. This means that all columns in the table and CSV file are used, and all elements within the XML file are used.

When creating the data source, it is best to keep things relatively simple. For our username and password data source, we will utilize a CSV file, which can be created with Microsoft Excel or any text editor.

Creating a data source for data binding

Let's start by creating a simple CSV file to provide a number of usernames and passwords to log in to our site. In Visual Studio, open the **File** menu, click on the **New File** menu option, select **Text File** from the dialog displayed, and select **Open**.

Enter the column headings *Username* and *Password*, separated by a comma. Next, enter a separate username and password, separated by a comma, on each line of the file. The file should look similar to this:

```
Username,Password

admin,password

test,password

viewer,password
```

Save this file within the same directory as your performance test project.

You will probably want the file to be included as part of your test project so that it is included with source control and forms a component of the project as a whole. This is not strictly necessary, but makes sense and allows better organization of your test projects.

In your test project, ensure the web test that you would like to add a data source to is opened in the main window, and click the **Add Data Source** toolbox button.

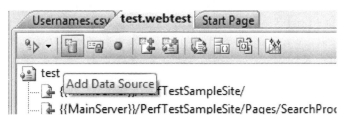

Figure 5.20: Add Data Source button.

A dialog is presented where you can specify the data source type and name. For our example, we will select the **CSV** file option and name the data source, appropriately enough, *UsernamesDataSource*.

Next, we choose the file that will actually be used as our data source. Either by browsing or by specifying the file path, select the data-source file you have created.

Visual Studio will parse the file, determine what data is present, and display it in the dialog window. Click the **Finish** button to add the data source to your web test. You should now see a **Data Sources** node within your web test, listing the data source you have just added, as in Figure 5.21.

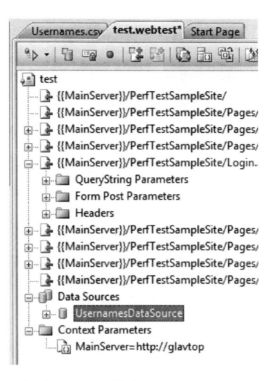

Figure 5.21: Web test with a data source added.

This data source can now be utilized within the test itself. In this case, we will use the usernames and passwords contained in the file to feed into the web test. First, expand the test action that requests the **login.aspx** page.

Figure 5.22: Expanded login test action showing form parameters.

This request will contain some form post parameters which the page will post to the server to log in. Currently, the values are assigned to exactly what was typed when the web test was recorded. Select the **Username** parameter and switch to the **Properties** window.

Properties	
Microsoft.VisualStudio.TestTools.WebStress.FormPostParame ▾	
Name	ctl02$UserName
Recorded Value	
URL Encode	True
Value	admin

Figure 5.23: Properties window displayed for Username parameter.

The **Value** property contains the value of the form parameter. Clicking in the **Value** property field will present a drop-down box, which you should expand to show the values which are options for this parameter. One of the options is the data source that was previously added.

Expand this node, and also expand the data source that we added. This should display the fields within that data source, which we can use to data bind to the form parameter.

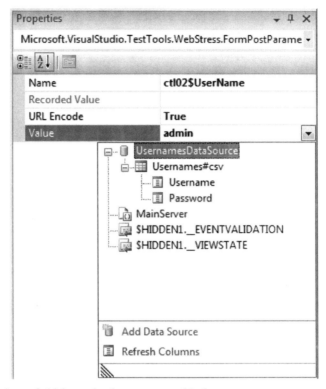

Figure 5.24: Select a field from the data source to bind to.

Select the appropriate field to data bind to the form parameter; in this example, the **Username** field. This binding will be reflected in the Properties window as well as in the web test action parameter.

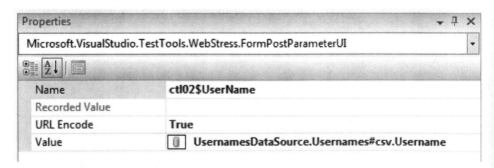

Figure 5.25: Data bound form parameter Properties window.

Now, each time this test is executed, the **Username** form parameter will be populated from the data source. By default, Visual Studio will start at the beginning and sequentially iterate through the data source each time the test is run.

Figure 5.26: Data bound form parameter request action parameter window.

If you like, this behavior can be changed by expanding the **Data Sources** node in the main window, selecting the relevant data source sub-node, and viewing its properties in the properties window. Expand the drop-down in the **Access Method** property, and as the property values suggest, the method of access for a data source can be changed from the default sequential access to random order, or ensuring that each selected value is unique and no duplicates occur (see Figure 5.27).

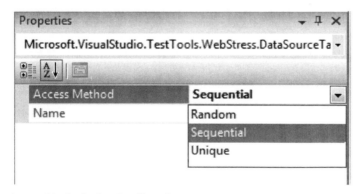

Figure 5.27: Access Method selection for a data source.

Since the data source has already been defined, the same technique can be used to assign a value to the password form element from the data source. Using a database is almost identical to using a CSV file, except that the connection to the database is specified, instead of the path to a CSV file.

Once the connection to the database is selected, a check box dialog is presented, allowing the user to select all the tables to be used as a data source. Any number of tables can be selected and added to the web test.

You may prefer to manage your performance test input data by having a single, separate database containing all the necessary tables for use as a data source. If you use this system, or indeed any databases as a data source, you must obviously ensure that all test agents can easily access the database during test runs.

Finally, XML data sources are something of a mix between CSVs and databases. Like a CSV file, the XML will contain the performance data input in text format, but it can also contain multiple tables. Take the following XML file as an example:

```xml
<?xml version="1.0" encoding="utf-8" ?>
<SampleData>
  <Users>
    <UserName>admin</UserName>
    <Password>password</Password>
  </Users>
  <Users>
    <UserName>test</UserName>
    <Password>password</Password>
  </Users>
  <Users>
    <UserName>viewer</UserName>
    <Password>password</Password>
  </Users>
  <Products>
    <Product>Widget</Product>
    <Quantity>3</Quantity>
  </Products>
  <Products>
    <Product>MegaWidget</Product>
    <Quantity>1</Quantity>
  </Products>
  <Products>
    <Product>Recombobulator</Product>
    <Quantity>16</Quantity>
  </Products>
</SampleData>
```

The XML file contains an arbitrary root node of <SampleData> and then subsequent child root nodes of <Users> and <Products> respectively. These nodes represent the tabular structure. The child elements of <Users> and <Products> represent the columns, extracted and used as the data source field. When adding the XML data source, the user specifies the location of the XML file and then selects a table to use from that data.

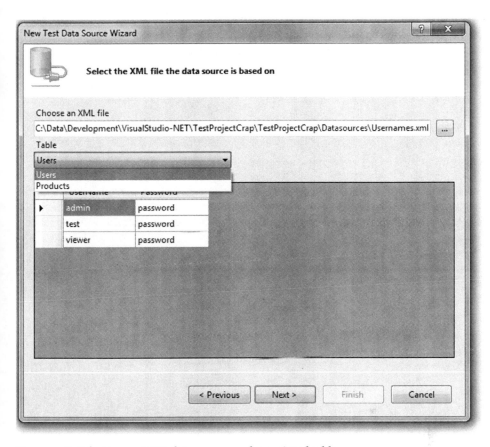

Figure 5.28: Selecting an XML data source and associated table.

While an XML file is more verbose, it does provide the advantage of being able to host multiple tables in one file.

Test deployment considerations

When a data source is used within a web test, that data source must obviously be made available to the test agents, so that the data can be extracted and used as context items during the test execution.

For a database, this means ensuring that the agents can connect to the database machine, and have the appropriate access to do so.

CSV and XML files must be deployed along with the tests in the compiled assemblies, otherwise the tests will not be able to locate the files. Indicating that the files need to be deployed as part of the test execution requires the test run configuration file to be edited. To do this, open the **Test** menu, then select the **Edit Test Run Configuration** option, and then the **Local Test Run** (`localtestrun.testrunconfig`) option.

Note

The name of your test run configuration may differ, or you may have multiple configurations. Ensure you apply the changes to the configuration that you will be using.

A dialog is displayed listing all the configuration categories. Select the **Deployment** option from the left pane. In the right pane, multiple files or entire directories can be added, and these items will all be included when tests are deployed to each agent during a performance test run.

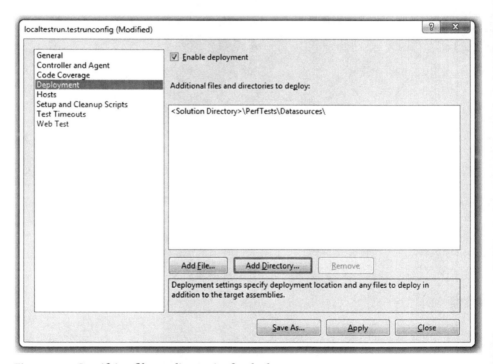

Figure 5.29: Specifying files or directories for deployment.

Having a single directory containing all the data sources means that the directory only needs to be defined once in the deployment configuration, and all files within that directory will be included in the deployment. If the director has been defined in this configuration, then any new data source files added to it later on will automatically be deployed. This is a really convenient deployment method.

Specifying singular files is certainly acceptable, as long as you ensure that each new data source file is added to the deployment configuration for all test run configurations that require it.

Web test code generation

Web tests provide a great deal of flexibility and a wide range of possibilities for customization and generating effective load. However, there may be instances where the supported customization methods are simply not enough, and more specific customization is required to create a valid test against the target system.

It is possible to generate code from web tests, and then simply treat that code like any other .NET development library component. You can then write whatever customization code is required. When code is generated for a web test, you will then have a separate copy of the web test, but in pure code. This will include any references to data sources, or other specific customization made to the test while it was still a web test.

Note

While relatively minor changes are often added to the generated code to achieve any desired effects, specifying data sources and modifying request properties is usually easier in web tests. For this reason, it's best to retain the original web test from which the coded test was generated.

To generate the code from a web test, select the **Generate Code** button from the web test toolbar in the main window.

Figure 5.30: Generate Code button for a web test.

A dialog will be presented, allowing you to specify a name for the generated coded test; once you've supplied that information, selecting **OK** will generate the code and add the file to the test project.

The code will contain the required attributes to define a data source (if one is used) and any other contextual items. The GetRequestEnumerator method will be overridden and will contain the execution path of the tests, as shown in the following code snippet:

```csharp
public class MyTest_CodeGenerated : Webtest
{

    public MyTest_CodeGenerated()
    {
        this.Context.Add("MainServer", "http://glavtop");
        this.PreAuthenticate = true;
    }


    public override IEnumerator<WebtestRequest>
GetRequestEnumerator()
    {
        WebtestRequest request1 = new WebtestRequest((this.
Context["MainServer"].ToString() + "/PerfTestSampleSite/"));
        request1.ThinkTime = 8;
        request1.Timeout = 60;
        yield return request1;
        request1 = null;

        WebtestRequest request2 = new WebtestRequest((this.
Context["MainServer"].ToString() + "/PerfTestSampleSite/Pages/
SearchProducts.aspx"));
        request2.ThinkTime = 2;
        request2.Timeout = 60;
        yield return request2;
        request2 = null;
...
```

This effectively shows one big method that yields requests for each web test action that was recorded. The WebtestRequest object represents the request being executed, and contains properties as you would see in the Visual Studio user interface through the Properties window.

It quickly becomes apparent that, with a large web test recording, the generated source file can become quite large. Performing modifications and maintenance to just one source file can be quite time consuming, as there is a tendency to refactor and clean up the code.

In general, the best practice is to leave the generated code as untouched as possible. Any customized actions should be factored out into separate classes and assemblies, with the generated code simply calling into the customized methods or classes. This way, the originally recorded web test can be retained, and code regenerated if required, with only minor changes being needed to call into the customized code.

Extensibility through plug-ins

Previously, we discussed the ability to modify the properties of a request within a web test. An example property was the **ParseDependentRequests** property, which determined if items such as style sheets and images could also be requested by the original test action. It would obviously be time consuming and inconvenient to have to do this for each request in a web test if you wanted to disable all dependent requests.

Extensibility is made possible in Visual Studio Team Test through plug-ins. A custom plug-in can be created quite easily and applied to the web test. In order to create a custom plug-in, the required steps are listed below.

- Create a new class in the test project, or in a referenced project.

- Ensure the class inherits from the Microsoft.VisualStudio.TestTools.Web testing.WebtestPlugin class.

- Override the appropriate method for your needs.

By way of example, let's create a plug-in to disable dependent requests for all requests in a web test.

- In your test project, add a new class to the project.

- Ensure the class is public, and that it inherits from the Microsoft.VisualStudio. TestTools.Webtesting.WebtestPlugin class.

The class should look similar to this:

```
using System;
using System.Collections.Generic;
using System.Linq;
using System.Text;
using Microsoft.VisualStudio.TestTools.Webtesting;

namespace TestProjectCrap
{
    public class TestPlugin : WebtestPlugin
    {
    }
}
```

- Override the `PreRequest` method.

- The `PreRequestEventArgs` parameter contains references to context elements such as the current request. In the implementation of the method, have the following code:
  `e.Request.ParseDependentRequests = false;`

- Compile the code.

The completed plug-in code should look something like this:

```csharp
using System;
using System.Collections.Generic;
using System.Linq;
using System.Text;
using Microsoft.VisualStudio.TestTools.Webtesting;

namespace TestProjectCrap
{
    public class TestPlugin : WebtestPlugin
    {
        public override void PreRequest(object sender,
PreRequestEventArgs e)
        {
            e.Request.ParseDependentRequests = false;
            base.PreRequest(sender, e);
        }
    }
}
```

This class is now a web test plug-in that can be added into any web test. To do this, click the **Add Web Test Plug-in** button, located in the web test toolbar above the test display window.

Figure 5.31: The Add Web Test Plug-in button.

A dialog will be presented showing a selection of available plug-ins to choose from.

Select the plug-in that was just created and click **OK**. The plug-in will now appear in the web test in a **Web Test Plug-ins** node as shown in Figure 5.32.

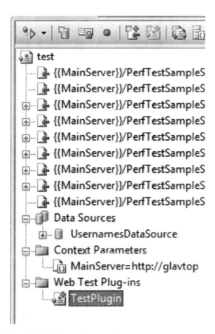

Figure 5.32: Web test plug-in added into the web test.

Now, each time the test is run, the plug-in will also take effect and set the parsing of dependent requests to "false" for every request. The changes are easy to see in these two screenshots showing a web test being run: Figure 5.33 without the plug-in added, and Figure 5.34 with the plug-in added.

Request	HTTP Status	Total Time	
⊘ ⊟ http://glavtop/PerfTestSampleSite/	200 OK	0.096 sec	
⊘ http://glavtop/PerfTestSampleSite/MainStylesheet.css	200 OK	-	
⊘ ⊟ http://glavtop/PerfTestSampleSite/Pages/SearchProducts.aspx	200 OK	0.039 sec	
⊘ http://glavtop/PerfTestSampleSite/MainStylesheet.css	200 OK	-	
⊘ ⊟ http://glavtop/PerfTestSampleSite/Pages/SearchProducts.aspx	200 OK	0.045 sec	
⊘ http://glavtop/PerfTestSampleSite/MainStylesheet.css	200 OK	-	
⊘ ⊟ http://glavtop/PerfTestSampleSite/Pages/SearchProducts.aspx	302 Found	0.200 sec	
⊘ ⊞ http://glavtop/PerfTestSampleSite/Login.aspx?ReturnUrl= %2fPerfTest	200 OK	-	
⊘ ⊟ http://glavtop/PerfTestSampleSite/Login.aspx?ReturnUrl=/PerfTestSampl	302 Found	0.049 sec	
⊘ ⊞ http://glavtop/PerfTestSampleSite/Pages/SearchProducts.aspx	200 OK	-	
⊘ ⊟ http://glavtop/PerfTestSampleSite/Pages/SearchProducts.aspx	200 OK	0.038 sec	
⊘ http://glavtop/PerfTestSampleSite/MainStylesheet.css	200 OK	-	
⊘ ⊟ http://glavtop/PerfTestSampleSite/Pages/SearchProducts.aspx	200 OK	0.030 sec	
⊘ http://glavtop/PerfTestSampleSite/MainStylesheet.css	200 OK	-	
⊘ ⊞ http://glavtop/PerfTestSampleSite/Pages/SearchProducts.aspx	200 OK	0.065 sec	
⊘ ⊞ http://glavtop/PerfTestSampleSite/Pages/ViewCart.aspx	200 OK	0.041 sec	

Passed Click here to run again Internet Explorer 7.0 LAN Edit run settings

Figure 5.33: Web test run without the plug-in.

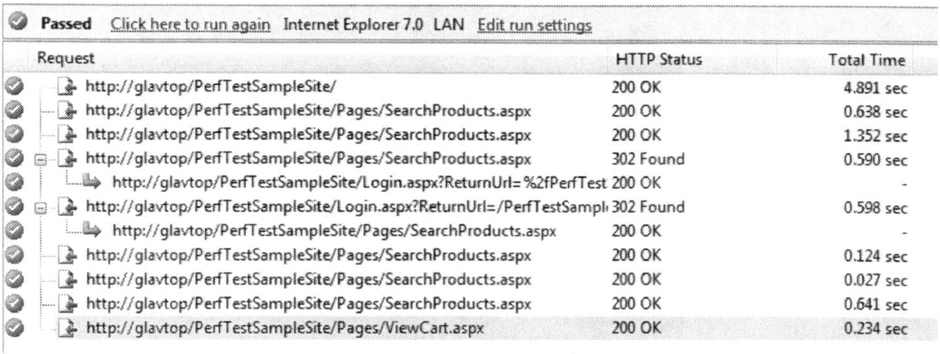

Request	HTTP Status	Total Time
✓ http://glavtop/PerfTestSampleSite/	200 OK	4.891 sec
✓ http://glavtop/PerfTestSampleSite/Pages/SearchProducts.aspx	200 OK	0.638 sec
✓ http://glavtop/PerfTestSampleSite/Pages/SearchProducts.aspx	200 OK	1.352 sec
✓ http://glavtop/PerfTestSampleSite/Pages/SearchProducts.aspx	302 Found	0.590 sec
✓ http://glavtop/PerfTestSampleSite/Login.aspx?ReturnUrl= %2fPerfTest	200 OK	-
✓ http://glavtop/PerfTestSampleSite/Login.aspx?ReturnUrl=/PerfTestSampl	302 Found	0.598 sec
✓ http://glavtop/PerfTestSampleSite/Pages/SearchProducts.aspx	200 OK	-
✓ http://glavtop/PerfTestSampleSite/Pages/SearchProducts.aspx	200 OK	0.124 sec
✓ http://glavtop/PerfTestSampleSite/Pages/SearchProducts.aspx	200 OK	0.027 sec
✓ http://glavtop/PerfTestSampleSite/Pages/SearchProducts.aspx	200 OK	0.641 sec
✓ http://glavtop/PerfTestSampleSite/Pages/ViewCart.aspx	200 OK	0.234 sec

Passed   Click here to run again   Internet Explorer 7.0   LAN   Edit run settings

Figure 5.34: Web test run with the plug-in.

As you can see, the web test with the plug-in added does not make any dependent requests for CSS resources.

There are numerous other methods in the `WebtestPlugin` class that can be overridden, and each participates in a different part of the request life cycle. All life cycle events that can be overridden follow the same pre- and post-condition pattern. Below is a list of those methods.

```
PostPage(object sender, PostPageEventArgs e)
PostRequest(object sender, PostRequestEventArgs e)
PostTransaction(object sender, PostTransactionEventArgs e)
PostWebtest(object sender, PostWebtestEventArgs e)
PrePage(object sender, PrePageEventArgs e)
PreTransaction(object sender, PreTransactionEventArgs e)
PreWebtest(object sender, PreWebtestEventArgs e)
PreRequest(object sender, PreRequestEventArgs e)
```

The naming of the methods makes it easy to understand at what point of the request life cycle they each take part, and this will factor in to how to implement the required plug-in to perform any desired custom actions. As you run more web tests, you will develop your own library of custom plug-ins to suit your personal needs or those of your organization.

Alternative ways of recording web tests

You don't necessarily have to use Visual Studio to record web tests. Having to install Visual Studio Team Test just for someone to record a web test may seem quite a high cost.

Luckily, there is an alternative; you can also use a tool called Fiddler to record web tests. Fiddler is an HTTP proxy which allows you to capture all incoming and outgoing HTTP traffic for analysis. It was written by Eric Lawrence, of Microsoft, and it is a very powerful tool indeed. What is even better is that it's freely downloadable from: HTTP://WWW.FIDDLER2.COM/FIDDLER2/VERSION.ASP.

After downloading and installing Fiddler, recording a web test is very simple. Start the Fiddler application, load Internet Explorer and perform the usual navigational steps to simulate the test you are recording. So far, this is no different from using Visual Studio to record test actions.

Once you have completed your actions, switch back to the Fiddler application, and you should have a screen with some recorded requests looking something like the screen in Figure 5.35.

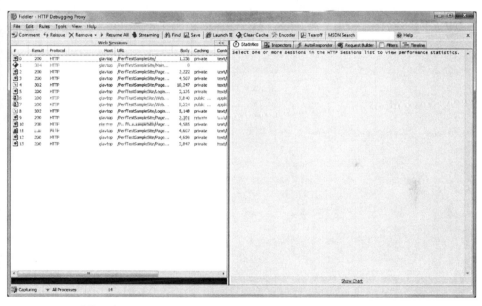

Figure 5.35: Fiddler showing captured requests.

Note

Once you have finished capturing requests for your test, it is best to either shut down Internet Explorer or stop Fiddler from capturing requests by deselecting the **Capture Traffic** *option from the* **File** *menu, or alternatively by pressing* **F12**. *This is advisable because sometimes toolbars and plug-ins in the web browser can make requests which have nothing at all to do with the site or the test.*

You will notice that selecting a request in the left pane of Fiddler shows the request details in the right pane. This is similar to Visual Studio, although the latter can show the request in a lot more detail.

To save the captured requests as a Visual Studio web test, select them all by clicking the **Edit > Select All** menu option, and then open the **File menu**, and select the **Save > Selected Sessions > as Visual Studio Web Test...** menu option.

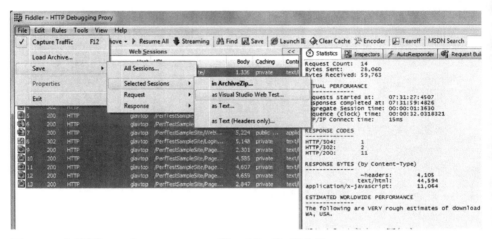

Figure 5.36: Fiddler, saving requests as a Visual Studio Web Test.

A dialog is then presented allowing the user to specify a name and location for the saved test. Before the test is saved, yet another dialog is presented, this time asking the user to specify the plug-ins used to execute against the recorded requests when saving. Simply accept the defaults and click **OK** to save the test.

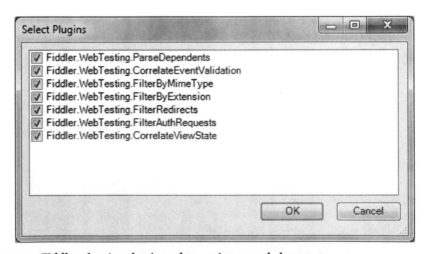

Figure 5.37: Fiddler plug-in selection when saving recorded requests.

The test is now saved as a normal Visual Studio web test that can be included in any Visual Studio test project. To do this, simply use Windows Explorer to copy the saved web test file and paste it into the test project within Visual Studio.

These tests are exactly the same as those recorded within Visual Studio. Using Fiddler just provides a convenient and low-cost (in terms of both price and installation effort) way of recording web tests to use for performance testing.

Considerations for load balancing / load balanced hardware

Production systems will often employ a technique called load balancing or load distribution. This is typically where more than one server is used to handle the load, or concurrent users, being applied to an application. This set of servers is often called a web farm, or a farm of servers. In order to achieve this, load balancing software or hardware is employed to take the incoming requests, and send them to one of the servers in the farm – typically the server that is experiencing the least amount of load, or doing the least amount of work at the time.

So the question is: when setting up the performance test rig, should the production scenario be replicated exactly, with load balancing in place while performing tests?

The answer to this question is "yes and no." It is important to test this scenario, but it is important to first test against a single server without load balancing in place. The reason for this is that a single server will produce a set of results which can be considered, if you like, as the "single measure of performance." That is to say, a single server is easier to identify as a known quantity because you are isolating results to within the specifications of that machine only, and that is useful information to have. Adding more machines via load balancing will typically produce better overall performance, but that performance is still essentially based on this single measure of performance, as well as the load balancing solution itself. Having this measurement based on a single server also provides an easy set of metrics for subsequent analysis when changes are made. Having load balancing in place introduces another variable into the environment in which changes are applied, and thus increases the "surface area" of change and effect – which is a rather grand-sounding way of saying that you'll have more things to account for when quantifying effects if you try and factor in load balancing.

Having said that, when a good idea of performance capability is ascertained from a single server, introducing a load balanced scenario is also important to gauge the effect of horizontal scalability. This will determine how much of an effect an extra server provides. An often incorrect assumption is that, if one server can easily handle, say, 1,000 concurrent users, then two servers will be able to easily handle 2,000 users. Unfortunately, load balancing doesn't usually provide a direct linear increase in the capability of a system to bear load.

The amount of extra capacity that load balancing will provide depends, for starters, upon the load balancing solution itself. Software-based mechanisms, such as Windows load balancing software (WLBS) are usually not as effective as hardware-based ones, although they are often a lot cheaper. Software-based mechanisms are often suitable for smaller-scale web farms, though.

Also bear in mind that the method of load balancing is important. How does the load balancer distribute requests and load to other servers? Various methods are employed to do this, such as:

- **Round robin style**
  This involves simply alternating between the available servers for each subsequent request coming in.

- **Connection based**
  An incoming request is forwarded to the server that has the least number of open connections servicing requests.

- **Load based**
  The server experiencing the least load will receive the next request. This brings up other questions of how the load balancer determines this information, and there are multiple ways to achieve that, as well.

Various load balancers will support at least one or more of the methods described above, some more efficiently than others. These variables make sure that the effects of load balancing are not as straightforward as expected.

Finally, the ability of the application to exist on multiple servers, with no affinity to any one server is also an important factor. This is referred to as being "stateless." Some load balancers can accommodate an application that requires "stateful" behavior, although I'll talk about this in greater detail in later chapters specifically covering optimization and load balancing.

This is why it's important to measure the effect of introducing load balancing. It will provide a more accurate gauge of expected performance, and allow better quantification of infrastructure requirements and system capability.

It is important to factor this consideration into your performance testing plan early on, so that the appropriate infrastructure tasks can be put into place to ensure testing can be performed against load balanced servers.

If you want to know more about load balancing, I'll cover it in the context of performance testing and application considerations later in the book.

Test automation

As the final part of creating a performance test rig, automation of test execution and collection of performance test results should be considered.

However, in order to automate a performance test, we first need a performance test to automate and, up until now, we have only discussed how to create and customize web tests. Web tests are the singular test items that will ultimately comprise a performance test using the functional scenario breakdowns mentioned earlier.

Now we need to create a performance test scenario and assign some web tests to it. For our purposes, we will create a basic performance test scenario to execute a series of web tests, and then automate their execution as well as the collection of the resulting performance data.

Creating a performance test scenario

Ensure you have a test project open in Visual Studio, containing some web tests that have already been recorded. Select the **Add Load Test** option from the **Project menu**, and you will be taken through the **New Load Test Wizard**.

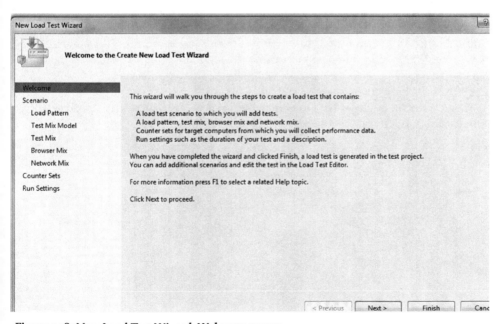

Figure 5.38: New Load Test Wizard, Welcome screen.

136

You will then be presented with a dialog around scenario settings. Enter a name for this load test scenario that will be simulated.

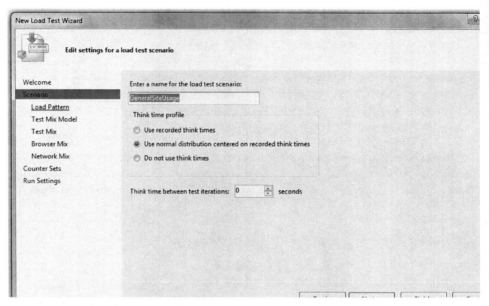

Figure 5.39: New Load Test Wizard, Scenario settings.

Leave the other settings at their defaults. The **Think time** settings determine whether the test will replay the idle periods where a user is thinking about what action to perform next; the default is to utilize an average distribution of think times based on the think times as they were recorded. Choosing the **Do not use think times** option incurs extra stress on the server and is useful for pure stress testing, but is not indicative of real world usage.

Next, you have the option to specify the initial settings for the concurrent user load to be simulated (see Figure 5.40).

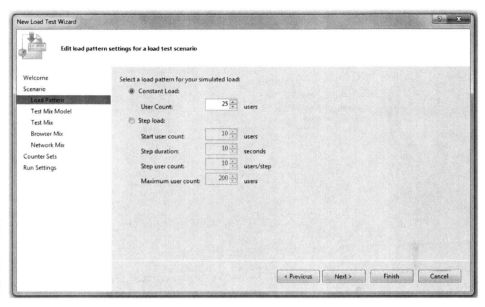

Figure 5.40: New Load Test Wizard, Load Pattern options.

If you are unsure of the concurrent user load to specify at this point, simply accept the default setting of a constant 25 concurrent users, as this can always be edited later on.

The **Step load** option allows for a steadily increasing load to be applied, starting at a set user level (**Start user count**), then progressively adding a number of users (**Step user count**). You can also control the length of time for which to execute each progressive step (**Step duration**), as well as the maximum number of users to simulate (**Maximum user count**).

Moving to the next screen (Figure 5.41) shows the **Test Mix Model** dialog, which (unsurprisingly) allows you to specify what kind of test mix is required. For most requirements, sticking to the default of **Based on the total number of tests** is best suited to most organizations, and will allow you to best model the needs of the business and assign percentage weightings of test based on functional paths and use cases.

If you want to investigate other available test mixes then, as each method is selected, an information box to the right will describe the option in detail.

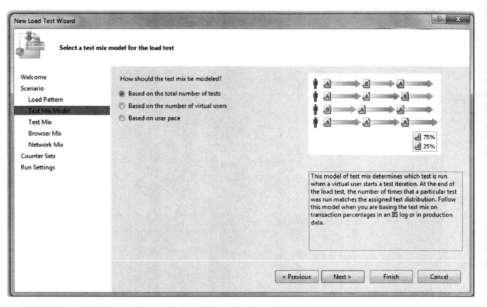

Figure 5.41: New Load Test Wizard, Test Mix Model screen.

On the next screen (Figure 5.42) you can select the tests that the load test will execute (known as the **Test Mix**), and assign percentage weightings to those tests to determine the ratio of their execution.

Basically, this means that a test with a weighting of 50% will execute twice as many times as a test with a weighting of 25%. Selecting the **Add** button will display a dialog where tests can be selected (or deselected) to participate in this load test using the arrow buttons between the two panes of the dialog.

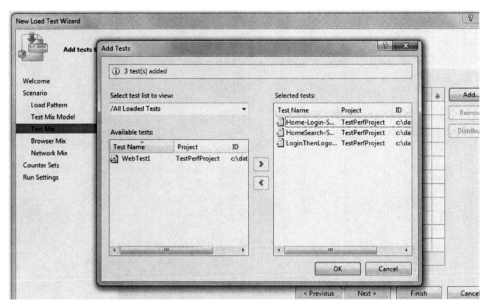

Figure 5.42: New Load Test Wizard with tests added.

Obviously, in order to run a performance or load test, there will need to be at least some tests selected to execute.

Once the tests are selected, clicking **OK** will show the tests added to the load test scenario with a default distribution (Figure 5.43). The distribution of the tests can be set to the required ratio required by the functional paths and use cases decided by the business, and they can also be easily modified later.

140

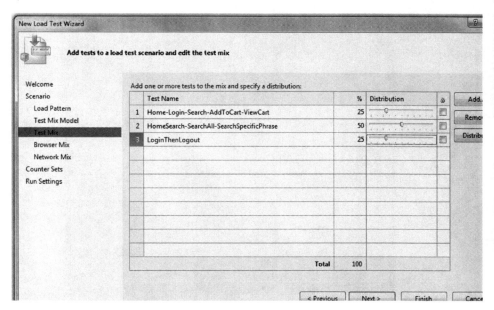

Figure 5.43: New Load Test Wizard, Test Mix defined.

At this point, you can click the **Finish** button to add the load test to the project with defaults attributed to the rest of the options. However, it's best to at least go through and confirm the default settings are appropriate for your needs.

The next step (Figure 5.44) involves adding browsers to simulate during the load test. If this is not a concern, then simply skip to the next step. Otherwise, the dialog will allow you to add a simulated browser by selecting the **Add** button and then distribute the weighting of browsers in the same way as was done for test weightings.

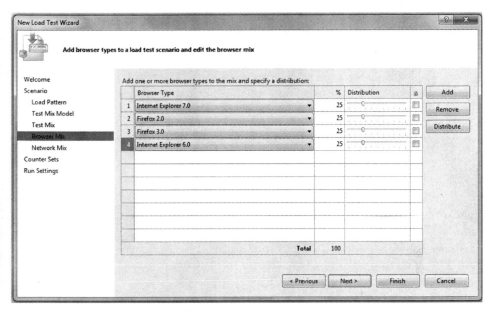

Figure 5.44: New Load Test Wizard, Browser Mix.

The next step (shown in Figure 5.45) involves adding simulated networks to the mix, with the now familiar weighting process. For most scenarios, leaving a single selection of LAN is best, as this will not reduce any of the simulated traffic to the server.

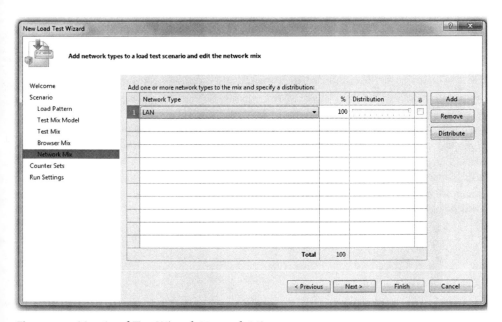

Figure 5.45: New Load Test Wizard, Network Mix.

Initially at least, this is best left at the default setting, with some tweaking performed at later stages when a good idea of raw performance is obtained.

The next, penultimate step (Figure 5.46) involves defining additional computers and associated counter sets for Visual Studio to monitor and collect during the performance test. For now, we can accept the defaults Visual Studio provides, as these cover the main metric points, such as the CPU, and memory for the test servers, load agents, and controllers.

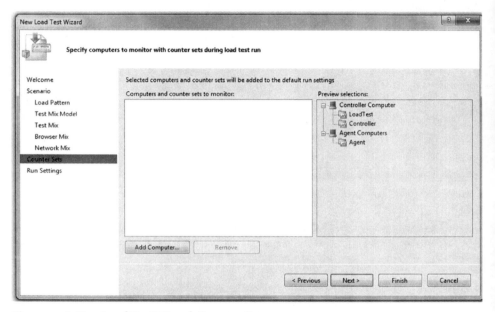

Figure 5.46: New Load Test Wizard, Counter Sets.

The final step in the process involves defining the run settings (see Figure 5.47). These are comprised of things like the time period for the performance test to run, including warm-up time, or the number of test iterations to execute. Additionally, the sample rate and the validation level are also specified. The validation level determines whether low validation rules, low and medium ones, or all validation rules are executed against the tests. A validation level of **Low** indicates only low validation rules are executed, whereas a validation level of **High** indicates all validation rules are executed. Initially, leave the run duration at a default, low time period of ten minutes, as this will allow us to perform a series of small tests to ensure everything is working as expected.

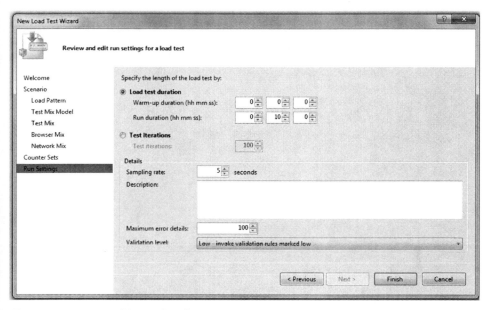

Figure 5.47: New Load Test Wizard, Run Settings.

Click on **Finish**, and the load test has now been added to the project.

Items can be selected in the main window and their properties edited using the property window, in the same way as any object in the test project.

To run the load test, the controller needs to be running as an absolute minimum. Agents are not strictly required to run the tests at low load levels, and are mainly used to distribute test generation to simulate high load levels.

With the controller running, the **Run Test** button can be pressed (Figure 5.49) and the load test will commence running, based on the run settings. If the defaults are used, then this will be for ten minutes.

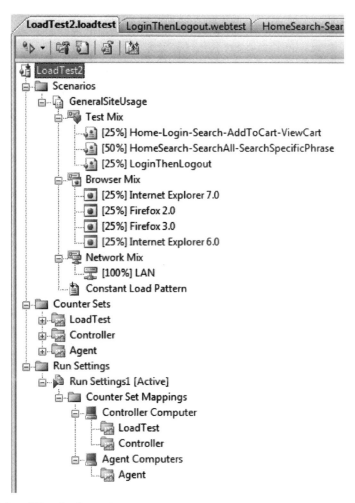

Figure 5.48: Load Test in the project.

Figure 5.49: Load Test, Run Test button.

When the load test is executing, a series of windows will be presented which show the current progress of the load test, together with some key counters and measurements. The display should look similar to that in Figure 5.50.

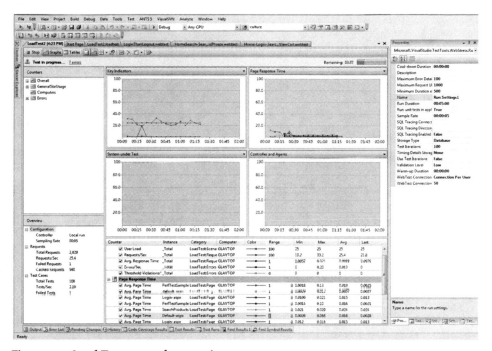

Figure 5.50: Load Test currently executing.

While the test is executing, additional performance metrics can be viewed by simply expanding and locating the desired metric in the left-hand **Counters** pane, and then either double-clicking or dragging the metric into the desired display window.

Once the load test has completed executing, a dialog is shown (Figure 5.51), asking if you'd like to view the detailed results.

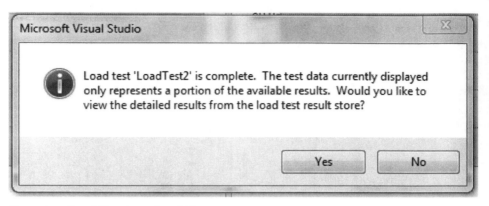

Figure 5.51: Load Test Complete dialog.

The dialog allows the user to load in all the performance metric data for evaluation if desired, as only a small portion is calculated and presented during the execution of the test. To get a full view of the metric data, more data must be loaded and analyzed.

Putting automation in place

Executing a load test and collecting results is a relatively trivial task when all the infrastructure is in place. Ideally, automating this manual task can allow tests to be run without manual intervention and/or during non-business hours. Cleaning up after a test run is another manual task that is a good candidate for automation.

All of this automation allows effort to be concentrated on the areas that provide value, such as result analysis, rather than on manual, mundane tasks like initiating execution and clean-up. Furthermore, the cost of performance testing is substantially reduced as a result of automating as much of the process as possible.

Executing the load test

Automating the execution of load tests is actually quite easy. Typically, a load test would be scheduled to run overnight, over a weekend, or even over the course of a few weeks. For these scenarios, it's useful to have the performance test execute without human interaction, so that regular performance runs can be performed and analyzed.

The easiest way to accomplish this is to simply have a batch file that executes the load test, and to use the NT Scheduler that comes with all current versions of Windows to schedule when this batch file is executed.

The batch file itself only needs to execute the standard Microsoft test application, MSTest executable (**mstest.exe**), and pass in arguments to allow MSTest to properly execute the tests. An example load test start script may look something like this:

```
"C:\Program Files\Microsoft Visual Studio 9.0\Common7\IDE\mstest.
exe" /TestContainer:ProdLoadTest.loadtest /RunConfig:"C:\Source
Code\LoadTest\PerfTestRun.testrunconfig"
```

In this example, the arguments below are passed to MSTest.

- **TestContainer**
  Represents the load test that should be executed. This contains all the details, such as Network Mix, run details, and so on, required to execute the test.

- **RunConfig**
  Represents the current test configuration which lists the controller to use, deployment options, test naming standards, etc., discussed earlier.

That is sufficient to start the load test executing. The Scheduler can be located in the Administrative Tools section of the Windows Control Panel.

Collecting performance monitor data

Previously, the PerfMon tool was discussed as a great way of collecting server performance metrics to validate and, indeed, of backing up the metric data collected by Visual Studio Team Test. However, if the load test execution is being automated, it makes sense that the beginning and end of the collection of performance data via PerfMon should also be automated.

The PerfMon tool already contains functionality to schedule starting and stopping the collection of performance data. Each version of PerfMon has a slightly different user interface, although the overall functionality is the same.

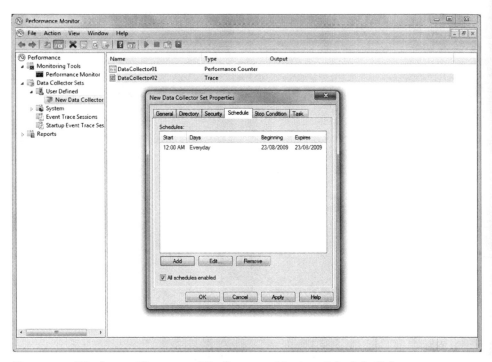

Figure 5.52: Windows 7 / Server 2008 Performance Monitor, Schedule dialog.

In both versions of PerfMon, you'll need to create a new counter set, select the properties of that counter set, and then select the appropriate scheduling options. Alternatively, select the **Data Collector** set and then select its properties. From the displayed dialog, select the **Schedule** tab to add, edit or remove a schedule, and define when it should start collecting, as shown in Figure 5.53.

In Windows XP, Server 2000, and Server 2003, the terminology is a little different, but the concepts are the same. Selecting the properties of an existing counter log, then selecting the **Schedule** tab, allows a user to define the start and stop times of the counter recording.

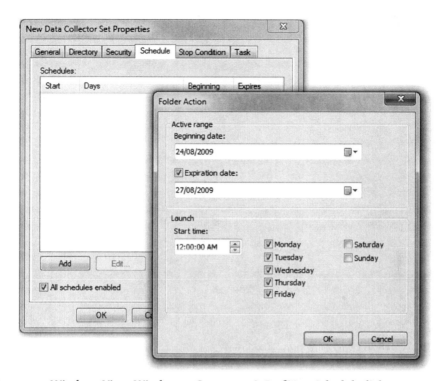

Figure 5.53: Windows Vista, Windows 7, Server 2008, PerfMon Schedule dialog.

Additionally, in more recent versions of Windows and Windows Server, selecting the **Stop Condition** tab provides options as to when the data collection should terminate.

When scheduling performance monitor collection and termination, it is best to generally start the collection a short period before the performance run commences, and then to terminate it a short period after the performance run has ended. This ensures that all data for the performance run is collected, but it will also clearly indicate what the idle or quiet times of activity on the system look like from a performance metric point of view.

It is important to note that, under Windows XP, Server 2000, and Server 2003, the scheduling features of PerfMon were somewhat unreliable. Occasionally, when scheduled to start, they simply wouldn't, and I have yet to find a good reason for this. Terminating collection has never seemed to be an issue. To prepare against this eventuality, you can use a command-line tool called **logman** to instruct PerfMon to start collection, and let the scheduling definition in PerfMon terminate the collection. **logman** is available on all Windows server operating systems, and to use it to start a PerfMon collection, use the syntax:

```
logman start MyPerfCounters
```

where MyPerfCounters represents the counter log set name. This tool can also be used to stop counter collection.

Collecting SQL Server usage statistics

Since the database plays such an important part in today's applications, it is useful to determine, not only how hard the database server is working but, ideally, what are the most expensive queries the database is running. This kind of information can be extremely useful in determining how the database is performing, and how the application is making use of the database.

SQL Server provides a convenient way to schedule the execution of scripts via the SQL Server Agent. Other database vendors offer similar methods. However, with SQL Server it is possible to define scheduled jobs in SQL Management Studio that execute scripts at specific times and output the result to a file or database table. There are, of course, many ways to schedule such an activity, but SQL Server Agent (managed via SQL Management Studio) provides one of the most convenient.

In order to determine what the most expensive queries are, the system tables in SQL Server need to be queried, as this is where SQL Server records its statistical data. An example SQL script to retrieve the most expensive queries would be this:

```
set nocount on;

select
    qs.total_worker_time,
    qs.execution_count,
    SUBSTRING(st.text, (qs.statement_start_offset/2)+1,
        ((CASE qs.statement_end_offset
          WHEN -1 THEN DATALENGTH(st.text)
          ELSE qs.statement_end_offset
          END - qs.statement_start_offset)/2) + 1
    ) AS statement_text
from
    (select top 100
        qs.plan_handle,
        qs.total_worker_time,
            qs.execution_count,
            qs.statement_start_offset,
            qs.statement_end_offset
    from
        sys.dm_exec_query_stats qs
    order by qs.total_worker_time desc) as qs
    cross apply sys.dm_exec_sql_text(plan_handle) as st
order by qs.total_worker_time desc;
```

This query will return results that look similar to those in Figure 5.54.

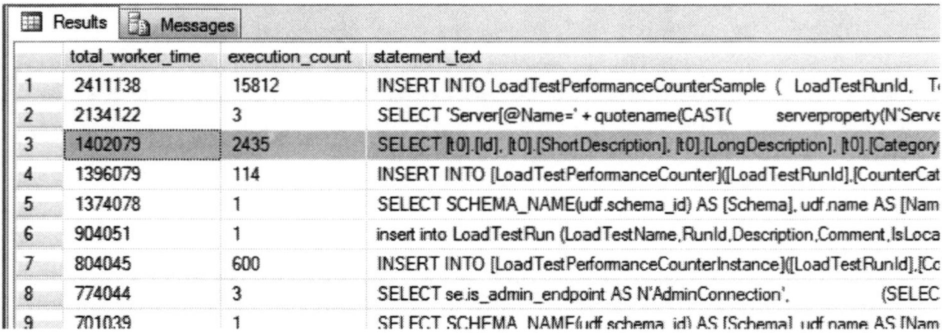

	total_worker_time	execution_count	statement_text
1	2411138	15812	INSERT INTO LoadTestPerformanceCounterSample (LoadTestRunId, T
2	2134122	3	SELECT 'Server[@Name=' + quotename(CAST(serverproperty(N'Serve
3	1402079	2435	SELECT [t0].[Id], [t0].[ShortDescription], [t0].[LongDescription], [t0].[Category
4	1396079	114	INSERT INTO [LoadTestPerformanceCounter]([LoadTestRunId],[CounterCat
5	1374078	1	SELECT SCHEMA_NAME(udf.schema_id) AS [Schema], udf.name AS [Nam
6	904051	1	insert into LoadTestRun (LoadTestName,RunId,Description,Comment,IsLoca
7	804045	600	INSERT INTO [LoadTestPerformanceCounterInstance]([LoadTestRunId],[Cc
8	774044	3	SELECT se.is_admin_endpoint AS N'AdminConnection', (SELEC
9	701039	1	SELECT SCHEMA_NAME(udf.schema_id) AS [Schema], udf.name AS [Nam

Figure 5.54: SQL Server most expensive query results.

The results of the query show the total worker time, execution count, and even the actual text of the query. The first two results are related to the performance tests and SQL server respectively, so these are not of immediate concern. The highlighted row (Row 3) represents a query from the sample application, (Rows 12 and 13 also represent queries generated from the application). This is determined by looking at the tables being used in the query text. Given the relatively few times that these queries are executed, the fact that they are appearing near the top of the result list may indicate an opportunity for optimization.

Results of this nature, when used in conjunction with performance tests, can quickly show less than optimal parts of the application from a database perspective. This is in contrast to the top-down perspective that Visual Studio adopts in reporting performance metrics. Using these two techniques can provide enormous insight into potential performance gains for your application.

Ideally, these scripts should be used after a performance run and then used comparatively as further runs are executed, in order to ensure that any applied performance changes are effective.

Another useful script to execute is one to determine the general index usage of the target database:

```
set nocount on;


use PerfTestSampleDB;
select
    obj.Name as ObjectName,
    ind.name as IndexName,
    ind.index_id,
    ind.object_id,
    isnull(user_seeks, 0) as user_seeks,
    isnull(user_scans, 0) as user_scans,
    isnull(user_lookups, 0) as user_lookups
```

```
from sys.indexes ind
    join sys.objects obj on (ind.object_id = obj.object_id)
    left join sys.dm_db_index_usage_stats st on (st.index_id =
ind.index_id and st.object_id = ind.object_id)
where obj.Type_Desc <> 'SYSTEM_TABLE'
order by obj.Name, ind.Name;
```

Note

If using this script, replace the **PerfTestSampleDB** *database name with the name of the target database to be analyzed.*

Executing this script produces an output similar to that in Figure 5.55.

	ObjectName	IndexName	index_id	object_id	user_seeks	user_scans	user_lookups
1	Category	PK_Category	1	357576312	3955	0	0
2	Country	PK_Country	1	2105058535	16836	3	0
3	Customers	PK_Customers	1	2121058592	4	0	0
4	filestream_tombstone_2073058421	FSTSClusIdx	1	2073058421	0	0	0
5	filestream_tombstone_2073058421	FSTSNCIdx	2	2073058421	0	0	0
6	Products	PK_Products	1	389576426	775	3955	0
7	queue_messages_1977058079	queue_clustered_index	1	1993058136	0	0	0
8	queue_messages_1977058079	queue_secondary_index	2	1993058136	0	0	0
9	queue_messages_2009058193	queue_clustered_index	1	2025058250	0	0	0
10	queue_messages_2009058193	queue_secondary_index	2	2025058250	0	0	0
11	queue_messages_2041058307	queue_clustered_index	1	2057058364	0	0	0
12	queue_messages_2041058307	queue_secondary_index	2	2057058364	0	0	0
13	Roles	PK_Roles	1	69575286	8	0	4
14	syscommittab	ci_commit_ts	1	2089058478	0	0	0
15	syscommittab	si_xdes_id	2	2089058478	0	0	0
16	UserCart	PK_UserCart	1	453576654	807	2389	0
17	UserRoles	PK_UserRoles	1	181575685	0	0	0
18	Users	PK_Users	1	229575856	1671	1	0

Figure 5.55: SQL Server database index usage statistics.

The results of the query show the general usage patterns of indexes within the sample application, with metrics around the number of scans, seeks, and lookups for each index. Optimization of indexes is a great way to reduce query execution times, and the metrics provided with this query can help to ensure that the index usage is always kept efficient.

Clean up tasks

When a performance run is executing, sometimes the test agents can experience low memory conditions, high CPU utilization and other resource issues. This is particularly likely at very high loads where the expectations placed on the test agents were not in line with their specifications. This usually happens early in the performance test phase, when the exact characteristics of test agents are only estimated.

Additionally, be aware that, after a performance test run has completed execution, even with the best intention and attempts by software, some memory may not be properly released. Eventually, this can lead to unstable test agents and, ultimately, failed or less-than-effective performance test runs.

For this reason, I recommend that you restart or reboot the test agent machines after each run. Fortunately, this can also be automated, using the included scheduling ability of Windows as described previously. We need to instruct each of the agent machines to restart, and this can be done using a command-line tool called **shutdown** which is available on all versions of Windows from Windows XP to Server 2008. To restart a remote machine, for example, the following syntax is used:

```
shutdown -r -t 0 -f -m \\testagent
```

Where:

- **-r** : instructs the machine to restart, rather than simply shut down

- **-t 0** : instructs the shutdown/restart process to happen after a timeout of 0 seconds, that is, immediately

- **-f** : instructs the machine to force all running applications to close without prompting any warning

- **-m \\testagent**: represents the machine to shut down / restart. In this case, the machine is named *testagent*.

Typically a batch file is created that restarts all agent machines that you may have in your performance test rig. This script could either be called directly after the scheduled performance test execution script, or it could be scheduled to execute at regular times during the day when it is known that the performance run has completed.

This way, the test agent machines are always in a known, clean state before each performance test run, which better ensures a successful performance test.

Note

This technique could also be applied to the controller if desired.

Conclusion

This chapter has provided an extensive walk-through of the following aspects of performance testing:

• architecture of a test rig

• setting up the various components of the performance test rig such as controller and agents

• troubleshooting test rig setup

• creating web tests and load tests, and parameterization of the tests

• automation of the execution of load tests, collection of performance data, and clean-up tasks.

The amount of setup and effort required to have a performance test rig running and automated is not small, and it is therefore important to have a good understanding of how a performance test rig operates and, more importantly, how to debug and diagnose it if, or when, errors occur.

Once the rig is running and automated, the cost of performance testing then just comes down to analyzing the results and any subsequent changes this may generate. This is exactly the situation you need to be in to effectively and continuously monitor your applications for performance issues. More importantly, this will allow constant metrics to be fed back to interested parties to ensure application development is going according to plan.

Chapter 6: Application Profiling

If you talk to teams of developers about performance profiling, someone will usually say something like, "We don't have time to profile our code, that's why we have load testers" or "If it runs slowly we just throw another server into the farm." Many developers see performance profiling as an extra piece of work to add to their existing workload, and yet another steep learning curve to climb.

Many developers enter the world of performance and memory profiling only when something has gone badly wrong. This usually means during system testing, load testing, and often (sadly) in production. Developers will download an evaluation copy of a profiler and try to isolate why the application is running slowly or keeps crashing. The pressure is on, and it's now the worst possible time to learn the skills required to be an effective application profiler.

Using profiling tools to look for potential bottlenecks *during* development can significantly reduce the number of problems that show up later. With the right tools and training, this can become a regular part of the development process without adding too much overhead.

Development profiling will never uncover all of the issues that a comprehensive load test would, but it can highlight parts of the code that have the potential to become bottlenecks when the application is stressed. Finding and fixing them early can make a big difference overall, especially if all the developers are testing the code they write.

This chapter, and the next two, are all about the tools and techniques that you can quickly master, and then use as part of your development process. Remember, it costs between 15 and 75 times more to find and fix an issue found during test than if that same issue was found during development (Boehm, 1981).

Types of profiling

Application profiling goes beyond the raw performance statistics obtained from system performance monitoring tools, and looks directly at the functions and allocated objects inside the executing application.

When profiling a .NET application, the execution speeds of its internal functions and the resources they use are recorded for a specific set of test transactions. The recorded data will give insight into where there may be performance bottlenecks and possible memory problems (such as memory leaks).

Profilers retrieve performance and memory information from .NET applications in one of three ways:

- **Sample based**
  The application function call stack is periodically recorded to give a low overhead, but equally low resolution analysis.

- **Events based**
  The Common Language Runtime can be configured to send notifications to specific profiler DLLs. Key information on function execution, CPU, memory, and garbage collection can be collected using this mechanism.

- **Instrumentation**
  Instrumentation code that measures the application is added to it at runtime, which can give very detailed and accurate results, but also comes with a high overhead.

A word about profiler overhead

Whichever profiler you use will add some overhead to the executing application it's measuring, and to the machine it is running on. The amount of overhead depends on the type of profiler.

In the case of a performance profiler, the act of measurement may itself impact the performance being measured. This is particularly true for an instrumenting profiler, which has to modify the application binary to insert its own timing probes to every function. As a result, there is more code to execute, requiring additional CPU and memory, causing increased overhead. Most profilers try to compensate by deducting the overhead of the instrumentation from the results.

The profiler also has to deal with the torrent of data it receives and, for a detailed analysis, it may require a lot of memory and processor time just to cope.

If your application is already memory and processor intensive, things are unfortunately only going to get worse, and it could be that it's just not possible to analyze the entire application. Thankfully, most tools allow you to limit the scope and depth of the analysis, which can help. In some situations, the only way to get results may be by writing test harnesses to exercise portions of the application in ways analogous to the full application.

Performance profiling

Performance profiling is all about discovering which parts of your application consume a disproportionate amount of time or system resource. For example, if a single function takes up 80% of the execution time, it's usually worth investigating.

Profiling will highlight small areas of code that would never otherwise be looked at again, and it makes developers ask some interesting questions. To be fair, most of the time the answer will be, "It has to do that and that's as fast as we can make it." The rest of the time, a potential bottleneck will have been uncovered.

What to profile

Profiling a multilayered networked application can be really difficult, simply because of the number of possible variables involved. The question that's difficult to answer is, "Which bit is slow?" Is it the client, the web server, the application server, the database server, or even one of the network links in between?

The first stage in profiling performance is to identify the "slow bit." Application server monitoring can help isolate the guilty layer, and will often help you determine if it is an application or a database problem. Sometimes the problem is even more complex, and a network monitoring tool will be required. These tools analyze packet journey times between the layers, and break down application transactions into server processing time and network time. They can help identify the layer responsible for slow-down, and determine if the problem is to do with a network issue, such as congestion, bandwidth or latency. Chapter 7 discusses this topic in more detail.

Once you have identified the layer responsible (or, if you like, the slow bit) that will give a clue as to the kind of profiler to use. Obviously, if it's a database problem, then use one of the profiling tools available for the products of the database vendor, or simply add another index (just kidding!). If it's a .NET application problem, then there are a whole host of profilers available, and we will be discussing some of the best ones later in this chapter, and when we look at more specific types of profiling later on.

Function analysis

To measure the performance of an application, you need to know how long specific test transactions take to execute. You then need to be able to break those results down in a number of ways. Specifically, function call and function call tree (the sequence of calls created when one function calls another, and so on).

This breakdown identifies the slowest function and the slowest execution path, which is useful because a single function could be slow, or a set of functions *called together* could be slow. Many tools create elaborate hierarchical diagrams which allow the developer to explore the call trees, and this can really help when trying to identify a bottleneck.

Line-level analysis

Profilers can accurately time individual code lines, allowing you to identify the slowest line within a slow function. For me, this is an essential feature because it gives you the best chance of coming up with workable optimizations.

However, line-level analysis does add a greater overhead to the profiling session and can normally be switched off, leaving the profiler to analyze at the function level only.

Wall-clock (elapsed) vs. CPU time

Most profilers measure wall-clock time and CPU time. The ability to distinguish between the two is important because CPU time is pure processing and excludes any waiting time. By contrast, wall-clock time is the total time taken to process a function, including any Wait time.

A function may take a long time to execute, but use comparatively little CPU time because it is actually waiting for a database / web service call to return or for a thread synchronization lock to free up. Identifying Wait time can help you identify where your application may benefit from asynchronous processing.

At the same time, a CPU-intensive function is usually a good candidate for optimization, because the CPU is a finite resource and a potential bottleneck.

Resource bottlenecks

Resources such as disk space, network bandwidth, server availability, graphics cards, and shared threads can all create bottlenecks in an application. Identifying functions causing high levels of resource activity and contention is a key goal in profiling. This kind of activity, when scaled, could quickly become a problem and reduce the scalability of the application.

Call count

Function call count is the easiest statistic to look at first, because a non-trivial function with a high call count often indicates an immediate problem. It's always worth validating the origins of the high call count.

Small optimizations add up and scale

The great thing about performance profiling an application during development is that a developer can immediately see where the main processing hotspots/bottlenecks in the code are. Optimizing the hotspots and asking intelligent questions about call counts can give small but significant improvements in performance and, if the whole team adopts this strategy, the gain can be significant.

With so much code executing on servers, small performance gains become significant because they quickly scale according to the number of users and the number of locations they affect. More to the point, identifying and eliminating potential bottlenecks will prevent them from ever becoming problems during load testing or in production.

Memory profiling

The way you write your code directly impacts how and when the objects you create are allocated and destroyed. Get it right, and your application will use memory efficiently as needed, with minimal performance impact. Get it wrong, however, and your application could use more memory than necessary, which will cause the memory manager to work harder than it needs to, and this will directly impact performance.

Even worse than that, your application could just keep allocating memory until no more is left, causing the application or the machine to crash. This is the memory leak, which every developer fears.

The good news is that there are plenty of tools out there which you can use to find and fix memory problems before they actually become problems. All you need is some background knowledge and a few basic techniques, and it will become second nature.

Checking that an application doesn't have memory leaks, and that it uses memory efficiently, together with fixing any issues found, will improve its overall stability and performance.

Garbage collection

The .NET memory management model ensures that any allocated objects which are no longer in use by the application will be reclaimed automatically. This relieves developers of the responsibility of having to free memory explicitly, which is something that was often omitted in native C/C++ applications, leading to memory leaks.

Garbage collection was invented by John McCarthy et al. in 1959 as part of the Lisp language, but gained most prominence when it was adopted as the memory management model for Java in 1995.

Instead of depending on the developer to manually de-allocate objects, garbage collection adopts an automatic model in which objects are monitored to determine if they are still in use. Those no longer used will have their memory reclaimed automatically. The automatic memory management model, of which garbage collection is a part, was adopted by Microsoft as the model for .NET. I will cover .NET's memory management model and how it works in detail in Chapter 7 but, for now, here is a brief overview.

The .NET CLR allocates objects (less than 85K) onto a managed memory heap, and ensures they are placed consecutively in memory with no gaps between objects. The garbage collector then periodically determines which objects are still in use, by looking to see if they are referenced by other objects, or from the stack, globals, statics, or even CPU registers. If no references are found, it concludes that the object isn't in use and can be "garbage collected."

When an object is garbage collected, it is simply overwritten by the objects above which are moved down in memory – a process known as compaction. This makes sure there are no gaps left in the heap. In truth, it's actually a bit more complicated than this, as objects are grouped into generations depending on how recently they were allocated. (For performance reasons the garbage collector always tries to collect the youngest objects first.)

Anything that keeps hold of a reference to an object will keep it alive indefinitely, and that can be the cause of a leak if it repeats continually. Memory profiling is all about finding suspiciously persistent objects, and tracing back to find the references in code that are keeping them in memory.

Using memory profiling techniques and tools, you can identify large objects that cause the application to have a larger memory footprint than necessary. You can also look for objects that are continually created and never garbage collected, causing memory leaks. I'll cover the garbage collector and associated concepts in much more detail in Chapter 8.

Profiler approaches

All memory profilers will track instances of allocated classes. Some will also track the allocation call stack, which means that they can report on a function's allocation profile and identify function "hotspots."

The ability to view allocations, in terms of both classes and functions, can be really useful. However, recording allocation call stacks can be very memory intensive and can sometimes limit the size and complexity of application that can be profiled.

Symptoms of memory problems

- **Memory leak**

  - Memory usage slowly increases over time.

  - Performance degrades.

  - Application will freeze/crash requiring a restart.

  - After restart it's OK again, and the cycle repeats.

- **Excessive memory footprint**

  - Application is slow to load.

  - After load, other application runs slower than expected.

- **Inefficient allocation**

  - Application performance suddenly degrades and then recovers quickly.

  - % Time in GC Statistic in PerfMon is greater than 20-30%.

I will be going through memory profiling in a lot more detail in Chapter 7.

When to start profiling

ıswer to this question is "profile when you feel you have achieved functional
.oding task." That means, after you have completed the requirement, and
ïrms it works as specified.

Profiling at this stage will highlight potential bottlenecks that should be investigated. Profile any earlier and you could be optimizing code that may significantly change.

Profiling usually occurs in one of three ways: reactive debugging, proactive analysis, or technique validation.

Reactive debugging

Reactive debugging happens when a problem has been found, typically during a load test or in a live system, and the developers have to react to this unwelcome news and fix the problem.

With load test debugging, you have a lot more data to work with because the results will describe the failing transactions in fine detail and give many detailed server statistics, which will help in isolating exactly where the problems are.

Production debugging is much more difficult, because really all you will get are some performance monitoring statistics and, if you are lucky, some anecdotal evidence about what might have been running when the slow-down occurred.

If you carry out load testing late in the life cycle, or if it's a production problem, a number of things now have to happen.

Developers have to:

*   isolate the tests to run to reproduce the problem

*   understand how to use the profiler

*   interpret the results

*   get familiar with the code again

*   fix the code

*   confirm the fix.

Production problems are inevitably accompanied by pressure from management to fix the issue. Developers are also usually caught off guard and are ill prepared for an in-depth analysis of a system they may have last worked with many months earlier.

This is all just an inefficient waste of time and resources, and it doesn't even include the time that would then be required for system testing in a production environment.

The earlier you start your application profiling and load testing, the better. Which is why my general recommendations are:

- Test your application transactions under load as soon as you can during development, and test regularly (as soon as you have something testable). Ensure issues are found and fixed early.

- Encourage a culture where developers proactively look for potential bottlenecks in their code using profiling tools (see next section).

You don't have to wait until the load test phase to begin load testing (although often the expense is too great to use these facilities too early). There are lots of tools out there that you can use to place stress/load on your application, and doing this as early as possible will highlight issues that single test profiling won't find. If you can, automate the stress testing and run it regularly, so that any code changes that impact performance are picked up quickly.

Proactive analysis

Proactive analysis, as the term implies, is all about the developer actively looking for performance and memory issues during the development cycle. It has the major advantage of being by far the quickest and cheapest type of analysis, because the developer already knows the code well, and is able to quickly make knowledgeable optimization decisions.

Proactive analysis takes place as part of the developer testing process, and should be an essential requirement before source code is checked back into the repository. It is 15–75 times quicker to fix an issue in development, than if it was found in later testing (Boehm, 1981).

The proactive approach does require an investment in tools and training, but it also results in more highly skilled development teams who are actively looking for problems in applications, and who are empowered with the skills necessary to find and fix these problems when they occur.

Technique validation

Profilers can really help developers choose the optimal algorithm to achieve a specific processing task. Questions such as, "Should I process it all on the server, or on the client in batches?" can be answered quickly and easily by running a few quick tests.

Finding the most efficient technique to process data can also be very difficult without a profiler. Searching online merely opens up a huge debate, and the only way to be sure is to write some test harnesses, and run a profile.

Tools used for profiling

Many of the available profiling tools combine both performance and memory profiling in one package. I will summarize the features of some of the main tools on the market and, in later chapters, I'll describe how to use them to carry out both performance and memory analysis.

CLRProfiler

The CLRProfiler is, at first glance, quite a basic memory profiling tool. On closer analysis, it's actually extremely powerful once you get the hang of it. Whilst it isn't the most intuitive or easy-to-use profiler you will find, it is certainly very detailed and comprehensive in the information that can be retrieved.

It can profile applications up to and including .NET Framework 3.5, although it only officially supports up to Framework 2.0.

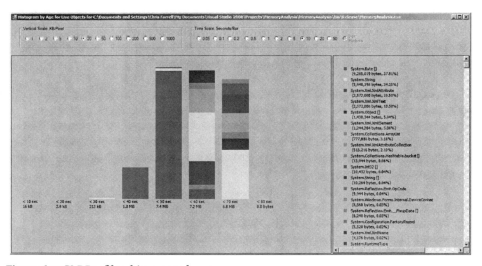

Figure 6.1: CLRProfiler, histogram by age.

CLRProfiler will monitor the executing application (exes, services and web applications) and then provide a number of histograms and call graphs. These can be used to track memory leaks, excessive memory usage, Large Object Heap issues and excessive garbage collection overhead; it's also possible to analyze Finalizer issues.

Unfortunately, CLRProfiler is one of those tools most developers have downloaded and tried out, but given up on after about twenty minutes because it is quite difficult to use.

166

It's free to download and, once you have mastered its quirky interface, and adopted a technique that works for you, it's possible to gain real insight into the memory state of the application.

CLRProfiler gets complicated really quickly and for that reason I will cover it in more detail in Chapter 8.

Red Gate's ANTS Memory and Performance Profilers

The Red Gate .NET Developer Bundle v5 works with .NET framework 1.1, 2.0, 3.0, 3.5, and 4.0, integrates into Visual Studio 2005, 2008, and 2010 at March 2010 release, and supports both 32-bit and 64-bit profiling.

The .NET Developer Bundle includes ANTS Performance Profiler Pro and and ANTS Memory Profiler and, at the time of writing, costs $795 for a single user license (*Red Gate, 2010*).

ANTS Memory Profiler

ANTS Memory Profiler (Figure 6.2) captures class instance allocation and has a low overall overhead. It provides an easy-to-use and flexible user interface.

ANTS also provides graphical insight into the heap with the memory timeline, which is a graphical representation of various performance counters including bytes on all heaps, private bytes and Large Object Heap size (other counters can be added in the options). The primary technique for using this tool involves the developer taking memory snapshots at relevant times. Snapshots can then be compared against each other and used to find classes requiring further investigation.

Filters allow the developer to filter out application noise and to focus on specific problems. Application noise refers to any object allocations that are irrelevant to our analysis but whose presence on the heap we may misinterpret. There are standard filters to eliminate general application noise, and specific filters that can be used to find common causes of memory leaks.

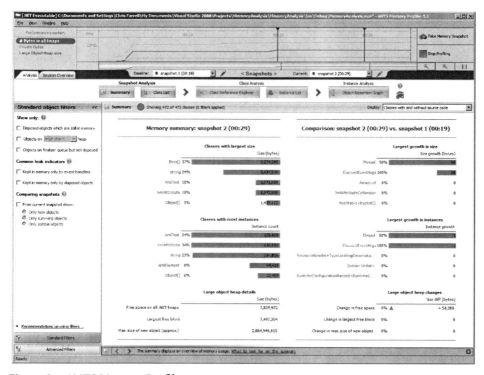

Figure 6.2: ANTS Memory Profiler.

Once a set of suspicious class instances has been identified, the Class Reference Explorer allows the developer to trace back into the tree of object references to find the exact references in the code which are causing the problem.

It's also possible to view a session overview of the snapshot, which gives insight into the state of both the Small Object Heap (including Gen 1 and 2) and the Large Object Heap.

ANTS Performance Profiler

When performance profiling an application, ANTS Performance Profiler (Figure 6.3) presents a performance graph with percentage processor time, plus a number of other performance counters which can be selected.

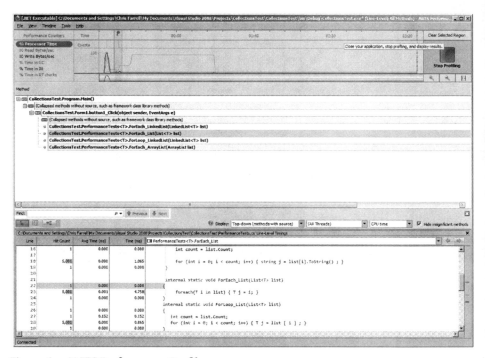

Figure 6.3: ANTS Performance Profiler.

Results can be viewed for the entire analysis, or for just a small portion using the trace graph and selecting an area of interest using the mouse (see Figure 6.4).

This can be really useful if you notice part of your trace for example with high CPU activity, and it allows you to focus on what was happening just for that tightly-defined period. The profile results for the trace can be viewed in Call Tree, Grid or Call Graph modes.

The Call Tree mode displays a hierarchical list of the slowest call trees for each execution path in the selected period, and highlights as the "hottest" the path that is most likely to be the bottleneck.

The grid mode displays the results in a classic grid format, giving:

• Time (CPU or wall clock)

• Time with children (CPU or wall clock)

• Hit count (number of times called).

A call graph can also be generated for every function, allowing the sequence of calls to and from a function to be traced.

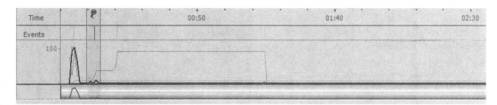

Figure 6.4: **ANTS Performance Profiler,** selecting a portion of the analysis trace.

Performance results can be viewed by CPU time or wall-clock time, which is a useful feature as it can help to quickly identify where the application may benefit from asynchronous processing.

ANTS also provides a number of analysis modes which change the amount of overhead that is added to the executing application:

• method level – lower overhead but less detailed

• line level – higher overhead, more detailed.

It is also possible to further reduce the overhead of both modes by selecting to profile only methods that have source code. That is often the most sensible course of action, since you can only optimize where you have source code to change.

Microfocus DevPartner Studio Professional 9.1

MicroFocus's DevPartner 9 is a suite of tools for .NET framework 2.0, 3.0, and 3.5, and Visual Studio 2005 and 2008. DevPartner pricing depends on the licensing model, but if you are buying from ComponentSource a single-user standalone license is $2,834.67 at the time of writing (*ComponentSource.com, 2010*).

The suite is a developer tool that integrates into Visual Studio 2005 and 2008, and can optionally also be run from the command line. It supports 32-bit profiling on both x86 and x64 systems, and includes a range of tools.

Memory Profiler

The Memory Profiler (Figure 6.5) can perform three types of analysis:

- RAM footprint analysis

- memory leak detection

- temporary object analysis.

DevPartner captures both the class instance allocation and the allocation call stack, so it's possible to view the results in terms of class hotspots and function hotspots.

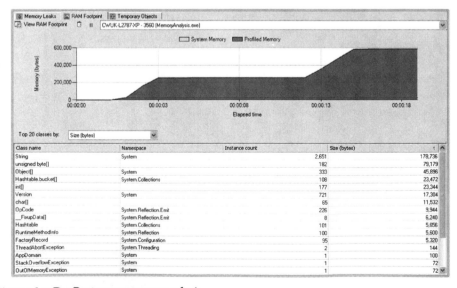

Figure 6.5: DevPartner memory analysis.

171

RAM footprint

RAM footprint looks at both the largest allocated objects and the methods and call trees responsible for allocating large amounts of memory. With these types of analysis it is possible to identify parts of the application that are causing its overall memory footprint to be larger than may be necessary. This often occurs when an application loads data and keeps it cached in memory for later use.

Temporary object analysis

Temporary object analysis looks at the allocation of relatively short-lived objects. These are objects that manage to stay around long enough to survive a couple of garbage collections, but then lose their references and become available for collection. These types of objects make full garbage collections run more frequently, which is inefficient. Having insight into where temporary objects are allocated can help a developer reduce object longevity and improve overall memory usage and performance.

Memory leak detection

The memory leak detection tool allows the developer to navigate through the application until they get to the point where they want to start tracking the leak. At that point, they press a button and all objects allocated from that point are recorded. When the developer has finished their test, they press a **View Memory Leaks** button, and the tool forces a full garbage collection before presenting the results of all of the classes allocated since tracking began and which survived collection.

The results can be viewed by class/object instance and also by function, as the call stack for each allocation is also recorded.

Performance Profiler

There are two separate performance profilers in DevPartner; one for function timing analysis, and the other, called Performance Expert, for function resource analysis, looking at the CPU, disk, and network activity.

The timing analyzer can profile both managed and native instrumented applications, though the resource analyzer is a pure .NET tool only.

Performance timing analysis

The timing analyzer can profile at the function and the code line level. It's also possible to profile both managed and native code at the same time, although the native code must be built with instrumentation.

Running a test is a simple matter of starting the application using the DevPartner Integration toolbar button within Visual Studio.

Figure 6.6: DevPartner toolbar buttons.

A couple of further buttons will appear on the toolbar, which will allow you to take performance snapshots, and the application will start.

The snapshot results are displayed within Visual Studio in a standard grid which can be sorted and filtered. It's also possible to reduce the scope of results by selecting to only view specific source or system modules. The main statistics provided per function (see Figure 6.7) include:

- Called (number of times the function was called)

- % in Method (% of time spent in function excluding time spent in calls to non-framework functions)

- % with Children (% of time spent in function including time spent in calls to non-framework functions)

- Average time (total time in function / number of calls).

The user can view the source for each function listed, giving them a timed line-by-line breakdown of the source code. Alternatively, it's possible to view the call tree for the function, and from here you can track backwards or forwards through the call tree to investigate the function's critical path (more on this later).

Method List	Source [Form1.cs]	Session Summary				

Method Name	% in ▽ Method	% with Children	Called	Average (us)
MemoryAnalysis.Form1..ctor(void)	0.6	22.3	1	159,031.6
MemoryAnalysis.Form1.InitializeComponent(v...	0.1	7.0	1	26,297.2
MemoryAnalysis.CurrencyManager.Start(void)	0.0	0.2	1	6,891.6
MemoryAnalysis.Form1.Form1_Load(Object, ...	0.0	0.3	1	5,208.0
MemoryAnalysis.Form1.AddOrder_Click(Objec...	0.0	0.2	5	626.2
MemoryAnalysis.Form1.button2_Click(Object,...	0.0	1.4	1	2,174.8
MemoryAnalysis.Form1.button1_Click(Object,...	0.0	0.8	1	1,735.8
MemoryAnalysis.Form1.AllocateLOH(Int32)	0.0	1.4	1	1,517.9
MemoryAnalysis.Form1.UpdateQueueLength(...	0.0	0.1	5	182.7
MemoryAnalysis.CurrencyManager..ctor(void)	0.0	0.0	1	394.5
MemoryAnalysis.CurrencyManager.add_OnPri...	0.0	0.0	6	4.2
MemoryAnalysis.Order..ctor(void)	0.0	0.0	5	4.3
MemoryAnalysis.CurrencyManager.Stop(void)	0.0	0.0	1	8.9

Figure 6.7: DevPartner Performance analysis.

Performance Expert Analysis

As with performance timing analysis, Performance Expert Analysis (Figure 6.8) is started from within Visual Studio, and additional buttons appear which allow you to take performance snapshots. This time, the application is being measured for CPU, disk, network activity, and Wait time, which are all potential bottlenecks.

When a snapshot is taken, the most CPU-intensive execution paths and functions are displayed, and various forms of analysis are available. Execution path analysis allows you to perform a call graph analysis on the execution path. The functions analysis displays a grid of resource statistics for each function, allowing you to sort by each column. From this view, you can quickly determine the most intensive functions in terms of CPU/disk, etc.

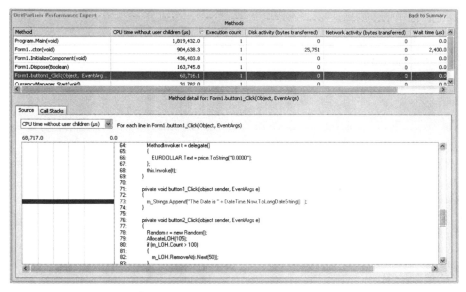

Figure 6.8: DevPartner Performance Expert analysis.

Other tools

In addition to the profiling tools, DevPartner also has:

- **Code review tool**
  Code quality, standards, security analysis

- **Code coverage analyzer**
  Determines how much of an application has been tested, and what hasn't been tested.

Microsoft Visual Studio 2008 profiling tools

Visual Studio 2008 Team Edition has a built-in performance and memory profiler, and you can choose to use either sampling or instrumentation methodologies. As well as the usual performance timing and memory allocation information, it is also possible to collect additional CPU counters, Windows events and Windows counters with these tools.

A profile report can be produced at any time, at which point a summary report is displayed from where you can drill into the data or select more detailed reports from a drop-down list. The report view provides a filter mechanism which allows for the creation of sophisticated queries on the available data. It's also possible to compare reports, which is useful, for example, to check that an optimization has been successful.

Performance Explorer

Visual Studio's profiler settings have a lot of options available, and so multiple performance analysis configurations can be set up for the same application in a Performance Explorer window. You may, for example, have separate configurations for Sampling and Instrumentation, and for Memory and Performance profiling. All of the reports for each configuration are stored together.

Performance Analyzer

On completion of a test, the performance analyzer will give a summary of the worst functions, as well as reports on most called functions, functions with the most individual work, and functions taking the longest.

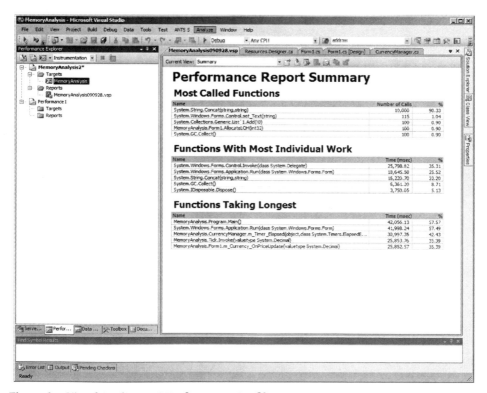

Figure 6.9: Visual Studio 2008 Performance Profiler.

From here, you can choose a function from the list and view its callers, its child calls, or you can view the source, if available. The profiler works well at the function level, but has only a crude reporting mechanism to give code line-level statistics. The next version of Visual Studio 2010 will address this issue, giving full line-level timings and source code visibility. Many other reports can be selected, including a function grid to determine the slowest functions, and a call tree to identify the slowest execution paths. It is possible, using a combination of the reports, to find function bottlenecks, which is naturally a good starting point to being able to correct these issues.

Memory Analyzer

To carry out a memory analysis (see Figure 6.10) you need to make sure that the Performance Explorer configuration you are using has the following .NET memory profiling options set:

- Collect .NET object allocation information

  - helps identify expensive allocated classes and functions.
- Also collect .NET object lifetime information

  - memory leaks
  - mid-life crisis detection
  - Large Object Heap issues.

The application can now be launched from within the Performance Explorer window.

Run your test transaction, then either press the **Stop** button on the Performance Explorer toolbar, or close your application.

The memory analyzer (see Figure 6.11) reports on:

- functions allocating the most memory

- types with the most memory allocated

- types with the most instances.

From the summary, you can view reports that detail:

- object allocation (largest allocated classes and the methods that allocated them)

- object lifetime (when objects are de-allocated)

- call tree (most memory expensive function call trees).

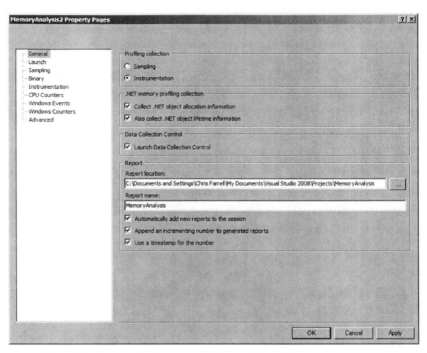

Figure 6.10: Visual Studio 2008 memory analysis configuration.

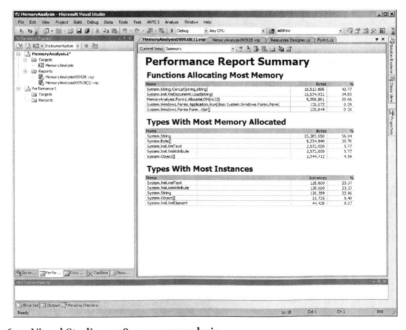

Figure 6.11: Visual Studio 2008 memory analysis.

What to look for

Let's now look briefly at some of the main types of problem that can be uncovered using the tools described above. As this chapter is just an introduction to the noble art of profiling, all of the techniques mentioned will be described in more detailed in subsequent chapters.

Performance analysis

The following key indicators can be used to identify potential bottlenecks and problems in your code. We will cover performance profiling in Chapter 7.

High call count

Functions with very high call counts should be treated with suspicion and investigated. Often the high call count is valid, but sometimes it's due to an error in event handling, and can be a major source of unintended processing

Resolution

Using the call graphing facility of your performance tool, it should be possible to trace back to where the calls to the function originate, and decide if it is acceptable behaviour. It's a very quick and easy check, and a very quick optimization if a problem is found.

I have actually lost count of the number of times I have found this issue in live code!

Slowest function excluding child calls

This is the slowest function where the body of the function itself is responsible for the time. It includes time spent calling .NET framework functions, but excludes time spent calling other source code functions. In other words, it's answering the question, "What's the slowest function we have written?"

Resolution

Identify the slowest functions excluding child calls and then, if available, look for the slowest code lines and determine if they are optimizable. You will often see slow lines waiting for database and web service calls to return.

Slowest function including child calls

This is the slowest function where the total cost of the functions, including time spent into calls to child functions (we have written), is accounted for.

Resolution

Use your tool's call graph facility to explore the slowest part of the call tree.

Functions with high CPU utilization

Any function with high CPU utilization is a prime candidate for optimization, as high resource demands can be a key bottleneck.

Resolution

Identify the most CPU-intensive lines of code within the function and determine if there are workable optimizations that may apply.

Functions with Wait time

Functions with Wait time can indicate performance problems in other application layers, or problems with thread locking (I'll discuss thread locking in Chapter 7, where it'll be more relevant).

Resolution

Identify which resource the function is waiting for, e.g. database or web service, then investigate the cause of the contention on that layer.

Functions generating disk activity

A function generating disk activity needs to be investigated further, as it is demanding resources and is therefore a potential bottleneck.

Resolution

Make sure the disk activity is necessary, particularly if this is a server application. Even if it is necessary, try to find an alternative if possible.

Functions generating network activity

A function generating network activity needs to be investigated further as another potential bottleneck.

Resolution

Make sure the network activity is valid and not an artifact left behind from prototyping or developer testing. Ensure that the number of times this network activity occurs is as low as possible, to reduce the effect of latency. If possible, get more data in one hit.

Memory analysis

When and where you create objects in your code has far-reaching consequences for the application as a whole. Allocating too early and for too long will increase the application's memory footprint. Leave references to objects in collections or from event listeners, for example, and they will stay in memory indefinitely.

We're going to look at memory analysis in a lot more detail in Chapter 8 but, for now, let's look at some of the key types of analysis that can help improve your application's memory profile.

Memory leak detection

Finding memory leaks is all about identifying objects that are allocated but never garbage collected. Memory leaks always get worse so, in theory, the longer the application runs, the bigger the leak will get, and the easier it will be to see. That doesn't really help when profiling, though, because you need to be able to identify a leak quickly.

Profiling tools help leak detection by allowing you to take memory snapshots. A snapshot usually involves forcing a garbage collection and then recording all of the objects that are left behind in memory. Objects that repeatedly survive garbage collection should be investigated further.

If objects of the same type continually survive garbage collection and keep building up in memory, you need to investigate the references that are keeping those objects in memory. Tracking object references back to source code allows you to find the cause of the leak in your own code, which means you can fix it.

Some profilers track memory allocation by function calls, which allows you to see the functions that are potentially leaking memory. This can also be a highly effective technique for finding a memory leak.

Excessive memory usage

Reducing the overall memory footprint can help an application to coexist with other applications on the desktop or server. It's always worth checking where your application is allocating and retaining large chunks of memory, just to ensure that this behaviour really is necessary. Often, it's done for performance reasons and is perfectly valid, as the memory overhead is worth the performance gain. Unfortunately, I have analyzed many applications where large amounts of data are held but then never used again, and this is the kind of behaviour you need to be on the lookout for.

Inefficient allocation and retention

Certain programming techniques, such as string concatenation, for example, can create large numbers of intermediate objects on the heap, which makes the garbage collector work harder than it needs to. The harder the garbage collector works, the greater the performance impact on the application.

Detecting when your application is allocating inefficiently will allow you correct the issue.

Large Object Heap fragmentation

The Large Object Heap is used to store objects that are greater than 85K in size. The trouble is, it can become fragmented, which can lead to the heap size expanding to larger than it needs to be. In severe cases, this can eventually lead to Out of Memory issues. See Chapter 8 for more detail on this.

Production / load test clues

Problems uncovered during load test or in production will usually be accompanied by a wide variety of performance metrics collected from multiple servers. Below are some of the most useful statistics that are widely regarded as key indicators of performance issues (Meier, Vasireddy, Babbar, Mariani, Mackman, and Microsoft, 2004). They are, at the very least, a starting point, and will help you identify where to begin your analysis and which tools to employ. For this article, go to HTTP://MSDN.MICROSOFT.COM/EN-US/LIBRARY/MS998579.ASPX.

General performance counters

The following performance counters can act as general guidelines for different performance problems. Please refer to Chapter 3 for a more detailed breakdown.

* `Processor\% Processor Time`

* `Memory\% Committed Bytes in Use`

* `PhysicalDisk\% Idle Time`

* `Network Interface\Output Queue Length`

* `.NET CLR Memory\% Time in GC`

* `.NET CLR Memory\# Gen 0,1,2 Collections`

* `.NET CLR Memory\# of Pinned Objects`

* `.NET CLR Memory\Large Object Heap Size`

* `.NET CLR LocksAndThreads\Contention Rate/sec`

* `ASP.NET\Requests Queued`

* `ASP.NET\Requests Rejected`

Managing profiling results

Each of the profiling tools stores the profile data in a proprietary flat file format, although some of the tools allow the data to be exported to XML or CSV files.

The main benefit to XML or CSV export is that you can use the data to generate your own reports and publish that data to other systems. This becomes more important when you begin automating your unit testing, because you can also analyze the executing tests using a profiler. Instead of just getting Pass and Fail for your tests, you could also collect performance and stability metrics. By comparing these metrics with previous test runs, it's then possible to identify problems as they occur.

Comparing analysis runs

Applications such as Visual Studio 2008 Profiler and DevPartner Professional have tools which allow various profiling results to be compared, and ANTS Memory Profiler allows for the comparison of memory profiling snapshots. This feature can help to quickly identify where there has been a performance improvement or degradation.

Pre-check-in requirements

In support of proactive analysis, it's a good idea to require developers to include evidence of performance and memory analysis results as part of a source code check-in procedure at the end of a unit of work.

This could be as simple as a manual procedure in which all of the profiler results files are zipped together and added (suitably labelled) to the project office. Alternatively, the source control system itself could be used to define a pre-check-in process requiring the addition of profile results files. This largely depends on how extensible the source control system is. Microsoft Team Foundation Server 2005 and 2008 allow custom check-in policies to be defined, allowing more complex check-in procedures.

Continuous integrated testing

Tools which support command-line execution and XML export can be incorporated into an automated testing framework, in which the automated tests are run and the executing process is profiled using performance or memory analysis.

The results are then extracted to XML and uploaded to a results server, along with the results for the control cases.

To make life even easier, an automated testing framework can be set up to identify when the performance of a test transaction has degraded, and report it to the development team.

Summary

Knowing how to profile an application, and understanding what the potential issues are, will help you write better code. Routinely testing the functionality you have written using a profiler, and looking for the common bottlenecks and problems will allow you to find and fix many minor issues that would otherwise become bigger problems later on.

Load testing as early as possible during development, as well as adding to these tests and running them regularly with the latest builds, will identify problems almost as soon as they occur. It will also highlight when a change has introduced a problem.

In the next two chapters, I will go through the performance and memory issues you might encounter, and techniques you can use to deal with them. I will also highlight how to use some of the most common tools to find and fix problems in your code.

Chapter 7: Performance Profiling

Applications are built from thousands, hundreds of thousands, and even millions of lines of code. Any one of those lines could be hiding performance bottlenecks. Chapter 6 covered how profilers can be used to identify bottlenecks by analyzing execution time and the use of resources such as the CPU.

Profiling is important because it focuses developer attention on lines of code that would otherwise go unnoticed in the mass of application complexity. Code may take a long time to execute, use a lot of CPU, or just wait for seemingly no reason. Once attention is drawn, the developer starts asking more searching and detailed questions of the code. It's during this process that either an optimization is discovered or a performance limitation is highlighted. Either way, the issue is discovered and its impact when the application runs at its peak load can be assessed.

.NET developers have a rich array of profiling tools available, from the basic to the advanced. The great thing about performance profiling is that, regardless of the tool, you will always use the same methodology to carry out your profile. This really boils down to a list of key performance metrics that you need to assess for every application method.

In this chapter, I will explain what the issues are in performance profiling, and what profiling can, and can't, do. We will go through where an application typically spends its time, and how an application competes for server and local resources. Next, we will look at the different types of profilers and what to look for when profiling your application. We will finish off by looking at how to use what are, in my view, some of the best commercial profiling tools on the market today, and also the profiling tools already included within Microsoft Visual Studio Team edition.

By the end, I hope you will agree that, once you understand the significance of the key performance statistics we will discuss, profiling an application test transaction can be carried out quickly and effectively. After profiling your first application, I hope you will also agree that the most surprising lines of code can turn out to be the bottlenecks!

A caveat

Performance profiling has two major flaws. The first is that it affects the performance of that which it measures. Just like checking the pressure of a tyre, you change what you measure. The second prevalent problem is that profiling on your workstation will never find the same issues that load testing will eventually uncover. The best we can hope for from profiling is that it may hint at potential bottlenecks for optimization.

I'm not advocating that developers should spend huge amounts of time "micro-performance-optimizing" code. What I *am* saying is that, with the right training and tools, they can identify potential problems and bottlenecks and fix them as part of their pre-check-in tests.

Spending time optimizing code is only worthwhile if the gain will be significant. Trying to optimize a loop currently taking 20ms may be academically interesting but ultimately pointless. Optimizing a loop taking 500ms in code executing on a server is a different story, because the optimization will be realized for every hit.

What the load test will tell you (and profilers can't)

Profiling will highlight the slowest / most CPU-intensive methods executed during a test. Bottlenecks are identified because methods responsible for the largest percentages of total execution and CPU time stand out.

A bottleneck identified during profiling is likely to be magnified when the application is running at full capacity with maximum application load. When an application is stressed in this way, other bottlenecks begin to appear as resources begin to max out. Memory, disk, network and database access can all cause problems, and further impact CPU usage in ways that were impossible to predict during a standard profile.

Load testing is designed to highlight these kinds of problems and load testing tools deliberately stress an application by firing large numbers of transactions at them.

Load testing

A load test will reveal lots of both cool *and* uncomfortable stuff about an application. Either way, saying, "Well it worked fine on my machine," doesn't really cut it any more.

Probably the two most important statistics or Key Performance Indicators (KPIs) from the load test for each test transaction are the **transaction response time under peak load** and the **maximum transaction throughput per second**. They are important because the response time, peak load, and transaction throughput will likely be key requirements for your project, and if the application doesn't meet them then there's a problem, and it's time to dust off that old copy of a code profiler and get to work!

The load test will give you a lot more data in addition to the main KPIs, namely the performance monitoring statistics (see Chapters 3 and 6) which can be collected from each of the different layers of the application architecture.

This is your starting point, since those KPIs will begin to show which servers were maxing out when the peaks and break loads were hit, and these indicators should at least point towards where the bottlenecks might be among CPU, disk, network, synchronization, memory, etc. If the bottlenecks are in .NET application servers, you can profile the relevant transaction using a code profiler. If it's a database, then using an appropriate database profiler will help.

This relatively simple approach can work, but the truth is that, in a complex distributed architecture, it often won't. In this case, you really need to get a good understanding of where your application transaction actually spends its time across the layers.

Where is it slow?

Timing an entire transaction of a distributed application doesn't really tell you a lot, because it hides the detail of what went on behind the scenes. I could just as well tell you that it took me 15 hours to get from London to New York City when, in fact, the flight only took 8 hours and the rest of the time was spent delayed. But even that's not the whole story.

- 30 minutes – travel to airport

- 2 hours – check in

- 4.5 hours – delay

- 8 hours – flight.

A typical application will have a distinct set of phases, each taking its own chunk of the elapsed time.

- Client processing time

    - CPU time

    - thread contention/Wait time

    - disk contention

    - graphics/painting/GPU contention.

- Client network send time (client to server)

  - time to wire (getting the data packets onto the card)

  - time on the wire (latency and error handling).

- Server processing time

  - request wait time / queuing (server queues request until ready)

  - CPU time

  - thread contention

  - disk contention

  - network contention

  - wait time making calls to other server resources.

- Server network send time (server to client)

  - time to wire

  - time on the wire.

With all of this happening, considering an elapsed time of (for example) 5,000 milliseconds, where is the bit that is slow? Is it all equally contributing or is there a definitive bottleneck?

To answer these sorts of questions, there are tools available that can identify exactly where the time for particular transactions is being spent. In most cases they involve installing probes onto each of the layers, and those probes then communicate with a central management tool that performs network packet analysis and matching. The result is a breakdown of how long each layer took to process, send and receive data to and from each of the other layers. Because such tools are operating at the network packet level, they can identify many common network problems as well, including latency, congestion, and errors/noise.

It's also possible to collect high-level performance data from some of these tools, which can include lists of the slowest methods and methods with possible memory issues. The leading vendors in this field include Compuware, DynaTrace and Opnet.

All of these tools provide additional information that can be used by developers to profile and debug their code in a more targeted and intelligent way.

When to start testing

In my view, the answer to the question, "When should you start testing?" is the same for performance, unit and load testing – that is, as soon as you can after development starts. Checking for bottlenecks using profiling tools will find many issues that would otherwise become load test or production issues later on, but it's the load test that will ultimately tell you if what you have written will meet the requirement.

Competing resources

All processes running on a machine have to compete for resources such as CPU, GPU, disk, network, memory, etc., and every time there is a scarcity, someone has to wait for their turn or time slice. In addition, every time an application asks another machine for some data, a whole new world of competition opens up, together with new opportunities to wait.

Add to that the fact that threads running within the processes have also to contend with each other to get access to shared resources, which can result in their having to wait for resources to become available.

The art of performance profiling is, in fact, to turn it into a science, and identify the methods executing in an application that:

- take a long time to complete

- use a lot of CPU

- create network activity

- create disk activity

- wait for other servers

- block or become blocked by other threads.

Ultimately, it's the code we have written that is doing the work. Sure, we make calls to .NET framework classes, but we can't change those so, if there is any optimizing to do, it's going to be in our code. Ideally, for each of the stats listed above, we need to know two things:

- what are the worst performing methods – excluding the impact from any calls made to other non-framework methods?

- what are the worst performing method call trees – the worst method, including the impact from any calls it makes to other non-framework methods?

Sometimes a single method can be really slow and a major bottleneck, but equally a sequence of method calls (call tree where one method calls another which calls another, etc.) can be a bottleneck when taken together, even though, individually, they're not.

With the issue of resource competition in mind, the profiler you choose should ideally capture the maximum amount of information whilst adding the minimum of overhead.

Types of profiler

There are four main types of profiler, that differ in their approach and in the impact they have on the application they measure. I'll give you a breakdown here.

Sampling profiler

A sampling profiler will periodically, usually based on a number of CPU cycles, record the application call stack. The call stack records the current executing method and the method that called it, etc. Recording the call stack therefore gives a snapshot of the methods that were in the process of being called.

Using a statistical approach to this information, it's possible to identify the most heavily-called methods and call trees. The overhead to this approach is relatively low, and can easily be configured by altering the frequency of stack sampling.

Key statistics such as call count and accurate measures of response time are impossible to find using sampling, but this method does have a low overhead, and it gives a surprisingly accurate snapshot of an application's "hotspots." Many server-based monitoring tools use sampling to give performance statistics without adding excessive overhead to the executing application.

Event-based profiling

The Common Language Runtime can be configured to send notifications to a specific DLL when memory allocation, garbage collection, and other events occur. This DLL can use the information provided to accumulate performance statistics.

Concurrency (thread contention) profiling

Increasing numbers of applications now use asynchronous processes and multi-threading. To cope with the problems caused by multiple threads accessing shared resources, developers employ synchronization mechanisms to control access to those resources. It's a nice idea in principle, but unfortunately this can lead to threads contending with each other for the same resource, causing locks.

Thread contention profiling analyzes thread synchronization within the running application and so identifies potential problems. There is obviously overhead involved with concurrency profiling, which basically hooks onto the .NET and native synchronization methods, recording when blocking occurs and for how long, as well as the call stack.

Instrumenting profilers

Instrumenting profilers actually modify the binary of the application by placing probes at the start and end of each application method, and around every system method. These probes are used by the profiler to time method execution speed and for iteration counting.

Instrumenting profilers give the most detailed results, but have by far the highest overhead and, as a result, are nearly always a developer-only tool and can't normally be used in a test or production environment.

Choosing a profiler

When choosing a profiler, you need to be sure that it will actually work with your key and future applications, and that you can actually use it effectively.

The first part is fairly easy, because most of the tool vendors allow you to download full evaluation copies of their tools, usually with limited-duration licenses. Take advantage of this and just make sure the thing works on your worst app.

The next question is whether the tool makes sense to you. You need a tool that you and your team can use quickly and efficiently, otherwise it won't be used and will become shelfware.

You also need to be sure the tool is affordable, because there is a wide diversity of pricing and licensing issues to consider. You don't want to have to put together a cost benefit assessment on performance analysis (although I have the PowerPoint slides if you need them!).

What profilers can measure

Let's look at some of the key metrics that many profilers collect for both methods and call trees.

- **Elapsed time / wall-clock time**: this is the amount of time a method or call tree took to complete if you timed it with a stopwatch. It includes processing time and time spent waiting for everything else to complete.

- **CPU/application time**: this is the time that was spent executing on the processor. This excludes any Wait time or time executing on other threads.

- **Network activity**: the number of bytes of network activity generated by the method or call tree. Often this statistic can be broken down into bytes read and bytes written.

- **Disk activity**: the number of bytes of disk activity generated by the method or call tree. This statistic can also often be broken down into bytes read and bytes written.

- **Wait time**: the time spent waiting for other resources or synchronization locks.

What to look for

Profiling is all about inspecting the slowest and most CPU-intensive methods in a test transaction relative to the rest of the methods that executed. You will normally see a list of five to ten methods which are significantly larger than the rest. They need inspecting line by line, and this is when your expertise comes into play, because you will start asking questions of your code. The most surprisingly innocuous lines of code can hide performance issues that can be easily optimized.

Knowing what is significant relies on your knowledge of the application, and depends on whether the application is client based or server based. Server-based applications need to optimize resource usage to cope with large transaction loads. Reducing the CPU time of a function by 200ms becomes a much bigger optimization when multiplied by a number of concurrent hits. The profiler statistics below are used to identify slow, frequent, or intensive methods.

High method call counts

This is both the simplest, and one of the most common, optimizations. A non-trivial method with an unusually high call count needs to be investigated, and nearly every application I have profiled has uncovered at least one example of this problem.

You've probably come across it whilst debugging with breakpoints in your code. You hit the breakpoint as expected, continue, and then immediately hit the breakpoint again. It's then that you realize there's a problem. For every one you find through using breakpoints, quite a few more are missed. It almost justifies code profiling on its own.

Once you have found a "problem method," your profiling tool should be able to trace backwards in the call stack to show you where the parent calls originated.

Slowest methods (excluding child time)

Identify the slow methods that exclude time spent in calls to your own methods and, if the tool allows it, identify the slowest line. If the line is a call to a web service or database, then there may be some optimization work to do on one of these layers.

A method could be slow simply because it is carrying out a complex processing algorithm. Now that you know it's slow, this could be a good time to re-evaluate the logic and look for optimizations.

CPU-intensive methods

CPU-intensive methods are identified using a statistic which excludes Wait time and just reports work carried out by the processor. If a method is CPU intensive, look for the worst line and determine if there is a possible optimization. If the whole method is responsible then, as with the slowest method, you should re-evaluate the algorithm.

Don't forget that CPU-intensive methods are accessing a scarce resource, and this could become a bottleneck under load in a server environment. A method with a disproportionately high CPU usage is an absolutely key target for optimization.

A method with low CPU time but high elapsed time has a high Wait time, and methods with high Wait times are often good candidates for asynchronous processing. ASP.NET pages can benefit particularly from asynchronous processing when they are waiting for I/O resources to return. Running asynchronously whilst waiting for a resource will free a worker thread to process other requests and help increase throughput.

Slowest call trees

For each of the slowest call trees, look to see if there is a single method that is responsible for a large proportion of the time. Many tools provide a "hot path" analysis feature that graphically expands a call tree down to its bottleneck method.

If there is a bottleneck method on the call tree, you can analyze it at the line level to find the slowest lines, and then look for algorithm optimizations.

CPU-intensive call trees

As with slowest call trees, use critical/hot path analysis to find the CPU bottleneck method within the call tree, then analyze at the line level to find the most CPU-intensive lines. Look for algorithm optimizations for the worst cases.

Slow database queries and procedures

Some profilers now give dedicated visibility into data access procedures and will highlight slow SQL queries and stored procedures. The same information is often uncovered with slow method analysis, where slow queries show up as the worst performing lines.

Excessive Wait time

Methods that have significant Wait time for resources or synchronization are often candidates for analysis, as the cause of the Wait time probably needs to be investigated. Often due to database or web service calls, Wait times can hint at problems elsewhere, and can also indicate thread-locking problems.

Methods with network activity

Network resource is a potential bottleneck, so methods with high levels of network read/write activity need to be identified and validated. Most of the time the activity is necessary, but it is worth checking the frequency of the calls and the latency statistics for the network link that will be used in production. A method with a high call count and network activity across a high latency network link is going to be a problem in production.

The other question to ask is whether the application is being too "chatty" – can the data requirements be satisfied with less frequent calls that return more data?

Methods with disk activity

Methods with heavy disk utilization need validation as they are potential bottlenecks. Often the speed of the disk controller is the rate-limiting step for a machine, so any method adding to disk overhead and contention is an optimization target. You will frequently identify disk activity accessing configuration or XML files that really should be cached after first access.

This check can also uncover where developer shortcuts or proof-of-concept work has been left in the code. On a number of occasions, I've seen code being left behind that had been put together quickly, with the intention of optimizing later.

Using the tools

Let's now go through some of the tools that are available for .NET performance profiling, and see how they can be used to uncover some of the problems we've discussed in this book.

ANTS Performance Profiler 5

With Red Gate's ANTS Performance Profiler, you can profile the following application types:

- .NET executable

- ASP.NET web application (IIS and WebDev)

- Windows service

- COM+ server

- XBAP (local XAML browser app).

You can record wall-clock and CPU time during the same profiling run, and switch between the two during results analysis, which is a really useful feature.

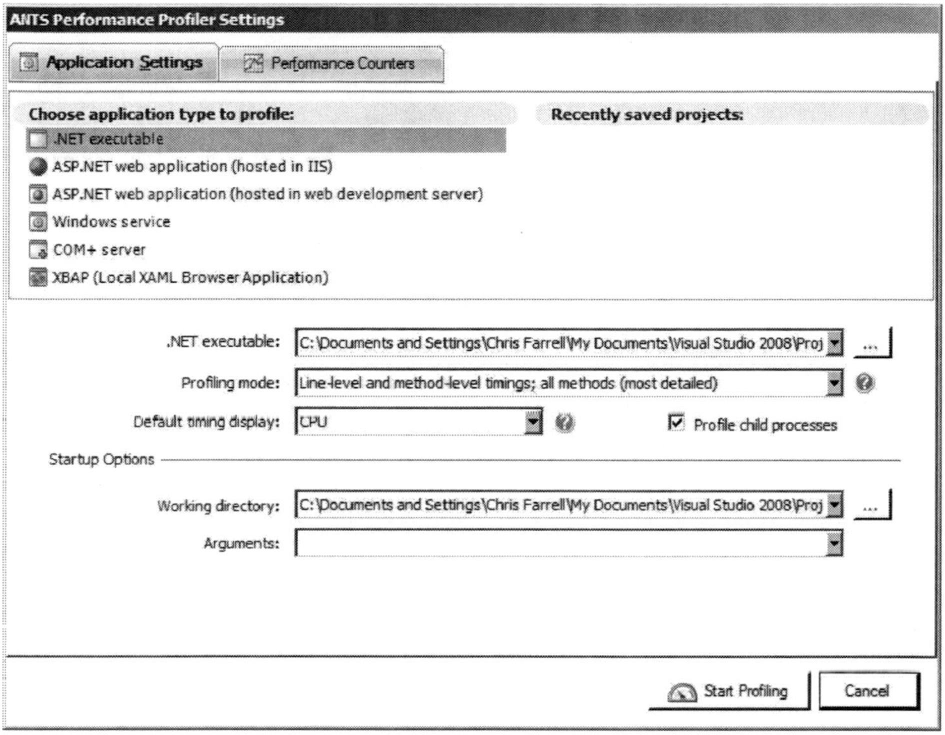

Figure 7.1: ANTS Performance Profiler settings.

Various performance counters can be added to the analysis, which will be displayed in the performance viewer after profiling starts. Typical counters include ones for various processor, memory, I/O, .NET and ASP.NET metrics.

Running an analysis

Choose the application to profile and press the **Start Profiling** button, and the performance analysis window will be displayed (Figure 7.2). The timeline graph at the top displays the % processor time along with the other performance counters you selected at startup.

The timeline is really important because you will use the various counters to identify regions of interest, which will typically involve high CPU usage, % time in garbage collection, and I/O read/writes. Wherever you see a spike in activity or a protracted period of processing, you can focus in on just this region and analyze what the application was doing. You can investigate any interesting region by dragging the mouse across it, selecting it for analysis.

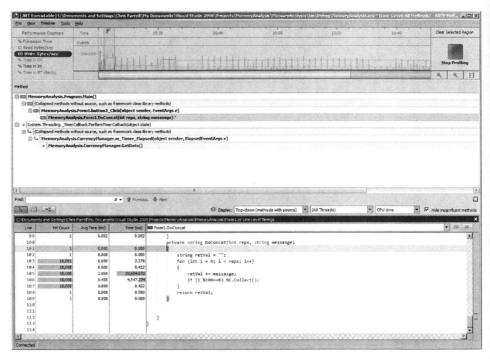

Figure 7.2: ANTS Performance Profiler window.

Interpreting results

The results for the selected region will be displayed in the call tree below, where all of the methods called will be displayed (Figure 7.3).

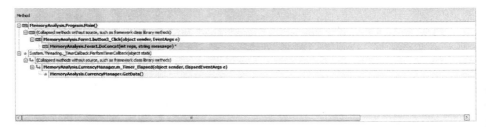

Figure 7.3: ANTS Performance Profiler, call tree.

You can choose to display the method results in a number of views: call tree, grid or call graph.

From the toolbar (in the middle of Figure 7.2) you can switch between viewing wall-clock and CPU timings. Another useful feature is the check box to **Hide insignificant methods** which hides methods responsible for less than 1% of the overall contribution. This will reduce some of the extra noise from the results that can sometimes make it difficult to see the real problems.

Call tree view

The call tree view (Figure 7.3) displays the method execution paths for the selected region, and will highlight the execution path contributing most in terms of either wall-clock or CPU time (hot/critical path analysis). You can choose to view the execution path in either top-down (caller to callee) or bottom-up (callee to caller) orientations.

Additionally, you can opt to view only methods with source code, which sometimes reduces the complexity of the call tree and makes it easier to see the contribution of your own code. Selecting an individual method displays the source code in the viewer below, together with line-level statistics for either wall-clock or CPU timings.

Hot path analysis is a great starting point in performance analysis because it immediately highlights the worst method in the worst execution path, taking you straight to the line-level code statistics.

Grid view

The methods grid view (Figure 7.4), displays every method called during the selected time frame. The list can be filtered to display only methods with source code, and can display either CPU or wall-clock time.

Namespace	Method Name	Time (ms)	Time With Children (ms)	Hit Count	Source File
System.Windows.Forms	Control.Invoke(Delegate method, object[] args)	0.005	851.400	3	
System.Threading	ExecutionContext.Run(ExecutionContext executionContext, Con...	0.004	2,344.567	6	
System.Threading	_TimerCallback.PerformTimerCallback(object state)	0.004	2,344.401	3	
System.Windows.Forms	Button.WndProc(Message m)	0.004	26,129.345	97	
System.Data.SqlClient	SqlDataReader.Close()	0.002	1,153.025	3	
System.Threading	_TimerCallback.TimerCallback_Context(object state)	0.001	2,344.430	3	
System.Windows.Forms	Control.Invoke(Delegate method)	0.001	851.401	3	
System.Data.Common	DbDataReader.Dispose(bool disposing)	0.001	1,153.005	3	
System.Data.Common	DbDataReader.Dispose()	0.000	1,153.006	3	
MemoryAnalysis	**Program.Main()**	0.000	26,133.814	1	Program.cs
System.Windows.Forms	Application.Run(Form mainForm)	0.000	26,133.814	1	
System.Windows.Forms	Application+ThreadContext.RunMessageLoop(int reason, Applica...	0.000	26,133.814	1	
System.Windows.Forms	Application+ThreadContext.RunMessageLoop(int reason, A...	0.000	26,133.814	1	

Figure 7.4: ANTS Performance Profiler, methods grid.

This view is the simplest yet, for me, the most powerful, because you can very quickly find out a number of crucial things:

- **Methods with high call counts** (hit count)

  - sort the grid by descending hit count

  - investigate methods with unusually high call counts using the call graph button.

- **CPU-intensive methods**

  - choose CPU time and sort by descending time

  - view the source for the slowest methods and look at the slowest lines

  - can they be optimized?

- **CPU-intensive method call trees**

  - choose CPU time and sort by descending time with children

  - use the call graph to investigate where in the call tree the most time is being spent.

- **Slowest method** – excluding time spent in calls to other non-framework methods (e.g. ones you've written)

  - choose wall-clock time and sort by descending time

  - view the source for the slowest methods and look at the slowest lines

  - can they be optimized?

- **Slowest method call tree** – including time spent in calls to child or other non-framework methods

  - choose wall-clock time and sort by descending time with children

  - use the call graph to investigate where in the call tree the most time is being spent.

By comparing methods between wall-clock and CPU time, you can identify methods with significant Wait time. A method with Wait time may be blocking due to thread synchronization, or it could just be waiting for a network resource to return.

Call graph

The call graph helps you to understand a method's calling relationships more clearly, and to trace execution paths in a more intuitive and explorative way.

You can drill into the call tree and investigate the most expensive paths for either wait or CPU time. You can also trace back into the call tree to find out where calls are coming from.

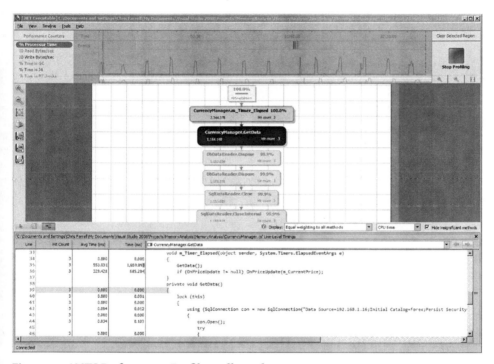

Figure 7.5: ANTS Performance Profiler, call graph.

The call graph is most often used from either the call tree or the grid view to investigate a method's calling relationships.

Optimizing analysis

Although it is already a low-overhead profiler, ANTS provides some additional options to reduce overhead even further.

Reducing tools overhead

ANTS can be configured to give method-level or line-level timings. Line-level timings add greater overhead but provide a much deeper level of analysis, as they allow you to find the slowest line of code as well as the slowest method. Overhead can be reduced further by restricting the profiler to only profiling methods that have source code.

You can also stop the ANTS Profiler tool from profiling child processes, which will reduce overhead even more. All of these features are set when starting an analysis (Figure 7.1).

DevPartner Studio Professional 9.1

DevPartner has two separate profilers, one for elapsed time analysis, the other for resource analysis. You can profile the following types of applications:

- .NET executable

- ASP.NET web application (IIS and WebDev)

- Windows service

- COM+ server

- JavaScript (timing analyzer only).

Performance timing profiler

DevPartner's timing profiler can analyze both managed and unmanaged native applications, and it requires instrumentation which, for managed applications, is carried out dynamically when profiling begins. Unmanaged applications need to be compiled and linked using a DevPartner-specific compiler/linker (wrappers to `cl.exe` and `link.exe` called `nmcl.exe` and `nmlink.exe`).

A combination of managed and instrumented native applications can be profiled together.

Running an analysis

The profiling session can be started from within Visual Studio using the DevPartner toolbar menu, in which case the application will immediately build and execute under the profiler. It can also be run from the command line using command-line switches or an XML configuration file. DevPartner can be configured, either to start the process or service to be profiled itself, or to wait for it to start.

Once the application has loaded, you can run your test transaction. When running under the profiler, a toolbar is displayed that has a drop-down list of all of the processes that are working with the running application. You can choose a process from the list and then use one of the toolbar buttons to take a performance snapshot, stop profiling, or clear all recorded data so far.

Pressing the **Take Snapshot** button or exiting the application will create the performance session report (Figure 7.6).

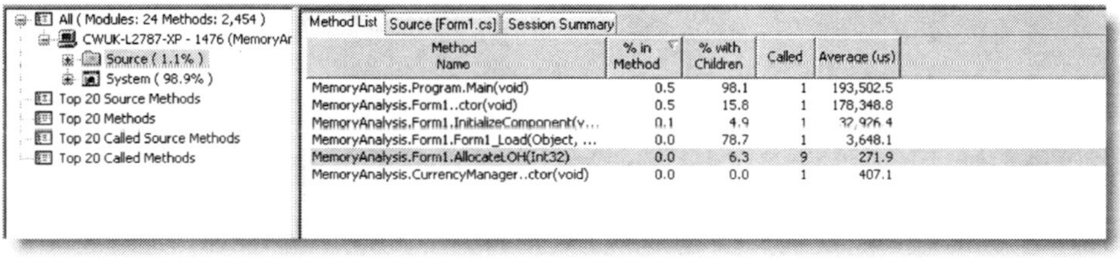

Figure 7.6: DevPartner performance profiler summary.

The default results columns displayed (you can choose additional columns) are shown in this table.

% in Method	% time spent in executing in method only – including system/ framework calls, but not in your own child method calls
% with Children	% time spent executing in method and all child method calls
Called	how frequently the method was called
Average	total time divided by the number of times called

Analyzing the results

- Sort the grid by the **% in Method** column to find the slowest methods.

- Right-click on the largest contributors and choose **Go to Method Source**, and the source view for the method will be displayed (Figure 7.7).

Count	% with Child...	Time ...	Source
			private void button2_Click(object sender, EventArgs e)
			{
			Random r = new Random();
			AllocateLOH(105);
			if (m_LOH.Count > 100)
			{
			m_LOH.RemoveAt(r.Next(50));
			}
			}
			private void AllocateLOH(int startSize)
100	0.0	84.5	{
100	0.0	2,471.0	Random r = new Random();
100	0.0	3,699.2	int siz = r.Next(10000) + (int)(startSize * (1024));
100	0.5	623,278.8	lblSize.Text = siz.ToString();
100	0.0	11,936.6	byte[] t = new byte[siz];
100	25.0	29,322,...	r.NextBytes(t);
100	0.0	1,218.3	m_LOH.Add(t);
100	0.0	399.8	}

Figure 7.7: DevPartner performance analysis source view.

- The source for the method will be displayed, together with timing information for each line, and the slowest line will be highlighted in red.

- Sort the grid by the **% with Children** column to find the slowest call trees.

- Right-click on each one and choose **Go to Call Graph**; the call graph for the method will be displayed (Figure 7.8).

- The call graph allows you to navigate through the call tree for the selected methods and investigate the method call relationships and where the time is being spent. The slowest call path is always displayed at the top with the critical hot path arrows highlighted in brown. Navigate along the critical path until you get to a method responsible for the largest majority of the time. This method will be highlighted in yellow and is the call tree bottleneck.

- Sort by the **Called** column to validate the most frequently called methods.

- To investigate high call counts for a method, you need to understand where the calls are originating. To do this, use the **Go to Call Graph** feature, described above, to investigate the callers of the selected method.

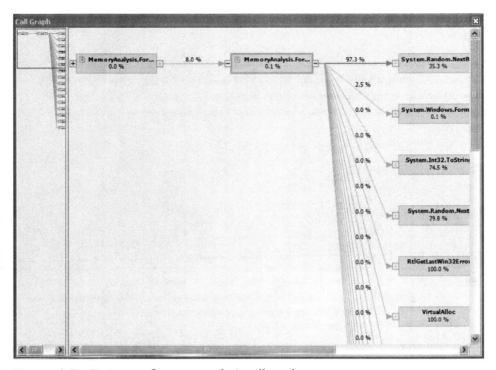

Figure 7.8: DevPartner performance analysis call graph.

Comparing results

DevPartner has a comparison tool that allows you to compare two performance traces and analyze the differences.

Optimizing analysis

DevPartner provides a number of different ways for you to reduce the level of overhead caused by profiling. You can exclude specific modules from profiling and reduce the level of information collected.

Isolating components

DevPartner allows you to add executables (exe, dll, ocx) as exclusions as part of the DevPartner Exclusions options within Visual Studio. They will not be instrumented at runtime (.NET) or monitored for performance. System Images can also be excluded with the DevPartner exclusions options, in which case performance data will only be collected for user code.

Reducing tools overhead

Each project can have the following optimization settings made:

Collect COM information	when set to "False," information won't be collected about COM interfaces/methods
Exclude others	when set to "True," will disregard elapsed time spent in other application threads, thus only reporting actual time rather than wall-clock time
Instrumentation level	as mentioned earlier, method level is lower overhead but lower detail than line level

Performance resource profiler (performance expert)

The resource profiler is a .NET-only tool and can collect CPU, network, disk, and synchronization/Wait time data, and it is really useful precisely because it can begin to highlight potential resource bottlenecks in your application. Always remember that small resource bottlenecks on a development machine can scale to a major bottleneck on a server under load.

Running an analysis

The profiling session can be started from within Visual Studio using the DevPartner toolbar menu, or it can be run from the command line.

Starting it within Visual Studio displays a performance graph where CPU, disk, and network utilization for the running application are traced. **Clear Recorded Data** and **View Results** buttons are also available on this menu.

After running the test transaction, you can either exit the application or press the **View Results** button, after which a summary report is displayed (Figure 7.9), giving the five execution paths and methods using the most CPU.

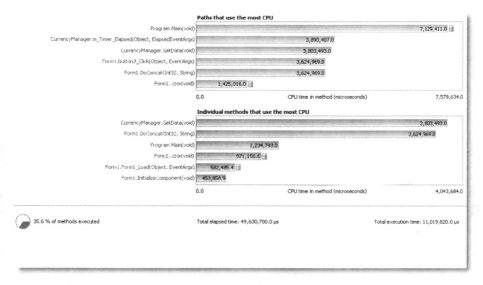

Figure 7.9: DevPartner Performance Expert analysis summary.

Analyzing the results

The method view is the most useful report with Performance Expert, because it allows you to quickly identify methods with potential resource bottlenecks. By clicking on one of the methods in the top five methods list, the method view will be displayed (Figure 7.10).

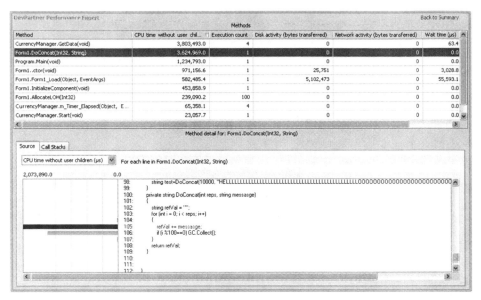

Figure 7.10: DevPartner Performance Expert method view.

All you need to do is sort by the following columns:

- CPU

- Disk activity (can be broken down further into Read/Write)

- Network activity (can be broken down further into Read/Write)

- Wait time/synchronization (synchronization errors, counts, waits).

Select each method listed with high or unusual activity, and the line with the highest activity will be highlighted in red and should be investigated further.

The most CPU-intensive call trees can be investigated by clicking on one of the trees in the summary to display a call graph for the chosen call tree (Figure 7.11).

The critical path is displayed at the top and can be traced to find the slowest method on the path. If there's more than one method on the path, a list of **Slowest methods along all called paths** is displayed and the slowest method can be chosen from here to identify the bottleneck method.

Unlike the Performance Timing profiler, Performance Expert doesn't have a comparison tool.

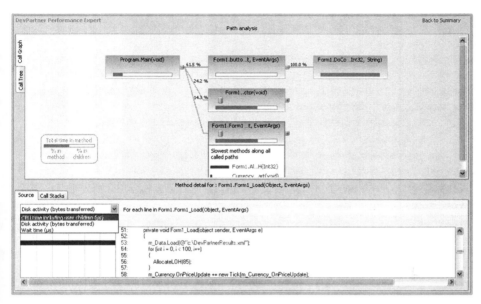

Figure 7.11: DevPartner Performance Expert call graph.

Optimizing analysis

To reduce the impact of profiling, individual projects can be excluded from analysis by setting the **Include in Analysis** property of the project's properties to "False."

Visual Studio Professional 2008/2010

Visual Studio 2008 Team Edition has a built-in performance profiler that can analyze your application using either sampling or instrumentation. You can access the profiler from the **Analyze** menu option from within Visual Studio, from where you can launch the **Performance Wizard**. This wizard will ask you to select the application to analyze and the profiling method to use (either sampling or instrumentation).

A session will be created in the Performance Explorer window from where you can change profiling properties, control the assemblies to be profiled and manage performance results.

Running an analysis

To start the analysis, press the **Launch with Profiling** button from within the Performance Explorer window and your application will launch, ready to run your test transaction. Alternatively you could press **Launch with Profiling Paused**, in which case the application will still load, but you can choose to start the profiler later on. This can be useful if you only want to collect data for a specific part of the application and need to navigate to it first.

Once your test transaction is complete, either stop your application, or press the **Stop Profiling** button from the Data Collection window. A summary report of the performance results will be displayed, which will vary slightly, depending on whether you chose a sampling or an instrumentation methodology.

From here, you can choose to view a number of detailed reports including method lists, call trees, and modules. On many of the reports you can apply noise reduction by selecting the **Noise Reduction Properties** button, which allows you to exclude from the report methods contributing less than a certain percentage overhead.

As sampling and instrumented profiles give you different data, let's go through them separately.

Sampling analysis

Sampling is a very low-overhead profiling option because it periodically samples the application, recording the method at the top of the call stack and its associated call tree. This is great for identifying methods and call trees with potentially high CPU usage, but not so good for processes that wait for other resources such as network, disk, or database calls to return. It's also clearly no use if you want to know exactly how many times a method has been called.

The more a method is found during a sample, the more CPU it is likely to be using. It's not precise but it is low overhead. You can change sampling frequency, and even the event that causes sampling to occur, to be any one of these:

- clock cycles

- page faults

- systems calls

- performance counter (selected from a list).

The results obtained from a sampling analysis can seem a little confusing because they are described in terms of samples, rather than something like milliseconds, as you would expect. A sample count is simply the number of times the method was being called when a sample event took place.

Visual Studio records two sample types:

- inclusive samples – number of times a method was in a call stack

- exclusive samples – number of times a method was top of the call stack.

Inclusive samples indicate that a method was either being called or was in the process of calling other methods. You can use this statistic to find the most expensive call trees.

Exclusive samples allow you to find the methods that are doing the most work.

Figure 7.12 shows a typical summary report for a performance analysis session.

Current View: Summary		

Performance Report Summary

Functions Causing Most Work

Name	Samples	%
[mscorwks.dll]	5,899	99.98
[mscoree.dll]	3,336	56.54
CLRStubOrUnknownAddress	2,433	41.24
MemoryAnalysis.Program.Main()	2,417	40.97
[USER32.dll]	2,410	40.85

Functions Doing Most Individual Work

Name	Samples	%
[mscorwks.dll]	4,109	69.64
System.String.wstrcpy(char*,char*,int32)	1,585	26.86
System.Random.InternalSample()	25	0.42
[rsaenh.dll]	21	0.36
System.Data.SqlClient.TdsParser.SkipRow(class System.Data.SqlClient._SqlMetaDataSet,int32,class System.Data.SqlClient.TdsParserStateObject)	13	0.22

Figure 7.12: Visual Studio 2008 performance analysis sampling summary.

The top five functions (methods) causing the most work, which includes calls to child methods and methods doing the most individual work, are listed in summary. From here, a number of different views can be analyzed, although the most immediately useful are:

- function view (slowest methods and call trees)

- call tree (hot path analysis)

- modules view.

Function view

The function view (Figure 7.13) is a sortable grid that lists all of the functions, both the inclusive and exclusive statistics, plus their percentage contribution overall.

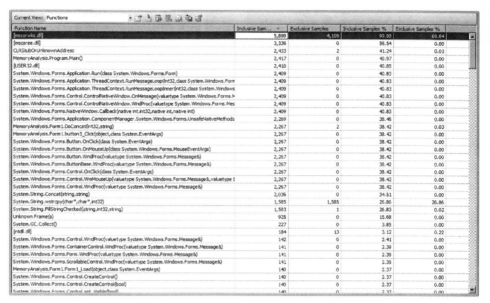

Figure 7.13: Visual Studio 2008 performance analysis function view (sampling).

Sorting by descending inclusive samples will list the methods creating expensive call trees, whereas sorting by exclusive sample lists the methods doing the most individual work.

213

Call tree

The call tree (Figure 7.14), as its name suggests, will display the captured execution paths and will allow you to identify the most expensive path and method.

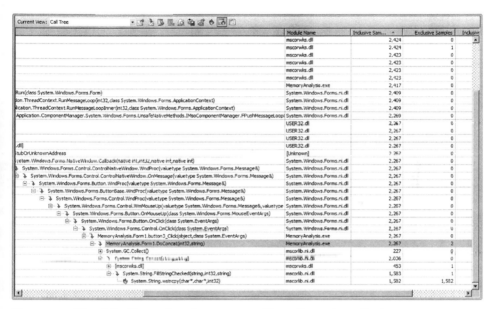

Figure 7.14: Visual Studio 2008 performance profiler call tree (sampling).

Each of the execution paths will be listed in a call tree, and you can navigate down through the call tree to identify bottlenecks. If you select **Show Hot Path Highlighting** and **Expand Hot Path** from the toolbar, the slowest execution path will be expanded and the hottest path and method will be highlighted.

Modules view

Modules view (Figure 7.15) gives you a big picture of where processing is occurring, and you can also use it to identify slow lines of code.

Current View: Modules				
Name	Inclusive Samples	Exclusive Sam... ▾	Inclusive Samples %	Exclusive Samples %
⊞ mscorwks.dll	5,899	4,109	99.98	69.64
⊞ mscorlib.ni.dll	2,418	1,630	40.98	27.63
⊞ System.Data.ni.dll	97	54	1.64	0.92
⊞ System.Xml.ni.dll	102	48	1.73	0.81
⊞ rsaenh.dll	22	21	0.37	0.36
⊞ ntdll.dll	184	13	3.12	0.22
⊞ dssenh.dll	11	11	0.19	0.19
⊞ KERNEL32.dll	40	3	0.68	0.05
⊞ [Unknown]	3,356	2	56.88	0.03
⊟ MemoryAnalysis.exe	2,519	2	42.69	0.03
⊟ MemoryAnalysis.Form1.DoConcat(int32,string)	2,267	2	38.42	0.03
⊞ Line 105	2	2	0.03	0.03
0x013318E6	1	1	0.02	0.02
0x013318E9	1	1	0.02	0.02
MemoryAnalysis.CurrencyManager.GetData()	98	0	1.66	0.00
MemoryAnalysis.CurrencyManager.m_Timer_Elapsed(object,cl	102	0	1.73	0.00
MemoryAnalysis.Form1..ctor()	8	0	0.14	0.00
MemoryAnalysis.Form1.AllocateLOH(int32)	38	0	0.64	0.00
MemoryAnalysis.Form1.button3_Click(object,class System.Eve	2,267	0	38.42	0.00
MemoryAnalysis.Form1.Form1_Load(object,class System.Even	140	0	2.37	0.00
MemoryAnalysis.Form1.InitializeComponent()	2	0	0.03	0.00
MemoryAnalysis.Program.Main()	2,417	0	40.97	0.00
⊞ MSVCR80.dll	2	2	0.03	0.03
⊞ System.Windows.Forms.ni.dll	2,412	2	40.88	0.03
⊞ ADVAPI32.dll	31	1	0.53	0.02
⊞ CRYPT32.dll	1	1	0.02	0.02
⊞ mscorjit.dll	9	1	0.15	0.02
⊞ mscoree.dll	3,336	0	56.54	0.00
⊞ schannel.dll	30	0	0.51	0.00
⊞ Secur32.dll	31	0	0.53	0.00
⊞ shell32.dll	1	0	0.02	0.00
⊞ SHLWAPI.dll	1	0	0.02	0.00
⊞ System.Configuration.ni.dll	1	0	0.02	0.00
⊞ System.Data.dll	31	0	0.53	0.00
⊞ System.Drawing.ni.dll	1	0	0.02	0.00

Figure 7.15: Visual Studio 2009 performance profiler modules view (sampling).

Sorting by exclusive samples and expanding your own assemblies and methods will highlight the slowest lines of code. You can then view the source on each line by choosing **View Source** from the context menu for the selected line.

Instrumentation analysis

Instrumentation inserts probes into the code, adding timing instructions to each method call and around every system call, increasing the overall size of the binary. It gives very high resolution timing information and can enumerate the number of times a method has been called, but increasing the size of the binary, and the overhead of executing and monitoring the profiler code adds significant overhead. The tradeoff is the amount of detail that can be retrieved. In addition, unlike with sampling, instrumenting profilers can work equally well with CPU and I/O-bound applications.

On completion of a performance test, a summary report will be displayed as in Figure 7.16.

Performance Report Summary

Most Called Functions

Name	Number of Calls	%
System.String.Concat(string,string)	6,738	87.51
System.Windows.Forms.Control.set_Text(string)	111	1.44
System.Random.NextBytes(uint8[])	100	1.30
System.Random.Next(int32)	100	1.30
System.Collections.Generic.List`1.Add(!0)	100	1.30

Functions With Most Individual Work

Name	Time (msec)	%
System.String.Concat(string,string)	7,503.12	51.77
System.GC.Collect()	3,925.19	27.08
System.Windows.Forms.Application.Run(class System.Windows.Forms.Form)	1,064.94	7.35
System.IDisposable.Dispose()	937.07	6.47
System.Xml.XmlDocument.Load(string)	374.82	2.59

Functions Taking Longest

Name	Time (msec)	%
MemoryAnalysis.Program.Main()	13,158.80	90.78
System.Windows.Forms.Application.Run(class System.Windows.Forms.Form)	13,103.93	90.41
MemoryAnalysis.Form1.button3_Click(object,class System.EventArgs)	11,469.74	79.13
MemoryAnalysis.Form1.DoConcat(int32,string)	11,469.20	79.13
System.String.Concat(string,string)	7,503.12	51.77

Figure 7.16: Visual Studio 2008 performance summary.

The summary lists the top five functions for:

- most called functions

- functions with the most individual work

- functions taking the longest to complete.

As with sampling, each method can be analysed from a number of different views, or the source code can be loaded if it is your own method.

Function view

The function view (Figure 7.17), as for the sampling analysis, lists all of the called methods together with their performance statistics.

216

Function Name	Elapsed Inclusive Time	Elapsed Exclusive Ti...	Application Inclusiv...	Application Ex...	Elapsed Inclusive Ti...	Elapsed Exclusive
MemoryAnalysis.CurrencyManager.Start()	63.45	43.31	42.66	42.66	0.00	
System.Windows.Forms.Control.set_Text(string)	20.93	20.93	16.01	16.01	0.00	
System.DateTime.ToString(string)	11.85	11.85	10.87	10.87	0.00	
System.Data.SqlClient.SqlConnection..ctor(string)	166.84	166.84	10.44	10.44	0.00	
System.Decimal.ToString(string)	4.89	4.89	4.82	4.82	0.00	
System.IDisposable.Dispose()	751,302.28	751,302.28	3.68	3.68	7.97	
MemoryAnalysis.CurrencyManager.GetData()	753,664.89	3.51	37.30	2.97	8.00	
System.Data.SqlClient.SqlCommand..ctor(string, class Syst	27.61	27.61	2.96	2.96	0.00	
System.Data.Common.DbDataReader.GetDateTime(int32)	7.25	7.25	1.90	1.90	0.00	
System.Data.Common.DbDataReader.GetDecimal(int32)	5.44	5.44	1.72	1.72	0.00	
System.Data.Common.DbDataReader.Read()	1.80	1.80	1.56	1.56	0.00	
System.Random..ctor()	6.06	6.06	1.03	1.03	0.00	
MemoryAnalysis.Form1.<>c__DisplayClass1.<m_Currency	22.74	0.98	21.05	0.94	0.00	
MemoryAnalysis.Tick.Invoke(valuetype System.Decimal)	187.13	1.67	1.95	0.75	0.00	
MemoryAnalysis.Form1.m_Currency_OnPriceUpdate(value	185.46	0.78	1.20	0.61	0.00	
System.Windows.Forms.MethodInvoker..ctor(object,nativ	0.62	0.62	0.60	0.60	0.00	
System.String.Concat(string,string,string)	0.55	0.55	0.49	0.49	0.00	
System.Threading.Monitor.Enter(object)	0.45	0.45	0.43	0.43	0.00	
MemoryAnalysis.CurrencyManager.m_Timer_Elapsed(obje	753,994.56	142.55	39.53	0.28	8.00	
System.Threading.Monitor.Exit(object)	0.28	0.28	0.27	0.27	0.00	
System.Int32.ToString()	0.16	0.16	0.15	0.15	0.00	
ControlCollection.Add(class System.Windows.Forms.Contr	8.40	8.40	0.10	0.10	0.00	
System.Windows.Forms.Control.set_Location(valuetype S	6.06	6.06	0.08	0.08	0.00	
System.Windows.Forms.Control.set_Size(valuetype Syste	0.21	0.21	0.07	0.07	0.00	
System.Collections.Generic.List`1.Add(!0)	0.08	0.08	0.07	0.07	0.00	
MemoryAnalysis.Form1.AllocateLOH(int32)	201.65	4.43	1.99	0.04	0.00	
System.Windows.Forms.Label..ctor()	0.14	0.14	0.03	0.03	0.00	
MemoryAnalysis.Form1.Form1_Load(object,class System.E	682.06	1.10	44.69	0.03	0.01	
System.Windows.Forms.Button..ctor()	0.10	0.10	0.02	0.02	0.00	
System.Windows.Forms.Control.set_Name(string)	0.03	0.03	0.02	0.02	0.00	
System.Random.Next(int32)	0.04	0.04	0.01	0.01	0.00	
MemoryAnalysis.Form1.InitializeComponent()	17.58	0.08	0.38	0.01	0.00	
System.Windows.Forms.Control.set_AutoSize(bool)	0.03	0.03	0.00	0.00	0.00	
System.Windows.Forms.Control.get_Controls()	0.00	0.00	0.00	0.00	0.00	

Figure 7.17: Visual Studio 2008 function view (instrumentation).

Notice that there are two kinds of timings: elapsed and application time. Elapsed time is how long it took if you timed it with a stopwatch (wall-clock time), whereas application time is a calculation indicating the amount of time actually spent processing.

The main statistics provided are:

Number of calls	number of times the method was called
Elapsed inclusive time	elapsed time including child calls
Elapsed exclusive time	elapsed time spent in method, excluding child calls
Application exclusive time	time spent processing method only
Application inclusive time	time spent processing method and children

You can now carry out a standard analysis:

- methods with high call count

- slow method call trees (elapsed inclusive)

- CPU-intensive call trees (application inclusive)

- CPU-intensive methods (application exclusive).

I/O-bound methods and call trees where there is a big difference between elapsed and application time are often due to I/O.

Call tree

The call tree view is identical to the one produced in the sampling session in Figure 7.14, except that the sampled statistics are replaced by:

- elapsed inclusive

- elapsed exclusive

- application inclusive

- application exclusive.

You can use the hot path analysis buttons to uncover the slowest execution path and the method bottleneck within.

Comparing analysis runs

When you have completed an optimization, it helps to make sure that the optimization has actually worked. Visual Studio has a comparison tool available from the **Analyze** menu which allows you to compare performance analysis results files.

On launching the tool, you have to choose the two files to compare before the comparison is displayed, as in Figure 7.18.

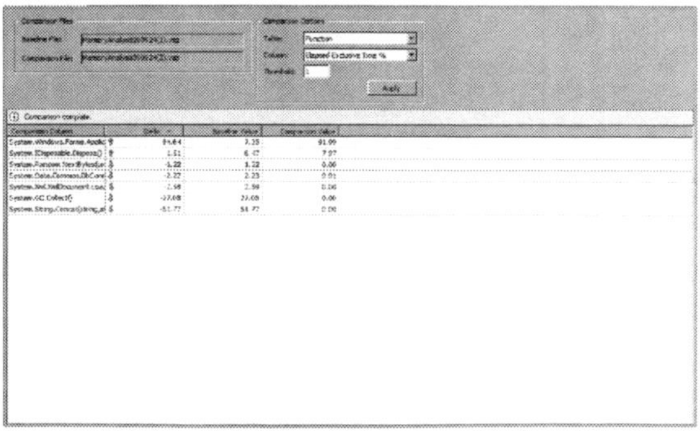

Figure 7.18: Visual Studio 2008 performance analysis results comparison.

Optimizing analysis

Profiling overhead can be reduced in Visual Studio 2008 by isolating components from profiling, and by choosing the type of profiler.

Isolating components

You can choose the assemblies to be included in the analysis from within Performance Explorer and, depending on the profiling mode, you can choose to either sample or instrument each assembly in the target list.

Instrumentation can be limited still further using the advanced properties of each assembly in the target list. By setting specific include or exclude switches, you can limit the namespaces and methods that will be instrumented.

```
/include Namespace::FunctionName or /include Namespace::*
```

Reducing tools overhead

As the profiler gives you the option to choose sampling or instrumentation, you can choose the level of overhead. As you should be aware by now, sampling gives a lower overhead analysis but is also less detailed, and the overhead of sampling can be reduced still further by reducing the sampling frequency within the Performance Explorer properties.

Visual Studio 2010 Team Edition

Visual Studio 2010 contains all of the functionality described in the 2008 product, and adds a number of new features.

The most obvious new feature is the performance summary report (Figure 7.19) which now allows you to view portions of the performance trace by selecting a region from the new performance graph, a feature which is, admittedly, already present in the ANTS Performance Profiler.

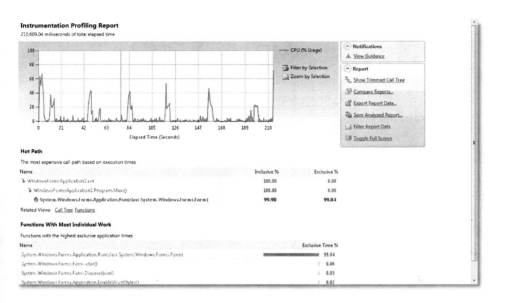

Figure 7.19: Visual Studio 2010 summary report.

Concurrency profiling

There is an additional profiling mode to allow concurrency profiling. Multithreaded applications are now very common, and both thread and resource contention have become a major problem for many developers. The concurrency profiler will allow you to detect when threads are waiting for other threads to complete.

Function Detail view

The new **Function Detail** view (Figure 7.20) will show the call stack for a method, and line-level statistics for the selected method.

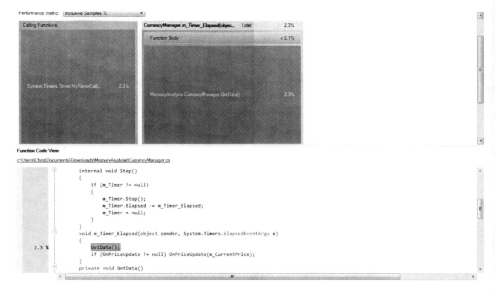

Figure 7.20: Visual Studio 2010 Function Detail view.

Tier interaction profiling

This allows you to view how long your code is spending within ADO.NET, performing SQL queries and stored procedures. This feature has to be switched on within the **Performance Explorer** properties, and the results can be viewed in the **Interactions** view.

JavaScript profiling

ASP.NET developers can now profile JavaScript running within Internet Explorer 8 browsers. With the advent of AJAX, browsers are executing more complex and demanding scripts than ever, and the ability to profile JavaScript code is increasingly important.

SQL Profiler 2005/2008

SQL Profiler installs as part of the SQL Management tools and is a simple, yet powerful, tool for identifying slow SQL and stored procedures on your database server. It's an extra tool you can use on top of code profiling to identify the root causes of bottlenecks.

Usually, for a slow SQL statement or stored procedure, the wall-clock time for the code line making the database access call will show as a bottleneck, and that will probably be your first hint.

Running the analysis

- Start SQL Profiler and create a **New Trace** from the **File** menu and the **Trace Properties** window will be displayed (Figure 7.21).

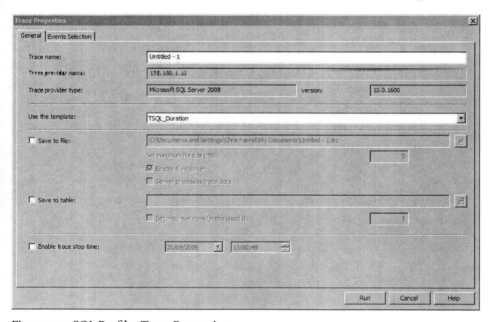

Figure 7.21: SQL Profiler Trace Properties.

- Choose the **TSQL_Duration** template on the General tab and check the **Save to file** option.

- On the **Events Selection** tab (Figure 7.22) check the **Show all columns** check box and opt to display the following columns:

  - Duration

  - TextData

  - CPU

  - Reads

  - Writes

  - StartTime

  - EndTime.

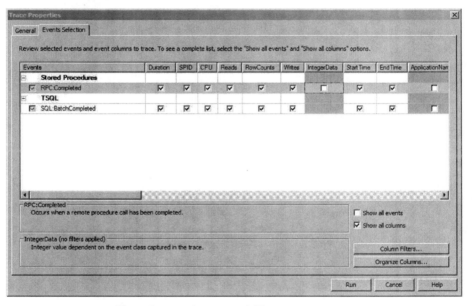

Figure 7.22: SQL Profiler column selection and filtering.

You can also use the **Column Filters...** button to filter the collected data based on any of the available columns. Typically, you could use this to restrict the profiling to a specific database, login, and possible durations, or CPU exceeding certain thresholds.

Once your session profile is configured, you can start the analysis by pressing the **Run** button. Stored procedure and SQL events will be logged to the trace, as in Figure 7.23.

223

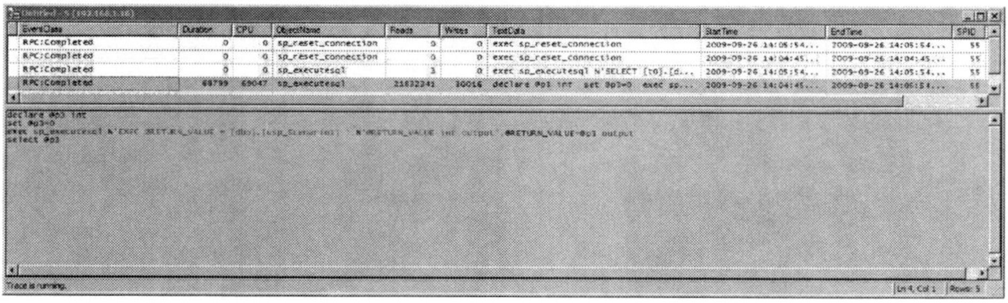

Figure 7.23: SQL Profiler results trace.

From the trace you will be able to identify the long running, CPU, and read/write-intensive calls that require further investigation.

Other predefined profile templates are available, including ones for lock detection and more detailed stored procedure analysis; you can even create your own templates. SQL Profiler is a simple tool to use and can quickly identify problems.

Summary

Regardless of the tool, the techniques are the same. Once you have found a bottleneck, you have to decide if it can be optimized. The important thing is that you now know it's there. Profiling your code will identify important issues that you can address before you ever check it into the source control system. The techniques I have described are quick and easy to run on any of the tools for any developer. You don't have to be some kind of code guru to do this.

Chapter 8: Memory Profiling

Why memory matters

Before getting into how to profile memory, it's worth going through how memory management in .NET actually works. Once you understand the issues you're likely to encounter, it's much easier to see what to look for while profiling.

The managed heap(s)

When an application executes, the .NET execution engine reserves two sections of memory called the Small Object Heap (SOH) and the Large Object Heap (LOH). As objects are created, they are allocated onto one of the two heaps based on their size. Objects greater than 85K are allocated onto the LOH and the rest on the SOH.

Detecting and essentially destroying redundant objects from those heaps is the job of the garbage collector (GC). It does this by periodically inspecting the heap and reclaiming the memory being used by objects no longer being used by the application. The goal of the GC is to avoid increasing the size of the heap, by reclaiming as much memory as possible, as efficiently as possible.

When the GC runs, it creates a list of all objects still in use by the application. If an object is still in use, its chain of object references will trace back to one of the application's root objects. Root references are just pointers to these root objects that reside on the heap. Root references can be found on the stack, from global variables, statics, and within the CPU registers. Every object pointed to by a root reference usually contains references to other objects, each of which then point to other objects, and so on. To work out which objects are still alive (rooted) the GC looks at every root object and lists every object they reference. For each of these referenced objects it lists all of their object references. The process is repeated until a complete list of all referenced objects is complete. The GC then applies a simple rule, "If you're not on the list, you don't survive." Anything not on the list is classed as garbage (or rootless) and so is available for collection.

Because the GC allocates and collects from the SOH and LOH differently, the two will be explained separately.

Small Object Heap

New objects are allocated onto the SOH consecutively; a reference called the Next Object Pointer (NOP) is held, indicating where the next allocated object should be placed (see Figure 8.1). When a new object is created, it is added to the SOH at the Next Object Pointer location, which is, in turn, incremented by the size of the object. Allocation is fast because it really only involves some address arithmetic.

As the application executes, objects are created, used, and eventually discarded. When the GC runs, the discarded objects are garbage collected.

In Figure 8.1 there are five objects allocated on the SOH. Object B has a reference to object C, and is itself referenced by a static class. Objects D and E are both referenced from the stack. The only object not referenced is Object A, which is therefore a candidate for garbage collection.

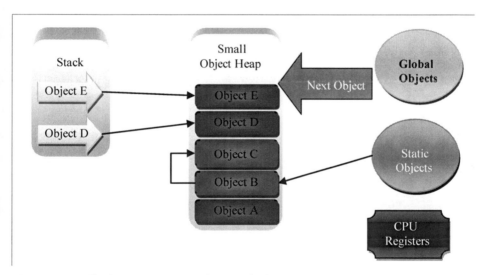

Figure 8.1: Small Object Heap with references before GC.

When the GC runs, it builds a reference list and determines that objects E, D, C, and B are "rooted." Everything else is assumed to be garbage, and so the GC moves the "rooted" objects down in memory, overwriting the "rootless" ones (in this case, Object A), and the Next Object Pointer will be reset to the new address at the top of Object E. Figure 8.2 illustrates what the heap will look like after a GC.

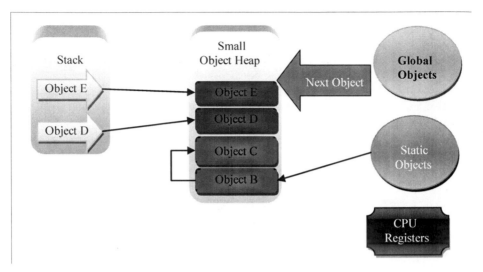

Figure 8.2: Small Object Heap with references after GC.

The point of all of this effort is to reclaim as much memory as possible. However, as it takes processing time to build the reference list and compact the heap, this can impact performance. The more your application garbage collects, the bigger the hit on performance. Thus, reducing the overhead of garbage collection is a crucial part of performance tuning an application.

Optimizing garbage collection

- Over time, the long-lived objects will reside at the bottom of the heap and the newest objects at the top. Because most objects are allocated within the scope of a single function call, the newer the object is, the more likely it is to be rootless. Conversely, the older an object is, the less likely it is to be rootless, given that whatever has been referencing it for such a long time probably continues to do so. When the GC runs, to avoid inspecting and reorganizing every object on the heap every time, it inspects the newest objects more often. To help with this process, the GC classifies objects into one of three generations.

- Gen 0 (youngest)

- Gen 1 (intermediate)

- Gen 2 (oldest).

Each time an object survives a GC, it is promoted to the next generation, until it eventually makes it to Gen 2, where it remains.

Figure 8.3 shows the SOH with objects logically grouped into generations. Objects Z and Y have recently been allocated and have never been inspected by the GC, classifying them as Gen 0 objects. Object X has survived one GC and so is classified as a Gen 1 object; finally, Object W has survived two (or more) GCs, and so is in Gen 2.

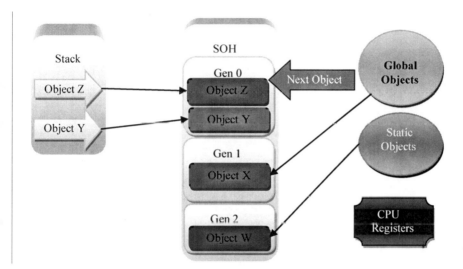

Figure 8.3: Small Object Heap with generations.

The GC will run under one of the circumstances below.

- When the size of objects in a generation reaches a threshold:

    - Gen 0 reaches 256K

    - Gen 1 reaches ~2MB

    - Gen 2 reaches ~10Mb.

- When the application receives a Low Memory warning from the OS.

- When the programmer calls **GC.Collect()** in code.

The above thresholds are approximate and the GC will, in fact, tune them to optimal levels depending on the allocation profile of the application.

Gen 0 garbage collection

When Gen 0 reaches its threshold, the garbage collector will run and the following events occur:

- a list of surviving (rooted) objects is created

- surviving Gen 0 objects are moved to Gen 1

- Gen 0 is now empty.

Figure 8.4 shows the end result of this garbage collection, where objects Z and Y move from Gen 0 to Gen 1.

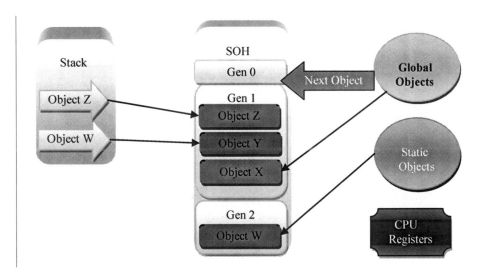

Figure 8.4: SOH after a Gen 0 GC.

It's important to remember that Gen 0 is always empty after a GC; all objects surviving the GC are moved to Gen 1 and the Next Object Pointer is set back to the start of an empty Gen 0. Any rootless objects left in Gen 0 are overwritten as new objects are allocated to the heap.

Gen 0 collections should occur ten times more frequently than Gen 1.

Gen 1 garbage collection

A Gen 1 garbage collection also collects Gen 0, and is the final step in deciding which objects make it to Gen 2, where objects can potentially persist for a long time.

In a Gen 1 garbage collection:

*   a list of surviving (rooted) objects is created

*   surviving Gen 1 objects are moved to Gen 2

*   Gen 1 is now empty

*   surviving Gen 0 objects are moved to Gen 1

*   Gen 0 is now empty.

It's worth noting that any Gen 1 object which is referenced by an *unrooted* Gen 2 object is not collected in a Gen 1 collection, but only in a Gen 2 collection, when its parent is collected.

Gen 1 collections should occur ten time more frequently than Gen 2.

Gen 2 garbage collection

Gen 2 garbage collection has the biggest impact on performance because it involves a full garbage collection of the Small Object Heap, where the entire heap is compacted, as well as the Large Object Heap (more later). The process is much the same as earlier, just with added steps for Gen 2:

*   a map of surviving (rooted) objects is created

*   rootless Gen 2 objects are overwritten by surviving (rooted) Gen 2 objects

*   rooted Gen 1 objects are moved to the top of Gen 2

*   Gen 1 is now empty

*   rooted Gen 0 objects are moved to the top of Gen 1

*   Gen 0 is now empty.

Large Object Heap

Any object of 85K or more is allocated onto the Large Object Heap. Unlike the SOH, because of the overhead of copying large chunks of memory, objects on the LOH aren't compacted. When a full (Gen 2) GC takes place, the address ranges of any LOH objects not in the rooted list are added to a "free space" allocation table. If adjacent objects are found to be rootless, then they are recorded as one entry within a combined address range.

When a new object is allocated onto the LOH, the free space table is checked to see if there is an address range large enough to hold that object. If there is, the object is allocated at the start byte position, and the free space entry amended.

Naturally, it's normally very unlikely that objects being allocated will be of a size that exactly matches an address range in the free space table. As a result, small chunks of memory will be left between allocated objects, resulting in fragmentation. If the chunks are <85K they will be left as they are, with no possibility of reuse. The result is, as allocation demand increases, new memory segments are reserved for the LOH when (admittedly fragmented) space is still available. Ultimately, the memory footprint of the application becomes larger than it should be.

This LOH fragmentation can cause Out of Memory exceptions even when there appears to be plenty of space available on the heaps.

Finalizable objects

Classes that access system services, such as file/disk, network, database or user interface resources, must ensure they are closed on completion. Failure to do so will cause resources leaks which are difficult to track from within .NET.

System resources accessed within a single function are typically cleaned up within a try-catch-finally block, but resources held at the class level and accessed over the scope of more than one function call must have a mechanism to close resources prior to class destruction.

To facilitate cleanup, .NET provides a destruction mechanism called "finalization." Placing a C++ style destructor in a C# class, or including a Finalize method in a VB.NET or C# application makes it a finalizable class. The GC will call the Finalize method or the destructor prior to collecting the object (unless the finalization for the object is suppressed), so putting your resource cleanup code in the finalizer makes sense. The problem is that adding a finalizer to a class will cause object instances to survive garbage collections even when they become rootless from application code.

When an instance of a finalizable object is created, the CLR adds a reference to the object on a queue structure called the "finalization queue" (see Figure 8.5). The reference's sole purpose is to prevent the object from being collected before the finalizer method is called. It acts as yet another root reference.

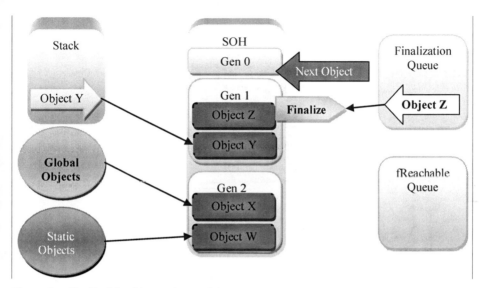

Figure 8.5: Finalizable object prior to GC.

If the GC finds objects whose only roots are in the finalization queue, it doesn't collect the object but, instead, copies those references to the "fReachable Queue" and promotes the object to the next generation. The fReachable queue just acts as a ToDo list containing references to all of the objects that are ready to have their finalizer method called. The GC doesn't call the finalizer directly because it's possible that the Finalize method itself may take time to complete while resources are unavailable, which would could significantly slow down the garbage collection.

As you can see in Figure 8.6, Object Z has been promoted to Gen 2 and its reference copied to fReachable, even though it has no other root references.

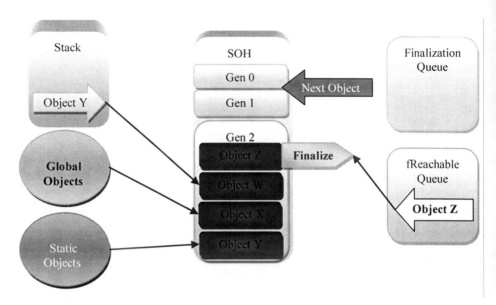

Figure 8.6: Finalizable object after GC.

The GC actually operates a separate thread that runs when items are added to the fReachable queue. For each object reference in the fReachable queue, it calls the Finalize method (or destructor if C#) on that object and deletes the reference. It's only when this is completed that a finalizable object is finally rootless, and thus an candidate for GC. This is why Finalizers can't have any thread-specific code within them, as the finalizer is called on a different thread.

In Figure 8.6, Object Z was promoted to Gen 2 in spite of the fact that it had no other references than the one in fReachable. Object Z can now be collected on a full garbage collection, since its Finalize method has been run.

Minimizing finalization issues

The best way to write finalizable classes is by implementing the IDisposable interface. Providing a Dispose method on a class allows the developer to explicitly destroy the object, as well as to explicitly suppress finalization where necessary. Code Example 8.1 illustrates the use of Dispose to clean up a finalizable class. Notice it has a call to **GC.SupressFinalize**, which effectively deletes the object's reference from the finalization queue, stopping its Finalize method being called, and also making it available for collection as soon as it is unrooted.

```
public void Dispose()
{
    Cleanup(true);
    GC.SupressFinalize(this);
}
private void Cleanup(bool disposing)
{
    if (!disposing)
    {
        // Thread specific code goes here
    }

    // Resource Cleanup goes here
}
public void Finalize()
{
    Cleanup(false);
}
```

Code Example 8.1: Minimizing finalization issues with Dispose.

Profiling memory

Memory profiling is all about understanding and then taking control of the class instances you allocate in your application. The allocation decisions, which include the scope you choose for variables and the way you define and clean up classes after use, will ultimately affect the memory footprint of your application. In many cases, the classes you choose to use in your application may have memory overheads that aren't initially apparent.

In .NET, the object reference is king. Without a reference, an object is destined for garbage collection, and that's a good thing. Memory problems occur when references to objects that are no longer being used persist longer than intended. It's so easy, for example, to forget to remove an object from a collection or unsubscribe it from an event and, once missed, it's almost impossible to find by just reviewing the code.

Running memory profilers against your main application test cases will highlight potential issues and make you revisit areas of the code long forgotten. You will (hopefully) ask questions, and want answers to the various anomalies raised, because any one of these anomalies could be a potential load test or production issue in the future. Finding and fixing those issues now will save you a lot of time and effort down the line.

With a good understanding of how memory is managed in .NET, let's now look at the kinds of memory problem that can occur, then how we can use different profiling tools to uncover these issues.

Finding memory problems isn't some kind of weird science; once you understand the garbage collector, and have established a basic method of analysis with your tool of choice, it's actually very straightforward. At the end of this chapter, that's where I hope you will be.

Memory issues

We'll now look at some common memory problems that can occur within applications. Later on we will consider how various profiling tools can be used to identify these issues.

Inefficient allocation

The managed heap makes allocation an extremely fast and efficient process, but the flipside to this is that garbage collection can be expensive. There are many things you can do in your code that will cause the garbage collector to work harder than necessary. Let's go through a few cases.

Excessive temporary object allocation

It makes sense to ensure that you allocate only what is necessary and set the scope to be small. Ideally, you should also try ensure that you understand the impact of the framework functions you use – many seemingly innocuous calls create unexpected intermediate object allocations.

One of the best examples occurs in string concatenation. Strings in .NET, once created, can't be changed because, amongst other things, they are allocated onto a consecutive heap. As a result, expanding or lengthening a string would involve reorganizing heap memory. Instead, when a string is altered, a new version is created and allocated onto the heap, leaving the old one to be collected.

```
string sHtml="<div>";
for (int i=0;i<100;i++)
{
    sHtml+="<span>" + i.ToString() +"</span>";
}
sHtml+="</div>";
```

Code Example 8.2: String concatenation causing excessive allocation.

Code Example 8.2 illustrates a typical string concatenation scenario. To create one string, 101 intermediate strings are created and discarded onto the heap. A more efficient way to approach code this would be to use a **StringBuilder** class.

```
StringBuilder sHtml=new StringBuilder();
sHtml.Append("<div>");
for (int i=0;i<100;i++)
{
    sHtml .Append("<span>");
    sHtml.Append(i.ToString());
    sHtml.Append("</span>");
}
sHtml.Append("</div>");
```

Code Example 8.3: Using a StringBuilder to reduce temporary object allocation.

Another example of a seemingly innocuous technique I have seen a number of times when optimizing code is the **GetChanges** method of the **DataSet** class (Code Example 8.4).

```
void Save(DataSet dsCustomers)
{
    if (dsCustomers.GetChanges().Count>0)
    {
    // Persist Customers
    }
}
```

Code Example 8.4: Temporary object impact of DataSet.GetChanges().

This is a misuse of the **GetChanges()** method which, depending on the size of the **DataSet**, can create a large number of temporary objects. In fact, the **DataSet** has a function called **HasChanges** for precisely this purpose, which returns "True" or "False," creating the same result with no temporary object impact at all.

Short story: the more you allocate onto the heap, the harder the garbage collector will have to work. Not always much harder, but these little additions can cumulatively become a more serious problem. Excessive temporary object allocation also runs the risk of causing other objects to be prematurely promoted to later generations, making the Gen 1 or Gen 2 collections work harder, and generally leaving you with a mess.

Mid-life crisis

Objects that make it to Gen 2, but lose their references soon after and become available for garbage collection are, put simply, inefficient. Because Gen 2 collections have a big performance hit, they occur as infrequently as possible, and objects that make it to Gen 2 only to die will potentially stay there for a long time. If this happens repeatedly, the size of the Gen 2 heap keeps getting bigger, and brings forward the time when another full Gen 2 collection will occur.

The more frequently a full Gen 2 collection runs, the bigger the impact on your application, and this is particularly true for a server application. All threads executing managed code are suspended during collection (in the case of a server GC) and this will severely limit scalability.

Long reference chains

To find out which objects are still in use, the garbage collector has to walk through the list of objects on the heap, starting with the root and then moving recursively through each object and its descendants. If you hold on to references to objects with large complex allocated object models, this process is going to have to work harder every time garbage collection runs. Imagine an ASP.NET application caching a complex DataSet in session state for every user, and you get the idea. The worst part is, I've actually found this running on a live web application at a customer site.

Memory leaks

Memory leaks are the problem that strikes fear into the hearts of most developers. They can cause the catastrophic failure of an application, and are seemingly impossible to find and fix.

The good news is that most memory leaks are actually extremely easy to find; you just need a good tool and a basic strategy.

Memory leaks are caused by your code repeatedly leaving behind references to objects, thereby keeping them in memory. Although this is mostly inadvertent, some of the time it's working as designed, but the impact of the design wasn't fully understood. Hey, software algorithms are complex, and it can be difficult to fully understand the impact of something by just looking at the code.

Finding a memory leak is simply a case of looking for object instances that are continually being created and never destroyed. Once identified, they can be traced back to where they were allocated in your code, and that's where they can be fixed.

Memory fragmentation

Memory fragmentation occurs when small, unallocated memory gaps are left behind during the process of allocation and deallocation. Over time, the gaps can add up to quite large amounts of memory, which is a problem that affects the both the large and small object heaps.

Large Object Heap

As mentioned earlier, because it is never compacted, the Large Object Heap can become fragmented (where lots of memory gaps are left behind after objects are collected). Often, the size of the heap is expanded even when there is apparently lots of space available (tied up in the gaps). Ultimately, an application can run out of memory when there are no free spaces of a sufficient size on the LOH and the application has reached its memory allocation limit.

If you create a single object larger than 85K it will be allocated onto the Large Object Heap. That means a single object, not a class plus its contents, as they are allocated separately. It's usually classes such as strings, byte arrays, and so on, that are the culprits. Objects of this size are allocated more frequently in your application than you might think. Typically, datasets and ViewState strings (which are very common in ASP.NET applications) can create strings larger than 85K without you ever being aware of it.

Small Object Heap

I know you're thinking, "Fragmentation is a Large Object Heap issue." That's true, but it can be a Small Object Heap issue as well.

SOH fragmentation can occur if the developer uses object pinning, which would typically happen when passing data to native code APIs. In this situation, the heap compaction and address reorganization of objects on the SOH will cause a problem, so it's possible to tell the GC to pin objects to fixed locations in memory. This prevents them from being moved during compaction, but can also cause memory fragmentation.

```
byte[] buffer = new byte[512];
GCHandle h = GCHandle.Alloc(buffer, GCHandleType.Pinned);
IntPtr ptr = h.AddrOfPinnedObject();
// Call native API and pass buffer
if (h.IsAllocated) h.Free();
```

Code Example 8.5: Pinning objects to fixed locations in memory.

238

Memory footprint

It's common practice to cache data structures that were expensive to create or retrieve and are frequently used. Caching can give large performance gains to an application and reduce the load on the application and database servers. However, caching naturally has a memory impact, which is worth investigating and validating. If implemented wrongly, caching can very easily turn into a memory leak.

Using tools to uncover memory problems

To uncover memory problems, you first need to find a tool you can use effectively for the size of application that you need to profile. You need to be able to develop strategies to filter out application noise, and interpretation skills to understand the results produced.

It's true that the best tool is the one that works for you, but ideally you want to get to a point where all the developers in a team feel comfortable profiling their own code before releasing it to source control. In this case, the best tool is the one that allows you to develop the easiest-to-use, most effective strategy. Anything else will simply fall by the wayside.

Test plans

Before you contemplate running an analysis, you need to have a test plan that describes the sequence of user interface actions or web service calls that you will make, and the data that will be passed. Memory analysis, particularly leak detection, involves comparing memory states, and using inconsistent test sequences or data can skew the memory state and make it less easy to spot patterns.

Let's now take a look at some of the main tools available for memory profiling .NET applications.

ANTS Memory Profiler 5

Red Gate's ANTS Memory Profiler can analyze .NET memory for the following application types:

- .NET Executable

- ASP.NET Web Application (IIS and WebDev)

- Windows Service

- COM+ Server

- XBAP (local XAML Browser App).

It focuses on how objects are laid out on the heap rather than tracking from where they were allocated. The overhead of tracking allocation call stacks can have a big impact on memory and the amount of data written to disk. As a result of ignoring that, ANTS has a low profiling overhead.

The tool allows you to take memory snapshots that list every allocated class on the heap. Before each snapshot is taken, ANTS forces a garbage collection, which means only rooted objects make it onto the list.

A number of predefined and configurable filters are available, which can be used to filter out objects that meet specific criteria from the results. This allows you to remove objects that are irrelevant to the analysis being performed. Once you have a filtered a set of results, you can use the class and object tracing tools to find the reasons why objects are still retained. Another really useful feature is the ability to compare snapshots. You can look for classes occurring in one snapshot but not the other, or classes that survived in both. Snapshot comparisons are particularly useful when looking for memory leaks.

The power of this tool really lies in the level of control and flexibility it gives you to filter, compare, and drill down. There are no predefined analysis types, but all the facilities are there for you to find key memory problems such as those mentioned above.

Memory leaks

To find memory leaks with ANTS, it pays to follow a basic strategy that starts with you defining your test transaction. I will now go through a basic strategy that you can follow to find memory leaks, but the techniques you will learn can be used to find many other memory issues.

Step 1 – Setting a baseline

- Start the application under ANTS Memory Profiler.

- Once it's loaded, take a baseline snapshot by pressing the **Take Memory Snapshot** button.

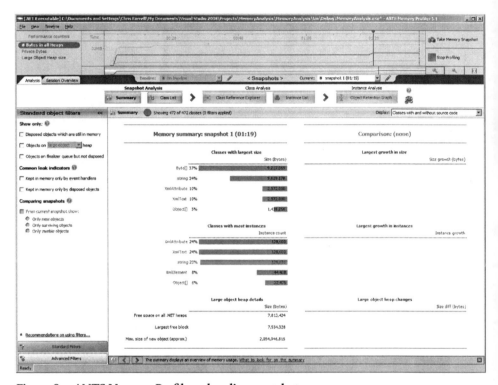

Figure 8.7: ANTS Memory Profiler 5, baseline snapshot.

Step 2 – Running the test transaction

The next step is to run your test transaction, which is the one you suspect may have a leak.

- Run your test transaction.

- Take another snapshot.

If there is a memory leak in your test it should leak every time. Repeating the test a number of times and taking a snapshot after each test should make it easier to see the leak when the snapshots are compared.

241

Step 3 – Applying filters

Before looking at the snapshots, it's a good idea to apply some of the filters to the results to eliminate as much application noise as possible. ANTS comes with a couple of filters designed specifically for two common leak causes.

- **Kept in memory only by event handlers**:

  - Caused by not removing a reference to an added event handler. This is the most common cause of leaks!

- **Kept in memory only by disposed objects**:

  - Often symptomatic of a leak.

Check these two filters individually first, and move to Step 4 for each one.

If no leaks are found using the common leak filters, you need to perform a more detailed analysis of the heap. To make this easier, it's a good idea to first eliminate object instances that are unlikely to be causing leaks from the results, and there are a number of filters available to help. I suggest setting each of the following filters before moving on to Step 4.

- **New objects** – you only need to see the new objects left behind since the previous snapshot, as they are possible leak candidates.

  - Using the **Standard object filters** section on the left-hand side, go to the **Comparing snapshots** heading.

  - Click on the **From current snapshot show:** check box and select **Only new objects**.

- **Finalizable objects** – eliminate objects waiting for finalization. These are waiting for .NET's finalization thread to run, they have no other references, and they will disappear from the trace anyway. Unfortunately, they appear as noise on our trace, but they can be easily removed.

  - Click on the **Advanced Filters** button at the bottom left of the screen.

  - Now, in the **Advanced object filters** section, click **Kept in memory only by GC roots of type:** and uncheck **Finalizer queue.**

- **Objects which are not GC roots** – a memory leak is extremely unlikely to be GC root.

  - Still on the **Advanced Filters** section, select **Objects which** and then **are not GC Roots**.

Step 4 – Comparing snapshots

We took a snapshot after each test, and we have also applied one or more filters. The next step is to compare each snapshot against the baseline. A memory leak should get worse each time you run the test and, by comparing each snapshot against the previous one, we should be able to see one or more classes that always appear. These classes warrant further investigation in Step 5.

Figure 8.8 is an example of a snapshot comparison where snapshots 2 and 3 are compared. The class list has been selected, and ANTS is displaying a list of all classes that have allocated and rooted object instances on the heap.

Figure 8.8: ANTS Memory Profiler 5, comparing snapshots.

In this example, the **Order** and **Tick** classes have consistently appeared in the snapshot comparisons, and are therefore selected for analysis in Step 5.

Step 5 – Tracking back to source code

Once a class is selected for analysis, we need to understand why it is being kept in memory – in other words, what is keeping a reference to it?

ANTS has a Class Reference Explorer to do this, and selecting a class from the class list and pressing the **Class Reference Explorer** button, displays a reference graph (Figure 8.9).

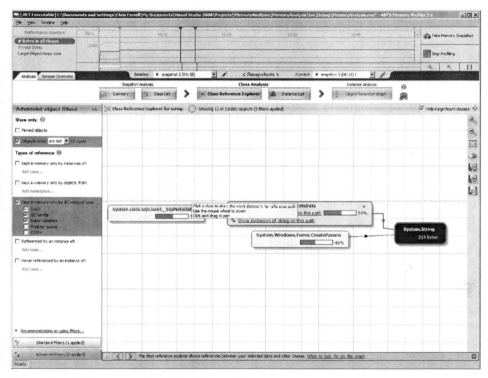

Figure 8.9: ANTS Memory Profiler, Class Reference Explorer.

From here, you can trace backwards to discover the classes that have instances holding references to the selected class. Usually the path with the highest percentage contribution is the one to follow first (in Figure 8.9, **SqlMetaData**, on the far left, is at 57%).

Ultimately, you should be able to trace back to a class you recognize. This could be one of your own classes, a third-party class library, or a framework-based caching class such as **HTTPApplicationState** or **HTTPSessionState**. It's now just a matter of viewing the leaking object instances being referenced by the suspect class, and inspecting the object retention graph.

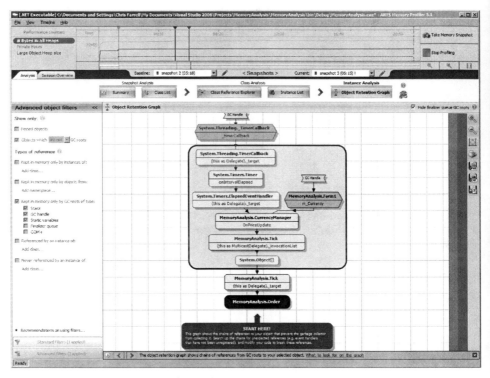

Figure 8.10: ANTS Memory Profiler, object retention graph.

Figure 8.10 shows an object retention graph. From it, you can see that the **MemoryAnalysis. Order** class instance is ultimately referenced by an instance of **MemoryAnalysis. CurrencyManager**, with a variable instance name of **m_Currency**. At this point, you can open up Visual Studio to view the source code, and so you see, by tracing back to the source, it's possible to fix the problem.

Surviving objects

The **Only new objects** filter will find many kinds of leaks and has the advantage of producing a small, focused set of classes to analyze. However, it won't work in a leak scenario where the application is designed to keep hold of a reference to the latest allocation of a leaked class, but forgets to drop reference to the old one.

To find this kind of leak, you need to run an analysis using the **Only surviving objects** filter instead of the **Only new objects** filter. Comparing an earlier snapshot against your latest test snapshot will reveal classes that exist in both snapshots (i.e. which have survived garbage collection). Classes in this list can now be investigated using the procedure described in Step 5.

Excessive memory usage

Objects that are constantly kept in memory can be tracked using the same technique as for memory leak detection except, instead of filtering **Only new objects**, select **Only surviving objects**.

Exactly the same snapshot comparison and objects tracking/tracing techniques apply. You should be able to trace long-lived large allocations back to their source references.

Heap fragmentation

As mentioned earlier, heap fragmentation can occur when the Large Object Heap can't reuse free space, or as a result of object pinning. The snapshot summary page in ANTS Memory Profiler can be used to identify symptoms of fragmentation. Three statistics are provided.

- Free space on all .NET heaps (total memory reserved).

- Largest free block (largest reserved memory block).

- Max size of new object.

If the **Free space on all .NET heaps** statistic is large and the **Largest free block** is small, this can indicate a fragmentation problem. It basically means that there are lots of small chunks of fragmented memory available. It doesn't necessarily mean there will be an Out of Memory exception, though. If the **Max. size of new object** is still large, then the size of the heap can still be expanded by reserving more memory, increasing the application footprint.

However, if **Max. size of new object** is also small, an Out of Memory exception is on its way! This is the classic fragmentation condition.

Object pinning

ANTS can help you gain some insight into object pinning issues by providing a filter helpfully called **Pinned objects**. Using this filter, you can view a list of classes with pinned instances on the heap, and then investigate their source.

Finalization issues

A filter is also available to display classes with instances on the finalization queue whose Dispose method wasn't called. A properly implemented Dispose pattern, together with a properly called Dispose method would avoid these references being left on the finalization queue.

Optimizing analysis

ANTS Memory Profiler can be optimized in either of the two following ways.

Isolating components

ANTS doesn't have a facility to exclude individual assemblies, namespaces, classes or functions (although you can use filtering to exclude them from results).

Reducing tools overhead

There are a couple of options to further reduce the overhead from the profiler, such as switching off the profiling of child processes and the monitoring of object disposal. This has to be configured at the start of a new profiling session, where the two **Profile child processes** and **Monitor disposal of objects** check boxes can be switched off.

Visual Studio 2008 Memory Profiler

Visual Studio 2008 and 2010 can perform memory analysis as part of the performance analysis tools built into the Team Suite edition. They have both an instrumenting and a lower-overhead sampling profiler. Sampling works well when all you need is a high-level summary view of allocation and deallocation. To gain more insight into the function call trees behind allocation, you'll require the detail given by instrumentation.

Getting started

You first need to create a new Performance Session in the Performance Explorer window, and then set the properties of the session (right click on **Properties**). The dialog in Figure 8.11 will be displayed.

- Choose **Sampling** or **Instrumentation** as the profiling method and check both items in the **.NET memory profiling collection** section.

  - .NET object allocation information helps identify expensive allocated classes and functions.

  - .NET object lifetime information is useful for tackling memory leaks, mid-life crisis detection and Large Object Heap issues.

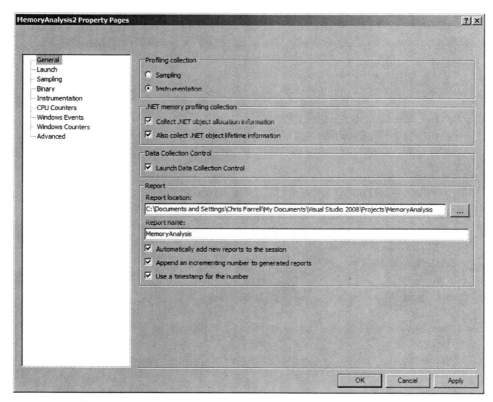

Figure 8.11: Visual Studio 2008 memory analysis configuration.

- The application can now be launched from within the Performance Explorer window, so run your test transaction, then either press the **Stop** button on the Performance Explorer toolbar or close your application, to end the test.

A summary report will be displayed (Figure 8.12), showing the top five functions and classes with the largest memory usage and the types with the most instances.

Performance Report Summary

Functions Allocating Most Memory

Name	Bytes	%
System.Xml.XmlDocument.Load(string)	15,534,931	61.85
MemoryAnalysis.Form1.AllocateLOH(int32)	9,094,608	36.21
System.Windows.Forms.Application.Run(class System.Windows.Forms.Form)	279,296	1.11
System.Windows.Forms.Form..ctor()	126,844	0.51
System.Random..ctor()	25,600	0.10

Types With Most Memory Allocated

Name	Bytes	%
System.Byte[]	9,140,587	36.39
System.String	5,879,776	23.41
System.Xml.XmlText	2,572,000	10.24
System.Xml.XmlAttribute	2,572,000	10.24
System.Object[]	2,054,480	8.18

Types With Most Instances

Name	Instances	%
System.Xml.XmlAttribute	128,600	23.11
System.Xml.XmlText	128,600	23.11
System.String	126,148	22.67
System.Object[]	51,946	9.33
System.Xml.XmlElement	44,438	7.99

Figure 8.12: Visual Studio 2008 Memory Analysis Summary.

A number of different views can be selected at this stage, including:

- **Object Lifetime** – good for mid-life crisis detection and Large Object Heap issues.

- **Call Tree** – good for most memory-expensive function call trees.

- **Allocation** – good for largest allocated classes, and the hottest function call trees responsible for allocating them.

Object lifetime view

The object lifetime (Figure 8.13) view displays where instances of each class were allocated, and in which of the generations they were collected. Knowing in which generation classes are collected helps in detecting midlife crisis problems. Classes with ever-increasing live instances could indicate memory leaks, and high levels of Large Object Heap allocation can lead to fragmentation problems.

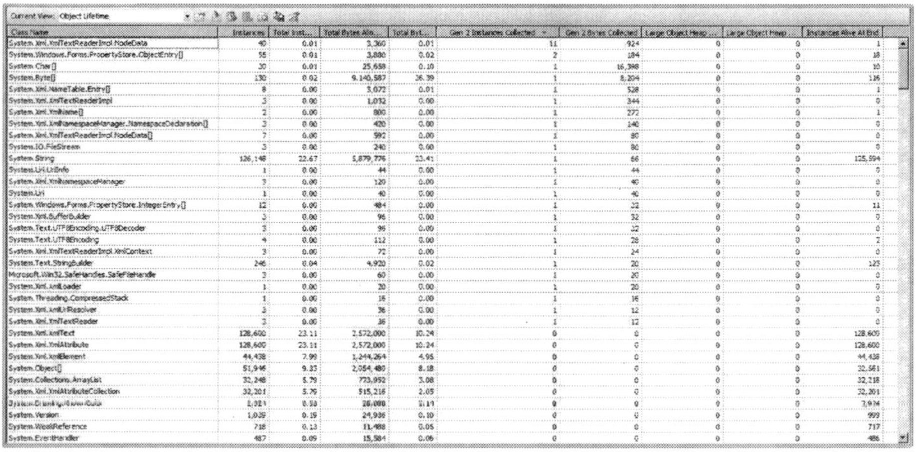

Class Name	Instances	Total Inst...	Total Bytes Allo...	Total Byt...	Gen 2 Instances Collected	Gen 2 Bytes Collected	Large Object Heap ...	Large Object Heap ...	Instances Alive At End
System.Xml.XmlTextReaderImpl.NodeData	40	0.01	3,360	0.01	11	924	0	0	1
System.Windows.Forms.PropertyStore.ObjectEntry[]	55	0.01	3,880	0.02	2	184	0	0	18
System.Char[]	30	0.01	25,658	0.10	1	16,398	0	0	10
System.Byte[]	130	0.02	9,140,587	36.39	1	8,204	0	0	116
System.Xml.NameTable.Entry[]	8	0.00	3,072	0.01	1	528	0	0	1
System.Xml.XmlTextReaderImpl	3	0.00	1,032	0.00	1	344	0	0	0
System.Xml.XmlName[]	2	0.00	800	0.00	1	272	0	0	1
System.Xml.XmlNamespaceManager.NamespaceDeclaration[]	3	0.00	420	0.00	1	140	0	0	0
System.Xml.XmlTextReaderImpl.NodeData[]	7	0.00	592	0.00	1	80	0	0	0
System.IO.FileStream	3	0.00	240	0.00	1	80	0	0	0
System.String	126,148	22.67	5,879,776	23.41	1	66	0	0	125,594
System.Uri.UriInfo	1	0.00	44	0.00	1	44	0	0	0
System.Xml.XmlNamespaceManager	3	0.00	120	0.00	1	40	0	0	0
System.Uri	1	0.00	40	0.00	1	40	0	0	0
System.Windows.Forms.PropertyStore.IntegerEntry[]	12	0.00	484	0.00	1	32	0	0	11
System.Xml.BufferBuilder	3	0.00	96	0.00	1	32	0	0	0
System.Text.UTF8Encoding.UTF8Decoder	3	0.00	96	0.00	1	32	0	0	0
System.Text.UTF8Encoding	4	0.00	112	0.00	1	28	0	0	2
System.Xml.XmlTextReaderImpl.XmlContext	3	0.00	72	0.00	1	24	0	0	0
System.Text.StringBuilder	246	0.04	4,920	0.02	1	20	0	0	123
Microsoft.Win32.SafeHandles.SafeFileHandle	3	0.00	60	0.00	1	20	0	0	0
System.Xml.XmlLoader	1	0.00	20	0.00	1	20	0	0	0
System.Threading.CompressedStack	1	0.00	16	0.00	1	16	0	0	0
System.Xml.XmlUrlResolver	3	0.00	36	0.00	1	12	0	0	0
System.Xml.XmlTextReader	3	0.00	36	0.00	1	12	0	0	0
System.Xml.XmlText	128,600	23.11	2,572,000	10.24	0	0	0	0	128,600
System.Xml.XmlAttribute	128,600	23.11	2,572,000	10.24	0	0	0	0	128,600
System.Xml.XmlElement	44,438	7.99	1,244,264	4.95	0	0	0	0	44,438
System.Object[]	51,946	9.33	2,054,480	8.18	0	0	0	0	32,561
System.Collections.ArrayList	32,248	5.79	773,952	3.08	0	0	0	0	32,218
System.Xml.XmlAttributeCollection	32,201	5.79	515,216	2.05	0	0	0	0	32,201
[illegible]	1,321	0.50	26,000	0.11	0	0	0	0	7,934
System.Version	1,039	0.19	24,936	0.10	0	0	0	0	999
System.WeakReference	718	0.13	11,488	0.05	0	0	0	0	717
System.EventHandler	487	0.09	15,584	0.06	0	0	0	0	486

Figure 8.13: Visual Studio 2008 memory analysis, object lifetime.

Mid-life crisis detection

Mid-life crisis can be easily identified by sorting the results grid by the **Gen 2 Bytes Collected** column; any classes with instances collected in Gen 2 are potentially a performance problem. They will make the garbage collector work harder and, with a bit of investigation, the code can often be altered to release references earlier.

Large Object Heap

The number and size of objects collected from the Large Object Heap is reported by class. A large collection size for a class warrants further investigation.

Call tree view

The call tree view (Figure 8.14) shows the most memory-intensive function call trees. By selecting the **Hot Path** button from the toolbar, the most expensive call tree will be expanded, and the most expensive function within the call tree will be highlighted. This is usually a good starting point, as it indicates the function is allocating a lot of memory and may benefit from optimization. This, of course, depends on the proportion of allocated objects that make it to higher generations.

Both inclusive and exclusive bytes and allocations are included in the statistics for this view. **Inclusive** includes allocations made by the function, and also includes calls it makes to child functions. **Exclusive** just includes memory allocated by the function body itself.

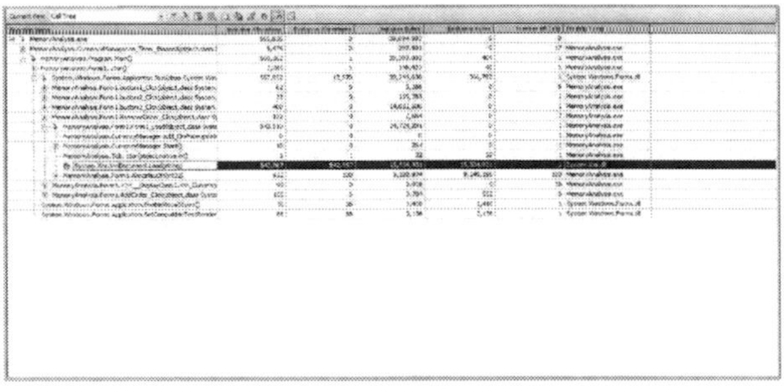

Figure 8.14: Visual Studio 2008 memory analysis call tree.

Allocation view

The allocation view (Figure 8.15) displays a grid of all allocated classes together with the function call trees that allocated them. It allows you to view the classes responsible for the largest proportion of memory usage, and then discover where that allocation is distributed across each contributing function call tree.

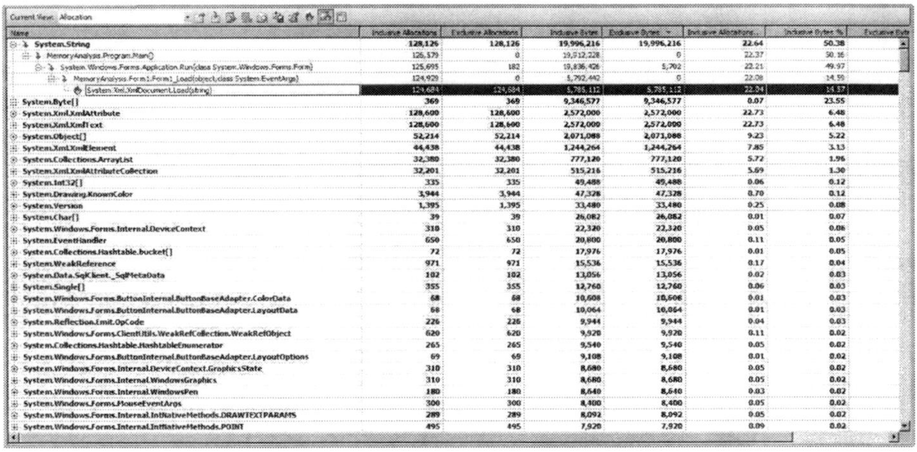

Current View: Allocation

Name	Inclusive Allocations	Exclusive Allocations	Inclusive Bytes	Exclusive Bytes	Inclusive Allocations...	Inclusive Bytes %	Exclusive Byte
System.String	128,126	128,126	19,996,216	19,996,216	22.64	50.38	
MemoryAnalysis.Program.Main()	126,579	0	19,912,228	0	22.37	50.16	
System.Windows.Forms.Application.Run(class System.Windows.Forms.Form)	125,695	182	19,836,426	5,702	22.21	49.97	
MemoryAnalysis.Form1.Form1_Load(object,class System.EventArgs)	124,929	0	5,792,442	0	22.08	14.59	
System.Xml.XmlDocument.Load(string)	124,684	124,684	5,785,112	5,785,112	22.04	14.57	
System.Byte[]	369	369	9,346,577	9,346,577	0.07	23.55	
System.Xml.XmlAttribute	128,600	128,600	2,572,000	2,572,000	22.73	6.48	
System.Xml.XmlText	128,600	128,600	2,572,000	2,572,000	22.73	6.48	
System.Object[]	52,214	52,214	2,071,088	2,071,088	9.23	5.22	
System.Xml.XmlElement	44,438	44,438	1,244,264	1,244,264	7.85	3.13	
System.Collections.ArrayList	32,380	32,380	777,120	777,120	5.72	1.96	
System.Xml.XmlAttributeCollection	32,201	32,201	515,216	515,216	5.69	1.30	
System.Int32[]	335	335	49,488	49,488	0.06	0.12	
System.Drawing.KnownColor	3,944	3,944	47,328	47,328	0.70	0.12	
System.Version	1,395	1,395	33,480	33,480	0.25	0.08	
System.Char[]	39	39	26,082	26,082	0.01	0.07	
System.Windows.Forms.Internal.DeviceContext	310	310	22,320	22,320	0.05	0.06	
System.EventHandler	650	650	20,800	20,800	0.11	0.05	
System.Collections.Hashtable.bucket[]	72	72	17,976	17,976	0.01	0.05	
System.WeakReference	971	971	15,536	15,536	0.17	0.04	
System.Data.SqlClient._SqlMetaData	102	102	13,056	13,056	0.02	0.03	
System.Single[]	355	355	12,760	12,760	0.06	0.03	
System.Windows.Forms.ButtonInternal.ButtonBaseAdapter.ColorData	68	68	10,608	10,608	0.01	0.03	
System.Windows.Forms.ButtonInternal.ButtonBaseAdapter.LayoutData	68	68	10,064	10,064	0.01	0.03	
System.Reflection.Emit.OpCode	226	226	9,944	9,944	0.04	0.03	
System.Windows.Forms.ClientUtils.WeakRefCollection.WeakRefObject	620	620	9,920	9,920	0.11	0.02	
System.Collections.Hashtable.HashtableEnumerator	265	265	9,540	9,540	0.05	0.02	
System.Windows.Forms.ButtonInternal.ButtonBaseAdapter.LayoutOptions	69	69	9,108	9,108	0.01	0.02	
System.Windows.Forms.Internal.DeviceContext.GraphicsState	310	310	8,680	8,680	0.05	0.02	
System.Windows.Forms.Internal.WindowsGraphics	310	310	8,680	8,680	0.05	0.02	
System.Windows.Forms.Internal.WindowsPen	180	180	8,640	8,640	0.03	0.02	
System.Windows.Forms.MouseEventArgs	300	300	8,400	8,400	0.05	0.02	
System.Windows.Forms.Internal.IntNativeMethods.DRAWTEXTPARAMS	289	289	8,092	8,092	0.05	0.02	
System.Windows.Forms.Internal.IntNativeMethods.POINT	495	495	7,920	7,920	0.09	0.02	

Figure 8.15: Visual Studio 2008 memory analysis, allocation view.

Optimizing analysis

There are a number of ways you can optimize the analysis by isolating analyzed components and reducing overhead.

Isolating components

You can choose the assemblies to be included in the analysis from within Performance Explorer and, depending on the profiling mode, you can also choose to either sample or instrument each assembly in the target list.

To achieve a good level of targeted detail without a crippling overhead, instrumentation can be limited using the advanced properties of each assembly in the target list. By setting specific **include** or **exclude** switches, you can limit the namespaces and functions that will be instrumented.

```
/include Namespace::FunctionName or /include Namespace::*
```

Reducing tools overhead

Sampling gives a lower-overhead analysis, although the cost of this is, as always, that it will provide a less-detailed call tree. The overhead of sampling can be reduced even further by decreasing the sampling frequency from within the Performance Explorer properties.

DevPartner Studio Professional 9

DevPartner Studio Professional 9 from Microfocus contains a .NET Memory Analysis profiler as part of its suite of tools. It also has a native memory profiler called BoundsChecker, which can be used to analyze native unmanaged applications.

The Managed profiler performs three types of analysis: **RAM Footprint**, **Temporary Objects**, and **Memory Leaks**. Each analysis tracks object allocation by class and function call, which allows the most expensive classes and functions for each type of analysis to be analyzed.

Using the tool

DevPartner provides a dedicated toolbar and menu within Visual Studio to allow for easy access to each of its tools, including the memory profiler. The application being tested is launched from the memory profiler toolbar button, which also displays the memory analysis window after the application has launched.

Each of the analysis types can be selected from the memory analysis window (Figure 8.16) and, depending on the analysis selected, there are options available for forcing garbage collections, clearing recorded data (temporary object analysis only), pausing analysis and generating a report snapshot.

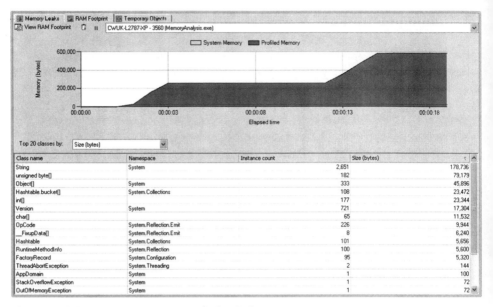

Figure 8.16: DevPartner memory analysis window.

A list of the top 20 classes, by size and instance count, is displayed by default, as is a memory allocation graph.

RAM footprint

RAM footprint analysis allows you to identify the largest allocated objects, and the functions that allocate the most memory. Using this analysis, you can reduce the overall memory footprint of your application.

To perform a RAM footprint analysis:

- Start your application from the DevPartner Memory Analysis toolbar button within Visual Studio.

- Perform your test transaction.

- Choose the **RAM Footprint** tab in the Memory Analysis window, and press the **View RAM Footprint** button.

You can now choose to view either **Objects that refer to the most allocated memory** or **Methods that allocate the most memory**.

Object analysis

Choosing **Objects that refer to the most allocated memory** will display a table of allocated objects sorted by size in descending order. Choosing an object will display its Object Reference graph, which can be used to investigate the references that are keeping that object in memory.

Method analysis

Choosing **Methods that allocate the most memory** displays a grid sorted by the live size of the functions allocating the most memory (Figure 8.17). Selecting a function in the list will display its call graph, which is the sequence of calls preceding the current one. The RAM footprint contribution for each function in the graph will also be displayed as a percentage.

It's also possible to view the source for a function, displaying its source code along with the allocation size information for each line of code.

Another useful feature is the ability to view live objects allocated by the selected function. This displays the object list, similar to the one in object analysis, from which the object reference graph can also be viewed.

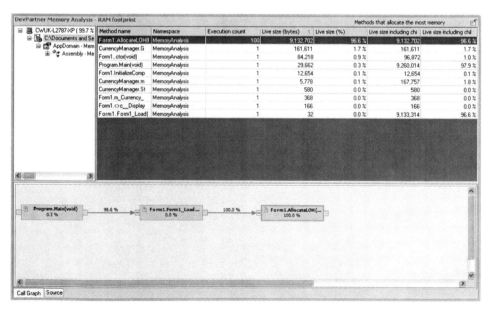

Figure 8.17: DevPartner RAM footprint analysis.

Temporary object analysis

- Temporary object analysis can be use to trace some of the inefficient allocation problems I described earlier. Temporary objects are objects which are allocated but which are collected after surviving one or two garbage collections, and can make the garbage collector work harder than necessary. DevPartner classifies temporary objects into one of three categories: short-lived (Gen 0), medium-lived (Gen 1) and long-lived (Gen 2).

DevPartner identifies which functions allocate the most memory in each of the three generations. A function that allocates objects that reside in later generations causes overhead due to compaction (the objects have had to be moved); therefore functions which allocate objects which are, on average, large and long-lived should be optimized if possible. To run a Temporary Object Analysis:

- Start your application from the DevPartner Memory Analysis toolbar button within Visual Studio.

- Perform your test transaction.

- Choose the **Temporary Objects** tab in the memory analysis window, and press the **View Temporary Objects** button.

The results are displayed in a grid (Figure 8.18), and can be sorted by average temporary size to reveal medium- and long-lived objects.

Selecting a function will allow you to view, via a tabbed window, either its function call graph or its source code. Viewing the source code will display the contribution each code line makes to medium- and long-lived distributions. If a single line of code is responsible for a large proportion of the temporary object allocations, it should be considered for optimization.

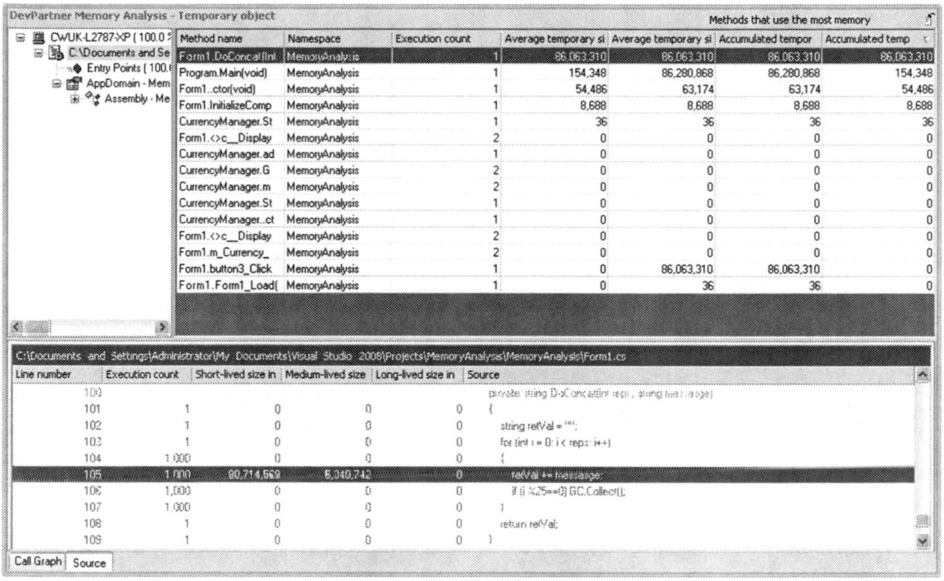

Figure 8.18: DevPartner temporary object analysis.

Memory leak detection

Memory leak detection can be carried out at any point after a memory analysis has started. To detect a memory leak:

- Start your application from the DevPartner Memory Analysis toolbar button within Visual Studio.

- Choose the **Memory Leaks** tab in the Memory Analysis window, and press the **Start Tracking Leaks** button.

- Perform your test transaction.

- Press the **View Memory Leaks** button.

As with all memory leak detection techniques, run your test transaction a number of times.

When the **View Memory Leaks** button is pressed, a garbage collection is forced and a report is produced, listing all the objects that were allocated since the **Start Tracking Leaks** button was pressed, but which weren't subsequently garbage collected. In addition, a summary is produced of the objects that refer to the most leaked memory, as well as the functions that leak the most memory. Both can be viewed separately.

Object analysis

Each potentially leaked object is listed in the **Objects that refer to the most leaked memory** report (Figure 8.19), along with various leak statistics. Selecting an object will display its object reference graph, which can be used to track the references that are keeping the object in memory.

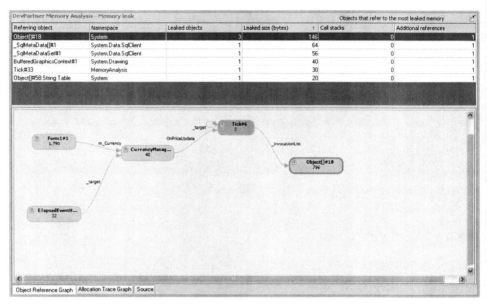

Figure 8.19: DevPartner Studio memory leak detection, object analysis.

Function analysis

The **Methods that allocate the most leaked memory** report (Figure 8.20) displays the functions that are potentially leaking memory, together with the leak statistics. Selecting a function will display, via a tabbed window, either its function call graph or its source code.

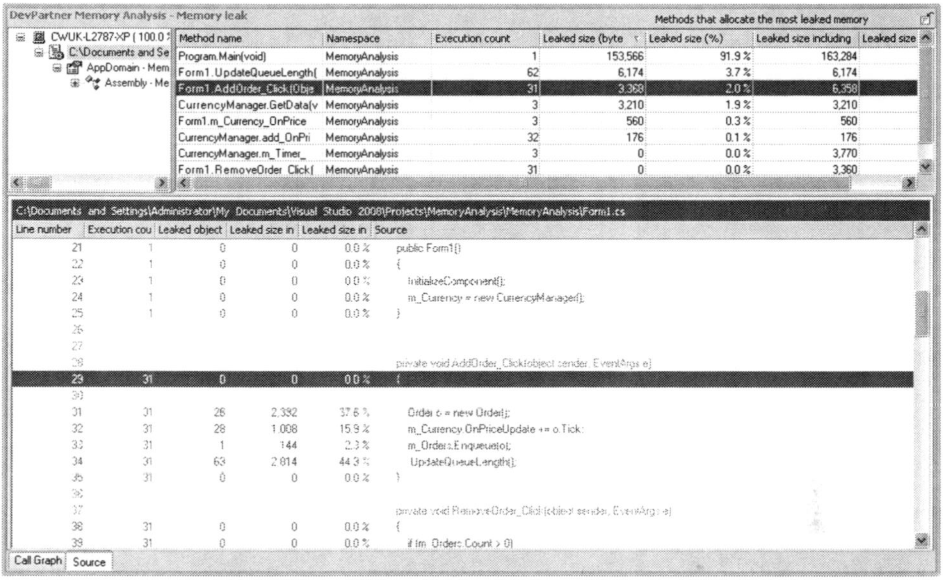

Figure 8.20: DevPartner Studio memory analysis leak detection, function view.

The call graph will display all parent and child function calls and their percentage leak contribution. You can trace the leak's critical path (worst allocation path) by following the call tree displayed at the top of the diagram until you get to the function highlighted in yellow. This is the function responsible for the majority of the leak.

The source view displays the source code for the selected function, and a per-code-line breakdown of leak statistics. If a single line of code is responsible for a large percentage of the leak size, then it is obviously worth investigating further.

When you're performing these various analyses it can be difficult to overcome the effects of application noise, especially when trying to detect small leaks. One way around this is to run a larger number of test transactions, which should raise the overall leak size, and so make it easier to see.

Optimizing analysis

Below are some ways to optimize the analysis, in much the same ways as the profilers we've already looked at.

Isolating components

DevPartner will collect allocation data from all of the loaded .NET assemblies.

Reducing tools overhead

The profiling overhead on an assembly can be reduced by switching off the tracking of .NET Framework objects. This restricts the analysis to just user classes, but could potentially obscure the source of a leak or problem. A memory leak is often most clearly identified by the buildup of multiple .NET framework classes referenced from a single user class.

This **Track System Objects** setting can be controlled via a project's properties, or as a switch from the command line.

CLRProfiler

The CLRProfiler has long been the workhorse of .NET memory analysis. It's a free tool and can be downloaded from Microsoft (or, for convenience, from HTTP://TINYURL.COM/ CLRPROFILER). It supports .NET framework 2.0 and earlier, although it does still work with framework 3.5 applications (which is, after all, just a collection of libraries running on the CLR 2). It isn't a particularly easy tool to use, but it does give a fascinating insight into the memory internals of your application.

Estimates as to the overhead added by CLRProfiler vary from it making your application anywhere from 10 to 100 times slower. You can profile WinForms applications, ASP.NET and even Services from a simple interface window (Figure 8.21). Profiling is very simply started and stopped using the **Profiling Active** check box.

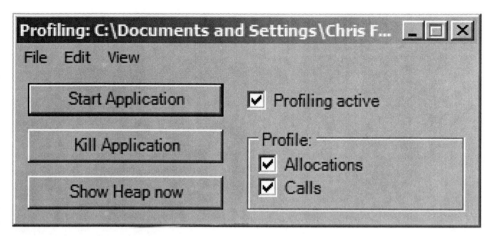

Figure 8.21: CLRProfiler main window.

Using the tool

- Choose the application type to profile from the File menu.

- Make sure **Profiling active** is checked, and check **Allocations** and **Calls**.

- Run your test transaction.

- Uncheck **Profiling active** to stop profiling and produce a summary.

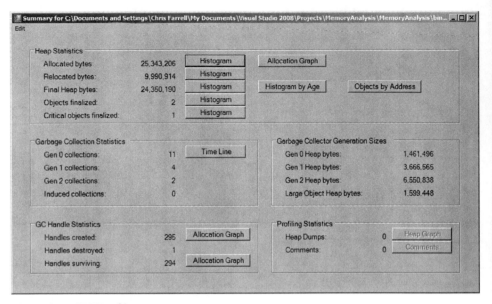

Figure 8.22: CLRProfiler summary.

Analyzing the summary

The summary window provides various statistics about the memory state after the last test transaction, and there are a couple of important statistics are always worth checking.

Generation ratio

The generally accepted guideline is that Gen 0 collections should occur ten times more frequently than Gen 1, and Gen 1 should occur ten times more frequently than Gen 2.

Checking the garbage collection statistics and calculating the ratios will indicate if there is a collection problem. You should particularly pay attention if Gen 2 collection is a lot more frequent than expected, as this could indicate a mid-life crisis issue and a temporary object problem.

Induced collections refers to garbage collections caused by the application calling **GC.Collect** to force collection. The general consensus is to avoid doing this, as it can upset the finely-balanced garbage collection algorithm, and lead to premature generational object promotion.

Relocated bytes / allocated bytes

If the proportion of relocated bytes to allocated bytes is high, this means the garbage collector is having to work harder copying bytes around memory. The higher this proportion is, the harder it has had to work, and the more you should consider looking for an explanation.

Allocation analysis

You can identify the source of the largest allocated classes by clicking on the **Allocated bytes Histogram** button in the **Heap Statistics** section shown in Figure 8.22. From the histogram displayed (Figure 8.23), you can view a list of the largest allocated classes and their distribution. Right-clicking on a specific class and choosing **Show Who Allocated** will display an allocation function call graph for the class.

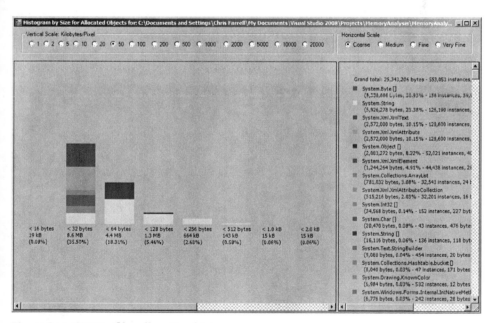

Figure 8.23: CLRProfiler allocation histogram.

The call graph can be used to discover where larger allocations are originating. The width of the lines and boxes on the graph are proportionate to the size of the allocation for which they are responsible.

Relocation analysis

You can use exactly the same technique I have just described (for allocation analysis), in order to find out where objects that are relocated are actually allocated. Reducing relocation overhead will reduce the burden on the garbage collector.

Object finalization

Finalizable objects can be investigated from the **Objects finalized** histogram button, and the allocation call stack for each class can be traced, just as for allocation analysis.

Heap visibility

Clicking the **Objects by Address** button provides a view of which heaps or generations objects are located on.

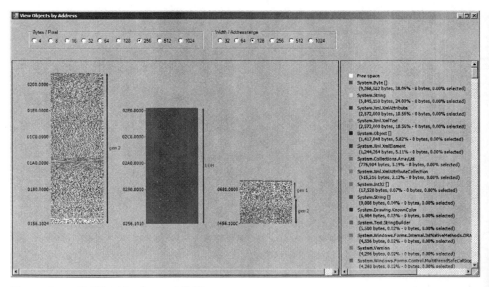

Figure 8.24: CLRProfiler heap visibility.

Each of the generations on both the Small Object Heap and the Large Object Heap can be inspected, the classes allocated to them can be viewed, and the allocation call stack traced.

Memory leak analysis

You can track memory leaks with the CLRProfiler using the **Show Heap now** button to take snapshots of the heap. After each snapshot, new objects are displayed in red, and older objects in faded pink.

The basic technique for finding leaks simply involves right-clicking on a snapshot and choosing **Show New Objects**. A graph of the allocation path of just the new objects will be displayed. You can also view **Show Who Allocated New Objects**, which will show the call stacks of functions that allocated new objects.

By repeating the heap snapshots and looking for classes and functions that consistently produce new objects after each iteration, a list of possible leak candidates can be drawn up.

Summary

Memory analysis is a key part of application profiling, and you can use the techniques described above to both validate the code you write and diagnose problems that have occurred in test or production systems.

The technique you will probably use the most is memory leak detection, but it is also worth remembering the impact that poor allocation patterns can have on performance and scalability.

The tool you choose is key, and should ideally allow every member of the development team to quickly and easily find problems, and confirm when there aren't any. With the right tool, and a simple set of techniques, that should be easily achievable.

Chapter 9: The Performance Testing Process

Development processes and scheduling tests

Previous chapters have shown how to record tests, how to automate the execution of the performance tests, and how to analyze the metric data that is gathered during this process.

How does performance testing fit in with various software development processes and methodologies, though? When should performance testing be scheduled during the course of a development project?

This chapter will discuss how performance testing can be integrated into your software development process. We will look at how performance testing can fit into a particular methodology, such as one of the many Agile variants or a more traditional, Waterfall-based process. It is important that performance testing should not impede the development process, but rather complement it and provide feedback into it.

Having such feedback into the development process is great, but we also need to be able to action this information in the event of performance issues. Managing the ongoing flow of data gathered from testing, and applying this data within the development process will also be examined.

In addition, we will look at how data gathered from performance testing can be communicated back to business stakeholders in a clear and concise form which is easily understood by technical and non-technical individuals alike. For a business, this is invaluable as it clearly demonstrates the value of performance testing in business terms, and allows full transparency of the entire process.

An ideal world

Of course we don't live in an ideal world, but we need to at least strive to get as close to it as possible. Let's examine what *should* happen, and then discuss the practical implications in real-world scenarios.

In an ideal world, performance testing is an integral part of the development life cycle, irrespective of what methodology is used (such as Agile/Scrum, or Waterfall). When a development project commences, some analysis and design may occur, project templates and iteration plans are detailed, and some code may start to be produced. It is at this point that the performance test rig should be estimated, designed, and built.

Factors to consider are:

- The needs of a web application compared to a desktop application. That is, what is being simulated, whether concurrent users or simply simulated load.

- The number of users that will need to be simulated, based on business requirements and projections. This will naturally impact how many test agents are required, and therefore affect licensing costs.

- Provision of hardware. Ensuring that there is an environment that can be used for performance testing, and that it is similar to the expected production environment. This could include virtual machine provisioning as well as web, application, and database servers.

- Ensuring that external systems are prepared for performance testing. For example, some external systems, such as payment gateway providers, will need to be informed about when performance testing will occur, so that they are aware of an impending load on their systems, and can provide potential test windows and test data to use.

- Setting up the automation aspects of the performance test run. If the performance test servers are shared systems, then other parties will need to be involved in the scheduling and execution of performance tests. For example, the performance test system may be a general test system during normal business hours, but be completely dedicated to performance testing after a certain time of day.

Once a performance test rig is in place, tests should be performed at regular, logical intervals. During initial development there may, initially, not be anything to test until the first deliverable but, as soon as there are usable pieces of the system, performance testing should commence.

Methodology

In an iteration-based methodology such as the many Agile variants out there, performance testing is best done near the end of each iteration, when a deliverable is ready for deployment. Iterations can typically range from one to two weeks in duration though, if they are longer, consider executing performance tests at points midway through the iteration.

In a milestone-based methodology, such as a Waterfall process, each milestone can be quite lengthy. In this scenario, it is best to execute performance tests at regular intervals during the milestone period, perhaps every week. Naturally, this period should be discussed and planned with the technical staff as well as the project manager, to ensure value is delivered and that it makes sense to execute performance tests at the specific stages of development.

In the early stages of the development life cycle, the application can be very dynamic, often going through periods where its functional aspects do not work as expected. This makes it difficult to performance test, and the value of performance testing against such code is quite small. Unless there are specific performance concerns against the application at this time, it is usually best to wait until a solid deliverable has been achieved, such as at the end of the iteration. At these stages of development, the time taken to record tests and then execute and analyze them can often be better spent ensuring quality code within the application. Performance tests written at this stage often have to be changed significantly, or even completely discarded, once the desired piece of functionality has been delivered in its near-final incarnation.

As the development cycle continues, the application matures and becomes less subject to major changes, and this is when it is possible to execute performance tests at more regular intervals. Ideally, this could be done daily, with performance reports sent to team members advising of any changes in performance. This way, the performance of the application is closely monitored during the entire development cycle, and this is an excellent way of keeping the entire team focused on the performance objectives.

The main point here is that performance should be measured early in the process, and in an ongoing manner throughout the entire development project. This provides the most insight into an application's performance very early in the development life cycle, and ensures that the development is undertaken with performance in mind. Regular performance reports can be distributed amongst the team for the benefit of everyone, and executive summaries of those reports can be distributed to key stakeholders to ensure complete transparency, and to keep everyone informed.

Automating the deployment of the application, combined with the automation of performance tests, can make this process as painless as possible, with little overhead to the development process. As mentioned previously, though, this may initially not be feasible early in the development phase, or at least until the product begins to take shape.

With test automation in place, there should be no reason why testing cannot occur every day. Typically this testing might occur overnight and run for a period of, say, 12 hours. Weekend runs can execute over the course of a few days to gain valuable insight into sustained load levels.This might begin at 7 p.m. on Friday evening, once everyone has gone home, and complete at 7 a.m. on Monday morning, meaning that your testing process has little or no impact on workflow from the point of view of the developers. However, analyzing the performance metrics does take time, and there may not be enough resource in the development team to spare a team, or even an individual, solely to look at performance test analysis. While having this analysis will provide enormous benefit, a value judgment must be made between that analysis and development velocity.

The reality

What has just been described is, without a doubt, an idealistic scenario, and this often does not occur. Quite often, performance tests may be executed close to the end of the development of the application, with the aim of fulfilling a preagreed objective to carry out performance testing.

This can be a dangerous approach, as the performance of the application may not meet the objectives and, if this analysis is performed too late in the development cycle, then the scope for change may be limited. Worse still, the changes required may be fundamental to the application, and require large-scale changes that simply cannot be accommodated at the late stage of development.

If the ideal scenario cannot be realized, then it is important to try and schedule performance tests at a few key stages of development, well before the final deliverable is required.

The scheduled times will depend on the available resources and willingness of everyone concerned to perform such testing. Obviously, the more tests, the better, but scheduling tests at a few key stages is, at the very least, a good compromise. As a minimum, executing performance tests midway through the development cycle, and then again when the application is 85% complete, is a reasonable compromise where regular periodic performance tests cannot be run. This approach can at least provide some warning if there are any performance-related issues, and it allows time for changes to occur.

A word about best practice

Even a team that follows best practices, adheres to accepted coding styles, and follows current development wisdom as well as possible, can still run into performance issues. One might glibly suggest that the current theory isn't perfect but, when creating complex applications that interact on a variety of levels, it is often not apparent what can have detrimental effects. Equally, individuals may work on components in relative isolation, and may not be able to accurately predict how efficient the component will work when it's attempting to service 3,000 concurrent users.

That being said, it is true that some aspects of best practice design and development are actually detrimental from a performance perspective. Loosely-coupled design is an objective for many solutions, and promotes a modular and componentized architecture. In some implementations of this design, a generic mechanism can be used to achieve the loosely-coupled architecture, and generic mechanisms can often require relatively significant amounts of computational power or multiple levels of abstraction, all of which can cost valuable processor cycles.

An example of this is the use of the `System.Reflection` namespace to reflect over classes and their associated methods and properties, perhaps to subscribe to events, execute methods or otherwise utilize aspects of the class without having a direct reference to it and its methods. While the methods within `System.Reflection` are very powerful, and a great way to achieve a loosely-coupled implementation, they are relatively slow and computationally expensive. This is not to say they should not be used, but just that you should bear in mind the net effects, and that the implementation of these techniques should be performed with due care and consideration.

The next chapter will examine common areas such as these, where performance issues can be encountered, and will then look at ways of avoiding them.

Managing and monitoring performance changes

The purpose of constantly measuring the performance of an application is to ensure that the performance remains a known quantity, and not a hypothetical guess based on how you think the application *should* perform.

We have already discussed at what points we should be performance testing, but how do we really know that the application is getting better or worse? Maintaining a database of performance test results is important, but is hardly a quick reference that can be compared against or, necessarily, consumed by all parties.

A type of executive summary is useful for this purpose, and should form part of the deliverable for each performance test. This should take the form of a concise, one- or two-page report on the main performance aspects of the application, a conclusion and, if applicable, some next steps.

An example template for a performance test executive summary is shown below.

Example performance test results – executive summary

Date/time	12/10/2009, 7 p.m.
Duration	12 hours
Concurrent user load	5,000 users

Run characteristics	commence at 50 users, increase by 100 users every 20 minutes, until 5,000 reached and sustained for duration of run
Peak operational period (sweet spot)	1,500 concurrent users, maintained 230 requests per second, all page times less than 3 seconds this is sufficient to meet current user volumes more work is required to meet projected/future user volumes
Operational ceiling	3,500 concurrent users; page times were excessive (> 40 seconds) but still responding; beyond this level, timeouts and service errors occurred
Slowest page	search; consistently slower than all pages
Fastest page	home page
Changes made to application from last test	addition of extensive data layer caching shrinking of image sizes implementation of async pages
Web server	high CPU utilization, averaging > 90% memory usage good, averaging 50% excessive number of exceptions being thrown per second
Database server	CPU usage good, averaging < 30% memory usage good, averaging < 25%
Conclusion	addition of data layer caching has alleviated load on database server and is no longer an issue web server now experiencing high CPU usage; need to examine ways of improving this some more work is required to ensure projected user loads are catered for search page is contributing to initial throughput issues and we need to examine better ways of performing searches

Next steps	high CPU usage on web servers is the main focus for performance improvement
	excessive exceptions being thrown is initial investigation point; event logs show pricing module is generating the most errors and will be profiled extensively
	extra caching will continually be introduced via output caching and further application level caching to reduce overall application work
	will revisit the search implementation to investigate the slowest point of the process

From this template it is easy to see the general performance characteristics of the application. This executive summary can be sent to all key stakeholders to ensure complete transparency in the performance of the application, and to allow team members to see how the performance of the application is progressing. It provides a clear indication of the current state of the application, as well as clearly defining future steps to achieve desired goals.

For non-technical business stakeholders, this is absolutely vital information, and immediately (not to mention proactively) answers the key questions they are likely to have:

- What is the current state of the application?

- Does it meet current and future business objectives?

- What is the plan, or next steps for ongoing improvement? (*This is especially important if the business objectives are yet to be realized.*)

These types of performance summaries should be committed to the project management repository (for example, the team SharePoint site), or source control repository (depending on what is being used to manage project artifacts). A history of the application's performance can then be easily viewed at any time, and any detailed performance metrics can always be recalled from the load test database, should a detailed investigation of any particular aspect of the application be required.

It may also be beneficial to provide a series of graphs to visually illustrate the performance trends of the application, and to clearly highlight the points at which high and low performance points are seen. These graphs should not form the main content of the executive summary, but should rather serve as further illustrations of your points should the reader wish to examine the report in more detail. Bear in mind that these types of reports will often be used by the management to report on the status of the application to their own, more senior management, so the concise summary is the more important facet of the report.

Introducing changes

Having said all this, making performance changes should be a carefully managed process. It is often tempting to implement a wide variety of performance enhancements into the application, in order to achieve a large and readily demonstrable performance gain. Yet this has risks associated with it. If a large number of changes are introduced, it is often difficult to determine which change offered the most benefit. In addition, the total aggregate of changes may actually be less effective than one singular change. To provide a simplistic example, two changes might be introduced to a performance run, the first one being a simple caching change that might yield a 30% increase in throughput. Yet the second change might be a code change performed at a more subtle level in the application, and could actually hamper performance; this will therefore reduce the overall performance gain to 20%. While this is admittedly still a gain, it is not apparent that one of these changes actually hampered performance, because the net gain is still positive.

Unless it is possible to easily identify the performance aspects of each change, it is best to keep sets of changes isolated to ensure the most value is realized and, more importantly, to ensure no negative effects are introduced.

Time and resources will play an important part here, and it may not be feasible to only implement simple, small sets of changes all the time. To move forward at a faster, more business-friendly pace, you'll need to be able to analyze the desired changes, fully understanding the expected benefits, and know how to measure and prove those benefits. For example, if the potential areas for change involve tweaking a computational algorithm and altering a much-used stored procedure, it would be possible to assess the changes to these areas individually even though both changes were applied at the same time. A computational algorithm may typically affect CPU utilization on a web or application server, and the tuning of a stored procedure will alter SQL execution plans and overall database throughput. These metrics may be isolated enough within the application to be able to assess in a single change set, but only a good understanding of the application can assess this risk.

Also, bear in mind that, the more changes you introduce, the harder it is to articulate those changes within a single summarized report. In these instances, it is tempting to leave out the seemingly smaller changes in favor of the perceived larger or, at any rate, more beneficial changes, but remember that having a history of performance summaries is extremely valuable for comparison and progress monitoring. Once details of changes are excluded from such reports, their value diminishes and a "colored" view of the performance history is all that is left.

The entire performance picture

With all the performance pieces in place, there is now a complete overview of the entire performance optimization path, giving you the ability to measure, analyze, plan, and predict the performance of your application.

Performance tests can be easily recorded, and subsequent improvements managed so as to be in line with business functional usage estimates.

Performance tests can be run at will, or completely automated over relatively short or sustained periods of time, simulating as much load as is required. Additionally, they can go beyond the estimated load to examine high volume effects, so as to cater for peaks or spikes in application load.

To achieve this:

- Detailed test results and metric data are recorded and kept for analysis and investigation at any stage of development.

- Periodic reports outlining an application's performance are produced and disseminated to business stakeholders and the technical development team, so that performance progress is well known at all phases of the project.

- Profiling of individual aspects of the application is undertaken to get a closer, isolated view of application components.

- Key questions around the ability of the infrastructure to serve the needs of the application and user-base are well known, quantified, and demonstrated through evidence and metrics, rather than through theory and guesswork.

- A history of the performance of the application as it has moved through development is easily available for analysis by all participants in the project.

It is the transparent, well-articulated and succinct provision of information that inspires confidence in key stakeholders of the application. This, in turn, provides positive effects to the team in general, as the business is more receptive when provided with open, honest communication about the project. Detailed technical metrics around performance are managed into an easily digestible form, with clear plans and risk mitigation strategies to achieve business objectives. This makes it easier to manage business expectations and to focus the development team.

It also means that a development team can prove that the application meets its requirements from a performance perspective. If the application interacts with other systems or components outside its control, and the performance suffers as a result, justification for the application's performance can be presented, and investigation can immediately target the other systems or components.

Later chapters will outline typical performance enhancements that can be made, as well as potential pitfalls in application performance that are not immediately apparent.

Chapter 10: Common Areas for Performance Improvement

Every application is different

Every application is different and has different combinations of criteria that affect its overall performance. It is very difficult to recommend specific performance improvements to an application without knowing how it works, how it interacts with the infrastructure around it, and other dependent systems. Quite simply, to understand where the most benefit, if any, can be gained by applying changes, there is nothing so beneficial as having a deep understanding of the application.

However, there are certain areas that are common to most applications which can typically benefit from scrutiny and potential modifications to increase application performance. At a minimum, these areas will provide a guideline as to which areas need to be investigated to ensure a performance concern is tackled early on in development, as well as a potential approach to the problem. This section will not provide exhaustive detail on each item, as that could be an entire book on its own. Instead, it'll provide enough information to enable you to properly determine whether these generic areas are relevant concerns within any given application.

A "ground-up" approach will be taken, first looking at the database, then moving up through the typical layers of an application, examining areas such as data access, business logic and network latency, and finally, for where a web application is concerned, the browser.

Database access

Many applications require some form of data access, which is typically, but not always, supplied using a database. Given that utilizing a database is the most common scenario, this discussion will concentrate on database access. That said, most techniques can be applied to non-database driven stores, such as XML files, message access systems or even cloud-based resources.

Any form of data store requires some resource to access it, whether in the form of SQL connections, TCP sockets, resource managers or a combination of all of three. It is usually quite costly for an application to acquire these resources, and even more so if it never releases the resources back to the system.

SQL database connections in particular are a finite resource, and so need to be carefully managed to ensure that there are enough available to the system to allow data access to take place. In addition, we need to ensure we are not constantly recreating these database connections, but are, instead, reusing them where possible.

The best and most efficient form of data access

The best and most efficient way of accessing your data store, is simply *not to access it at all*.

The idea here is to cache your data where possible. Data access will initially be required to populate the cache, but reference data, which is data that never really changes, should be loaded only once, and stored in memory. Subsequent requests will then only need to access the data from memory, and the database will be spared from servicing requests to return the same data over and over again. This technique is a great way to improve application performance relatively easily, but it may not be practical or even possible in all instances, depending on the data needs of the application. This has to be assessed at a functional and architectural level. For example, data requiring real-time accuracy is generally not a good candidate for caching.

Obviously, this approach places an extra burden on memory usage, so simply loading all your data into memory may not be practical. This is why you should design a caching strategy. Typically, this should involve analyzing the application to form an idea of how data is being used, and to assess the value of storing it in memory as opposed to having to retrieve it from the database.

In its most simple form, caching would involve storing data in a variable or object that is never released from memory for the lifetime of the application. This assumes the data never changes and that the data size makes it feasible to fit into main memory. A simple cache could look similar to the following class:

```
public static class PostcodeCache
{
    private static Dictionary<int, string> _postcodes = new
Dictionary<int, string>();

    static PostcodeCache()
    {
        LoadPostcodes();
    }
```

```
    private static void LoadPostcodes()
    {
        // Typically load from th database or datastore here....
        _postcodes.Add(2000, "Sydney");
        _postcodes.Add(3000, "Melbourne");
        _postcodes.Add(4000, "Brisbane");
    }

    public static string GetPostcode(int postcode)
    {
        if (_postcodes.ContainsKey(postcode))
            return _postcodes[postcode];
        else
            return null;
    }
}
```

The code sample above shows a very simple class that, when it is first constructed, loads postcodes into a private field (typically from a database). The .NET runtime ensures that this is only performed once because of the static nature of the class and, from that point, all postcode data can be retrieved directly from memory. The usage of this class is even simpler:

```
[TestMethod]
public void TestExistingPostcode()
{
    Assert.AreEqual<string>("Sydney", PostcodeCache.
GetPostcode(2000));
    Assert.AreEqual<string>("Melbourne", PostcodeCache.
GetPostcode(3000));
    Assert.AreEqual<string>("Brisbane", PostcodeCache.
GetPostcode(4000));
}
[TestMethod]
public void TestPostcodeNonExisting()
{
    Assert.AreEqual<string>(null, PostcodeCache.
GetPostcode(1234));
}
```

This example shows a very simplistic implementation, and assumes data that may never need to be changed or invalidated during the lifetime of the application.

Naturally, data doesn't always fit this easy model. Data will typically need to be invalidated at some point, and any data requiring real-time accuracy clearly cannot be cached. This analysis needs to be done carefully to ensure that stale data does not become an issue in the application.

Once the lifetime characteristics of segments of data have been established, it is then a matter of implementing appropriate caching in the application. If the requirements are simple enough, time-based expiry, event-based expiry and other forms of triggered invalidation of cache data can be implemented using a custom solution. Often, a number of different expiry schemes are required, and tools such as the Enterprise Library Caching component offer just such cache management features, although there are also other third-party components that can be used to implement your caching requirements. In ASP.NET, things are a little easier as the provided ASP.NET cache can be used to manage all the application's caching needs.

What to cache?

At this point it is worth discussing what types of data should be cached. Unfortunately, there is no single answer to apply to all situations, but there are some general rules.

- **Static, or reference data**: this data either never changes or, at least, only changes very rarely. This can be cached indefinitely or for relatively long periods of time, for example a day or more. As discussed earlier in this chapter, postcodes or zip codes would be a good candidate for this.

- **Read many, write few**: this data is typically read a large number of times, but may be written or updated infrequently. The data itself could be cached until an update occurs on it, in which case it could be invalidated. Later, we will see how cache dependencies can help achieve this.

- **Write many, read few**: data that is written or updated very often is generally not a good candidate for caching.

- **Search queries**: in some cases, often-used search query results can be cached where the data itself is not updated very often. Once the data is updated, then the query results can be invalidated. We'll look at how SQL Caching Dependencies can help with this later.

- **Real-time data**: this is typically where the most current version of the data must be used at all times, and is often updated quite frequently. In many cases, this data cannot be cached. In some cases, with a careful caching strategy, some caching may be possible, but this needs careful assessment by the business and technical stakeholders.

ASP.NET cache

The ASP.NET cache is one of the most powerful caching mechanisms available to .NET developers. In ASP.NET versions 3.51 and below, the ASP.NET cache was only usable within ASP.NET applications, but since the latest release of ASP.NET (version 4), the powerful caching features can also be used within traditional desktop applications.

Cache dependencies

.NET supports a variety of options for cache invalidation via dependency objects; in basic terms, cached data will depend upon certain criteria and, when the criteria are rendered invalid or stale, the data is removed from the cache. .NET provides support for a host of dependency mechanisms such as:

- **File based**: when a file system change occurs, the associated cached item is invalid.

- **Time-based**: when a cached item has been in the cache for a specific amount of time, a specific date/time is reached, or the cached data has not been accessed for a certain time period, then the data is removed from the cache.

- **SQL-based**: when the result of a query in a SQL database changes, the associated data is removed from the cache.

- **Cache item-based**: when an associated item that is also within the cache is removed, any other associated cache items are also removed.

Here's an example of how to add data to the ASP.NET cache:

```
var data = GetDataFromStore();
if (System.Web.HttpContext.Current != null)
{
    System.Web.HttpContext.Current.Cache.Add("TheData", data,
null,
            DateTime.Now.AddSeconds(30),
            Cache.NoSlidingExpiration, CacheItemPriority.Normal,
null);
}
```

The previous code sample starts by retrieving data from the data store, then adding to it the code with the TheData key and an absolute time limit of 30 seconds. The result is that, after 30 seconds, the data is automatically removed from the cache. To retrieve that data, the following code can be used:

```
ModelContainer data = null;
if (System.Web.HttpContext.Current != null)
{
    data = System.Web.HttpContext.Current.Cache["TheData"] as
ModelContainer;
    if (data == null)
        data = GetDataFromStore();
}
```

This code fragment first checks to see if retrieving the data from the cache using the `TheData` key returns null. If so, then the item has been removed from the cache and the data must be retrieved from the data store.

`SqlCacheDependency` is a particularly powerful mechanism for detecting changes in your data, and automatically invalidating cached data whenever a table or query changes in the database. It exists in the `System.Web.Caching` namespace and, instead of relying on a time-based mechanism, we can ask the SQL database to notify our application whenever there is a change in data within a table, or in the result of a query.

Implementing `SqlCacheDependency` takes a little more setup work than a traditional in-memory cache but is still relatively easy. Before we can use this mechanism, the database and associated table must be enabled to provide SQL cache dependency notifications. This can performed from the command line using the `aspnet_regsql` tool:

```
aspnet_regsql -t {table} -et -C {connection-string} -d {database}
-ed
```

> **Note**
>
> There are many variations available to enable SQL cache dependency on specific database objects. For example, rather than using the command line options shown above, providing **"-W"** as a command line switch will invoke wizard mode and guide you through the process. Similarly, supplying **"-?"** as a command line parameter will display all available options.

Alternatively, this can also be performed programmatically in code, provided the context of the code has sufficient security privileges:

```
SqlCacheDependencyAdmin.EnableNotifications("{database-table}");
```

The code to utilize a SQL cache dependency is identical to standard cache usage, with the exception of setting up a `SqlCacheDependency` object when inserting the data item into the cache. The following code illustrates this:

```
var cacheData = Cache["MyRecord"] as DataEntity;
if (cacheData == null)
{
    SqlConnection conn = new SqlConnection(ConfigurationManager.
ConnectionStrings["sql"].ConnectionString);
    SqlCommand cmd = new SqlCommand("select CustomerName from
Customer",conn);
    SqlCacheDependency cacheDependency = null;
    try
    {
```

```
        cacheDependency = new SqlCacheDependency("test-
database", "Customer");

        using (var dc = new DataStoreDataContext(ConfigurationMan
ager.ConnectionStrings["sql"].ConnectionString))
        {
            var records = dc.Customers.Take(1);
            if (records.Count() > 0)
            {
                cacheData = new DataEntity() { Name = records.
First().CustomerName, RetrievalTime = DateTime.Now };
                Cache.Insert("MyRecord", cacheData,
cacheDependency);
            }
        }
    }
}
```

Using this code, SQL Server will notify the web application whenever the contents of the **Customer** table change, and will cause the cached data to be cleared, forcing the data to be reloaded from the database next time it is requested.

Windows Server AppFabric

Windows Server AppFabric (formerly known as Project Velocity) is a relatively new initiative from Microsoft that provides a highly scalable caching infrastructure that can span across multiple servers in a farm, with the ability to synchronize the cache state across all servers in the farm automatically. Microsoft provides technical documentation, downloads and samples for Windows AppFabric at HTTP://TINYURL.COM/APPFABRIC.

Up to this point, discussions around caching have been focused on single machine scenarios; that is, a single cache on a single machine. Obviously if there are multiple machines in a typical web farm, then a cache on one machine may not be the same as a cache on another, and so some efficiency is lost.

Windows Server AppFabric aims to mitigate this issue by providing its own cache farm, together with the ability to synchronize caches across the farm as changes are made. Its function is modeled from the ASP.NET cache, so usage patterns are very familiar to most developers. Windows Server AppFabric provides a seamless integration with ASP.NET, which enables ASP.NET session objects to be stored in the distributed cache without having to write to databases. It offers the speed and efficiency advantages of an in-memory cache, but coupled with the benefits of a distributed, synchronized cache across a farm of web servers.

AppFabric presents a unified memory cache across multiple computers to give a single unified cache view to applications. Applications can store any serializable CLR object without worrying about where the object gets stored. Scalability can be achieved by simply adding more computers on demand.

Windows Server AppFabric is an excellent choice for any web application wishing to achieve high performance, and should be seriously considered.

Indexing

Indexes on database tables can significantly speed up database access and reduce query execution time. There are many aspects to indexes and query optimization that would take a book in themselves to explain in their entirety (and there are many such books available), but essentially, optimizing the indexes can be a quick win for comparatively little effort.

In some cases, database use continues over time and indexes can become fragmented and inefficient. Ideally, maintenance tasks should be scheduled to defragment and rebuild the indexes in a database to avoid the problems this can cause. The DBCC and ALTER INDEX SQL commands can be used to achieve this.

Creating good indexes is just as important as having them in the first place, as a badly designed index can actually lead to worse performance. Providing a well-designed index during system design requires a good understanding of the application and how data will be accessed. Once the application has been accessing data for a decent period of time, retrospective analysis and changes can then be performed to ensure indexes are optimal.

What is even better is that SQL Server provides a tool to do just that. In SQL Server 2008 Management Studio (SSMS), the Database Engine Tuning Advisor can be run against the database to provide a report on what areas need to be improved. This is an invaluable tool for a low effort, potentially high value, gain.

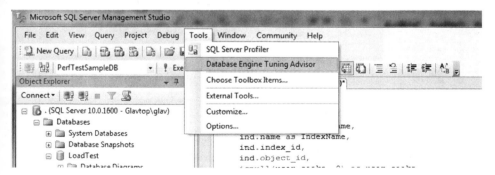

Figure 10.1: Database Engine Tuning Advisor menu option.

An easy way to ensure that indexes are properly optimized is to produce daily or weekly reports on their statistics. The following SQL script is a simple way to look at overall usage of indexes, such as which ones are most used, and how they are used.

```
set nocount on;


Use PerfTestSampleDB
select
      obj.Name as ObjectName,
      ind.name as IndexName,
      ind.index_id,
      ind.object_id,
      isnull(user_seeks, 0) as user_seeks,
      isnull(user_scans, 0) as user_scans,
      isnull(user_lookups, 0) as user_lookups
from sys.indexes ind
      join sys.objects obj on (ind.object_id = obj.object_id)
      left join sys.dm_db_index_usage_stats st on (st.index_id =
ind.index_id and st.object_id = ind.object_id)
where obj.Type_Desc <> 'SYSTEM_TABLE'
order by obj.Name, ind.Name;
```

The SQL script produces output similar to that in Figure 10.2 and indicates how many seeks versus scans are being performed on the indexes. This shows you which are the most used indexes, as well as whether they are being used efficiently, and where seeks are much more efficient than scans. This information is like gold when it comes to optimizing your indexes and database design.

	ObjectName	IndexName	index_id	object_id	user_seeks	user_scans	user_lookups
1	Category	PK_Category	1	2105058535	0	0	0
2	Country	PK_Country	1	2121058592	6	9	0
3	Customers	PK_Customers	1	2137058649	0	0	0
4	filestream_tombstone_2073058421	FSTSClusIdx	1	2073058421	0	0	0
5	filestream_tombstone_2073058421	FSTSNCIdx	2	2073058421	0	0	0
6	Products	PK_Products	1	5575058	20	0	0
7	queue_messages_1977058079	queue_clustered_index	1	1993058136	0	0	0
8	queue_messages_1977058079	queue_secondary_index	2	1993058136	0	0	0
9	queue_messages_2009058193	queue_clustered_index	1	2025058250	0	0	0
10	queue_messages_2009058193	queue_secondary_index	2	2025058250	0	0	0
11	queue_messages_2041058307	queue_clustered_index	1	2057058364	0	0	0
12	queue_messages_2041058307	queue_secondary_index	2	2057058364	0	0	0
13	Roles	PK_Roles	1	21575115	0	0	0
14	syscommittab	ci_commit_ts	1	2089058478	0	0	0
15	syscommittab	si_xdes_id	2	2089058478	0	0	0

Query executed successfully.   (local) (10.0 RTM) | Glav

Figure 10.2: Simple index statistics SQL Script output.

Database access abstractions

When building today's business applications, an abstraction layer is often placed around the database access mechanism to make it easier to use or to make it fit easier into the object model of the application. There are many variants that can be used, ranging from Microsoft technologies such as LINQ to SQL and Entity Framework, all the way to a number of third-party and Open Source products such as nHibernate. As with all abstractions, there can be negative effects on performance if these are used without caution. Each product or technology has different ways of ensuring performance is acceptable, and these methods are typically specific to that product. For this reason, an in-depth discussion ranging across all the currently popular mechanisms is beyond the scope of this book, but here's information around some of the techniques that can cause potential issues.

LINQ to SQL, Entity Framework, nHibernate, etc.

Object relational mapping frameworks such as LINQ to SQL, Entity Framework and nHibernate all provide good abstractions over a relational database to allow for easy working with a traditional object model, and easy mapping of objects to the relational data.

As with all abstractions, this can incur a performance cost, especially if used without a reasonable knowledge of the potential effects of implementing these frameworks.

To illustrate this, let's look at a very simplistic example. The following diagram shows two tables that are linked by a foreign key relationship between the **CustomerId** field in the Order table and the **Id** field in the Customer table.

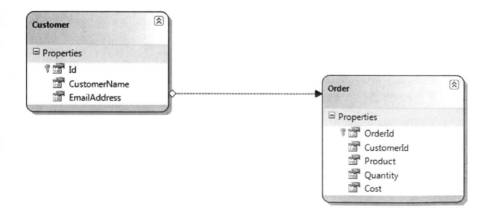

Figure 10.3: Two tables linked by CustomerId.

This very basic schema will store customers and their associated orders. For this example, we'll use LINQ to SQL to provide the relational mapping layer, as it's a comparatively simple framework to work with. Generating a set of LINQ to SQL classes for this schema will enable us to manipulate the records in the database.

To iterate through the customer records in the Customer table and show the number of orders a given customer has, we could use code similar to the following snippet:

```
using (var dc = new DataStoreDataContext())
{
    var customers = from c in dc.Customers
                    select c;

    customers.ToList().ForEach(c =>
    {
        Console.WriteLine("Name: {0} has {1} orders.",
c.CustomerName,c.Orders.Count);
    });
}
```

The code is very clean and simple to understand. We are referencing the Customer object (which maps to the corresponding Customer table) and the Orders object collection *within* the Customer object, which was generated by LINQ to SQL because of a relational constraint on the Orders table. However, if we look at the query produced, using SQL Server Profiler, we will see the following:

First, a query is performed to obtain all the customers

```
SELECT [t0].[Id], [t0].[CustomerName], [t0].[EmailAddress] FROM
[dbo].[Customer] AS [t0]
```

Then, multiple similar queries are executed in succession to retrieve all the orders for each customer as we iterate through the customers:

```
exec sp_executesql N'SELECT [t0].[OrderId], [t0].[CustomerId],
[t0].[Product], [t0].[Quantity], [t0].[Cost] FROM [dbo].[Order]
AS [t0] WHERE [t0].[CustomerId] = @p0',N'@p0 int',@p0=1

exec sp_executesql N'SELECT [t0].[OrderId], [t0].[CustomerId],
[t0].[Product], [t0].[Quantity], [t0].[Cost] FROM [dbo].[Order]
AS [t0] WHERE [t0].[CustomerId] = @p0',N'@p0 int',@p0=2

exec sp_executesql N'SELECT [t0].[OrderId], [t0].[CustomerId],
[t0].[Product], [t0].[Quantity], [t0].[Cost] FROM [dbo].[Order]
AS [t0] WHERE [t0].[CustomerId] = @p0',N'@p0 int',@p0=3
```

The list continues for each customer ID.

It is not immediately obvious that the previous code fragment, which iterates over the customers and produces an order count, actually performs multiple distinct SQL queries, dependent on the number of customer records. In a small table, this may not be noticeable, but as the number of records on both tables grows, it will reveal significant performance issues.

These kinds of problems can be tackled in a number of ways depending on the application requirements, such as by creating separate views and functions, or perhaps a dedicated stored procedure to return only the required results. In our simplistic example, a stored procedure such as the one shown in the following SQL fragment could be used to return the desired results in a single call:

```sql
select distinct(C.CustomerName), (IsNull(O.CustomerId,0)) as
"OrderCount"
        from dbo.Customer C
left outer join [dbo].[Order] O on O.CustomerId = C.Id
```

While this example is specific to LINQ to SQL, the concept being presented is applicable to all products that supply similar functionality, such as nHibernate and Entity Framework. Each framework has specific characteristics, and it is essential to understand what the potential costs of utilizing their powerful features are. It is beyond the scope of this book to go into detail on the many products in the object relational mapping space, but it is important to ensure that even seemingly simple queries are at least examined using a tool like SQL Server Profiler to give the resulting SQL statements a "sanity check."

Reflection

Reflection is a way for application code to examine assemblies, classes, fields, and almost anything else that is within its domain at runtime. Reflection methods exist within the System.Reflection namespace and, using them, we can find out what methods and properties a class has, or we can dynamically load an assembly, look for a constructor matching a particular signature, and then invoke it.

Reflection is a very powerful mechanism, and is often employed to allow dynamic invocation or runtime querying of type information. This can allow a great degree of loose coupling within an application which, from an architectural perspective, is a good thing.

That being said, using reflection does come at the cost of performance. It is quite a computationally intensive process and, when overused, can lead to performance issues such as high CPU utilization. That is not to say that it should never be used, but just that it should be used with full knowledge of its consequences, and its implementation carefully monitored.

To illustrate this, we will use reflection to provide descriptive titles for an enumeration. First, we create the attribute that we will use to decorate our enumeration:

```
[AttributeUsage(AttributeTargets.Field, AllowMultiple = true)]
public class DescriptiveTitleAttribute : Attribute
{
    public DescriptiveTitleAttribute() { }
    public DescriptiveTitleAttribute(string displayTitle)
    {
        DisplayTitle = displayTitle;
    }

    public string DisplayTitle { get; set; }
}
```

The DescriptiveTitleAttribute class simply provides a string DisplayTitle member.

We then create an enumeration that uses this attribute as shown in the following code:

```
public enum SongType
{
    [DescriptiveTitle("Contemporary Rock")]
    Rock,
    [DescriptiveTitle("Pop, Teeny Bopper")]
    Pop,
    [DescriptiveTitle("Rap and Hip Hop")]
    Rap,
    [DescriptiveTitle("Heavy Metal")]
    HeavyMetal,
    [DescriptiveTitle("Classical and Opera")]
    Classical
}
```

As you can see, using attributes to associate with enumerated members in this manner is a concise and easy way of providing extra metadata (in this case a display title) that is associated with the fields or properties of a given type. For this contrived example, we shall create a simple dictionary that will contain a song title and the song genre using the SongType enumeration previously shown.

```
Dictionary<string, SongType> songs = new Dictionary<string,
SongType>();
songs.Add("Lots of heavy guitar", SongType.HeavyMetal);
songs.Add("Oh Baby", SongType.Pop);
songs.Add("Baby Baby", SongType.Pop);
songs.Add("Oooh baby oooh", SongType.Pop);
songs.Add("Shake till it falls off", SongType.Rap);
```

To iterate through this collection and extract the display title enumeration associated with the element will require some reflection. Using reflection, the method shown in the following code will take a SongType enumeration value, and extract the DisplayTitle attribute value:

```
private static string GetDescriptiveTitle(SongType enumItem)
{
    var typeOfEnum = enumItem.GetType();
    var field = typeOfEnum.GetField(enumItem.ToString());
    var attribList = field.GetCustomAttributes(true);
    if (attribList.Length > 0)
    {
        var attrib = (DescriptiveTitleAttribute)attribList[0];
        return attrib.DisplayTitle;
    }
    return string.Empty;
}
```

Iterating through our dictionary collection of songs and extracting the song type is simple, as shown below:

```
foreach (var item in songs)
{
    var songType = GetDescriptiveTitle(item.Value);
    Console.WriteLine("{0} - {1}", item.Key, songType);
}
```

The code shown so far is all very easy to understand, with the exception of the reflection code itself, which represents the most complexity. For comparative purposes, we shall also use a very simple alternate method that does not use reflection to retrieve the display title of the SongType enumeration members. For this, we will use another dictionary collection to hold the DisplayTitle values, as shown in the following code:

```
Dictionary<SongType, string> songTypeDescriptions = new
Dictionary<SongType, string>();
songTypeDescriptions.Add(SongType.Classical, "Classical and
Opera");
songTypeDescriptions.Add(SongType.HeavyMetal, "Heavy Metal");
songTypeDescriptions.Add(SongType.Pop, "Pop, Teeny Bopper");
songTypeDescriptions.Add(SongType.Rap, "Rap and Hip Hop");
songTypeDescriptions.Add(SongType.Rock, "Contemporary Rock");
```

To extract the display title for each enumerated member, we can simply access the keyed element of the dictionary:

```
foreach (var item in songs)
{
    var songType = songTypeDescriptions[item.Value];
```

```
    Console.WriteLine("{0} - {1}", item.Key, songType);
}
```

In order to demonstrate the computational difference, we will iterate over each collection 10,000 times. The results are:

- using reflection took approximately 768 milliseconds

- not using reflection took approximately 18 milliseconds.

While the times taken here are certainly not excessive, the relative difference is very large. In a more typical and complex application, it is not inconceivable that substantially more reflection might be used. It is with this in mind that the effects of using reflection must be understood, especially in a web application where multiple concurrent requests are being processed.

As mentioned previously, that is not to say that reflection should not be used. In many cases, reflection can be used with little detrimental effect to performance. In the simple example we just went through, using an attribute on the enumerated members can still be employed, with the initial call to access a display attribute triggering a call to populate an internal cache of descriptive values. The internal cache can then subsequently be referenced in code, bringing the benefit of fast access to the descriptive attribute, but also the clean aspect of using attributes on the enumerated members.

This solution obviously does not apply to all situations, but it does illustrate that a happy middle ground can be achieved. The key point is to understand that reflection does incur a performance penalty, and the process of assessing the impact of any potential issues and mitigating them will be unique to each application.

String manipulation

When it comes to strings in .NET, the classic performance trap is that of the immutable string. To cut to the core of the issue: if performing more than approximately three string operations or manipulations, use a StringBuilder object instead of a string.

The number of string operations is dependent on the size of the string and type of operations, so your mileage may vary; but in general, any more than three string operations are better performed with a StringBuilder. To illustrate this point, have a look at a very basic class to concatenate a string:

```
class MyStringManipulator
{
    const string SomeStringData = "QWERTYUIOPASDFGHJKLZXCVBNM";
```

```
    public int UseRegularString(int numberOfOperations)
    {
        string myStringData = null;

        for (int cnt = 0; cnt < numberOfOperations;cnt++ )
        {
            myStringData += SomeStringData;
        }

        return myStringData.Length;
    }
}
```

To exercise this class, a simple console application is created to measure and display the time taken to perform the task:

```
static void Main(string[] args)
{
    const int NumberOfOperations = 10000;
    var worker = new MyStringManipulator();
    var watch = new System.Diagnostics.Stopwatch();
    int numChars = 0;

    watch.Start();
    numChars = worker.UseRegularString(NumberOfOperations);
    numChars = worker.UseStringBuilder(NumberOfOperations);
    watch.Stop();
    Console.WriteLine("Your String Data totalled: {0}
chars in length in {1} milliseconds.", numChars,watch.
ElapsedMilliseconds);

    Console.WriteLine("Press ENTER key");
    Console.ReadLine();

}
```

The code simply performs a string concatenation 10,000 times and displays the time taken, producing the output shown in Figure 10.4.

Figure 10.4: String concatenation using a regular string object.

Now let's try exactly the same operation using a `StringBuilder` by slightly changing the concatenation implementation, as shown below:

```
public int UseStringBuilder(int numberOfOperations)
{
    StringBuilder myStringData = new StringBuilder();

    for (int cnt = 0; cnt < numberOfOperations; cnt++)
    {
        myStringData.Append(SomeStringData);
    }

    return myStringData.Length;
}
```

Now when the program is executed, the output shown in Figure 10.5 is produced.

Figure 10.5: String concatenation using a StringBuilder object.

The time taken was reduced from 2,176 milliseconds to just *1 millisecond*, which is a substantial increase in execution speed. To further illustrate this, let's examine the memory usage of the program. Using CLRProfiler and running the program that utilizes a standard string object, the profiler reports approximately 1.8 Gigabytes of memory being allocated for strings (see Figure 10.6).

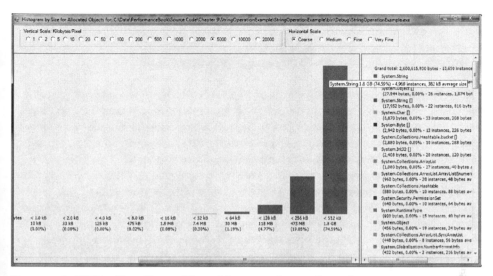

Figure 10.6: CLRProfiler allocated bytes histogram for regular string usage.

Using CLRProfiler to report on the memory usage when using the StringBuilder, we can see a meager 512 kilobytes of memory being used to create exactly the same result, which is a huge difference (see Figure 10.7).

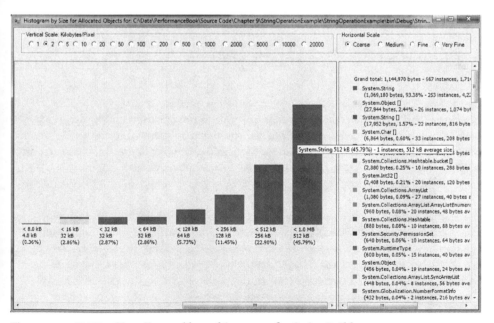

Figure 10.7: CLRProfiler allocated bytes histogram for StringBuilder usage.

292

A regular string object is immutable and cannot be changed once created. This means that when a string is modified, a new string object is created in memory that represents the modified string. The original string, being immutable, is never modified. The end result to the developer is that it simply looks as if the original string is modified.

Internally, when a concatenation (or any string operation) occurs on a regular string object, memory is first allocated to contain the resulting string, then the original string object plus any modifications are copied into the newly allocated area of memory. This newly allocated string object is then returned to the user as the result of the string operation. Doing this many times obviously results in a lot of work and memory consumption. In contrast, a `StringBuilder` is optimized to *not* do this work when manipulating strings, so the extensive re-allocation of data and memory is not performed. Internally, a string builder is *not* immutable and performs string operations on the original data. There is no need to allocate memory for a copy of the original string and copy the original instance of the string into it to perform modifications. A string builder will retain the original character data, only allocating what is necessary to perform the modifications on the original data.

Finally, remember that the .NET garbage collector will also have to work very hard to reclaim memory in the regular string object example. The reclaiming of memory will only happen at a later time when the GC performs a collection. If the system is busy, then this may not happen for some time. This will further hamper the performance of the application and the system overall.

Cryptographic functions

Performing cryptographic functions in code is a computationally expensive function. Encrypting and decrypting data requires complex algorithms, and this is more pronounced when using asymmetric cryptography, which forms the basis of Public Key Infrastructure (PKI). Secure Sockets Layer (SSL) communication utilizes this technique, and there are many hardware solutions that are available to offload the encryption and decryption of data to a separate dedicated device (this will be discussed in the final chapter, on HTTP optimization).

The `System.Security.Cryptography` namespace in .NET provides a number of classes that encapsulate this functionality. In the case of encrypting and decrypting data, all of the classes allow a particular keysize to be specified. Generally speaking, the larger the keysize, the stronger the encryption; that is, the harder it is to break. With that in mind, there is a tendency to choose the biggest keysize supported by the algorithm, but this can naturally have a significant computational cost. With symmetric encryption, the effects will be marginal, but still present; with asymmetric cryptography, the computational cost can be huge. Indeed, the cost of choosing a keysize of 1,024 bits could be as much as 5-10 times more than a 256 bit keysize, depending on the data and algorithm used.

It is worth noting that using the cryptographic classes supplied in the .NET framework is generally a much better approach to custom implementations. The .NET framework has gone through extensive testing and optimization and, as a result, framework-supplied implementations will be faster and more secure.

The main point here is to choose the keysize carefully if you're implementing cryptographic functions in your applications. Security is important, but the effect of implementing the highest level of cryptography needs to be carefully thought out to ensure it does not adversely affect the entire application, and reduce the ability of the system to perform adequately as a whole. This is particularly important in web applications, or services that have the potential to process a large number of requests concurrently.

Network call latency

Applications often need to call external services such as web services, payment gateways, or other non-local resources. This typically involves using some form of transport protocol to communicate with the external resource. Web services are one of the most common forms of communication between systems, but it can also involve traditional TCP/IP, FTP, or even proprietary protocols. Regardless of the protocol, these points of integration act as potential performance bottlenecks and should be carefully managed.

Even though the network in question may seem quite fast, such as an organization's 100 Gb/s intranet, calling a web service or connecting to a TCP socket is still much slower than calling a method on an assembly residing in the same application domain. Any time a network "hop" is performed, the data being transferred needs to be serialized and eventually deserialized, protocol packets must be created and synchronized, with source and destination ports coordinating threads to accept and marshal the data to the correct destination.

It is good practice to build in a level of isolation between your application and the external resources. Architecturally this may involve defining and implementing interface contracts between the systems, and communicating via these APIs. Doing this has the advantage of making it possible to then provide alternative implementations of the external resource, such as a "dummy" or "mock" version of the resource.

Being able to provide mock implementations of an external resource allows a performance test to focus purely on the application. With those metrics recorded, we can then examine end-to-end functionality by using the proper external resource implementation and measuring the "delta," or change in performance. This provides an accurate view of the effect that the external resource has on overall system performance, making it much easier to isolate any performance bottlenecks in either the application or the resource being accessed.

Providing this mock interface layer obviously requires more work up front and consideration when designing the system. However, it does provide great benefits, not just from a performance metric perspective, but also in removing external dependencies during the development phase.

The ability to provide a mock implementation is also very dependent on the resource itself. Web services are relatively easy to work with since interfaces are a part of web service contract design and development. Other forms of communication will require specific implementations, and the key is abstracting that communication to encapsulate the component, and thus provide an easy way to implement a mock version.

Irrespective of design, though, there are some key considerations when calling external resources over a relatively slow link, such as an intranet or the Internet.

Key considerations when calling external resources

Protocol

HTTP is one of the most common forms of network communication, but is also one of the least efficient in terms of performance, due to its verbose nature and typically string-based representation. TCP/IP is a far more efficient protocol and typically uses binary to communicate over the network, resulting in much faster communications. TCP/IP implementations are usually proprietary, though, and are mostly used where both the sending and receiving party are under your direct control and do not require interoperation with other external systems. Basically, HTTP and its derivatives are more standards compliant and interoperable than TCP/IP or other forms of binary communication.

Size of payload

The more data that is sent and received, the more time is taken to send that data over the link. Data Transfer Objects (DTOs) are often employed so that large object graphs are not sent over the link; only the necessary data is put into the DTO object and transferred over the link. All types of information being sent and received should be carefully analyzed to ensure they are sent in as efficient a form as possible.

Serialization/deserialization

Whenever data or an object is sent through a communications protocol, it needs to be serialized into a form where it can be sent. This process is then reversed on the receiver, where the data is deserialized and the original object form is restored. Not only does this take time to send and receive, but the actual serialization and deserialization processes can be relatively time consuming. This is very prevalent in web service communication where objects are sent over the wire (i.e. over a network) and the objects are typically serialized into string form using an XML format. XML is a very verbose protocol, and the size of the XML representation of the object is often much larger than its native binary form. In this scenario, large objects become even larger when sent to the external resource, which can significantly impact performance. Technology stacks such as Windows Communication Foundation (WCF) provide ways of utilizing binary serialization, which is far more efficient than traditional XML serialization in some cases, but these are non-standard. Generally speaking, if you have control over both sending and receiving parties, it is best to use the most efficient form of communication, such as binary serialization. If interoperation with other systems is a requirement, then verbose protocols such as Simple Object Access Protocol (SOAP) and higher-level protocols such as WS-Security may be required.

Chatty vs. chunky

If a link is slow, then it is best practice to ensure that the number of calls performed is kept to a minimum. This often means that communication patterns need to be designed so that calls are not "chatty," performing an excessive number of calls with small amounts of information. It is best to adopt a "chunky" approach, where more data is initially transferred over the link, but fewer calls are made overall. With large numbers of small calls, each segment or packet of information that is transferred needs to have a header and contextual information surrounding the data payload itself, so that the protocol can interpret the data correctly. This means that, when transferring a given set of information, the total data size of many calls with small payloads is often larger than one or two calls with larger payloads. This applies to any protocol but is especially important to web services. TCP/IP utilizes a header to describe a packet of information, and always performs an initial handshake consisting of a series of requests and acknowledgements by the communicating parties. Large sets of data are broken into smaller packets to be transferred via TCP/IP. Web services are a higher-level protocol, that is, a protocol built on top of another protocol, which has its own way of packaging and structuring its data payload in addition to what is provided through lower-level protocols such as TCP/IP. For web services, it is generally best to avoid multiple web service calls and try to design the communications interface to return the necessary data in a single web service call.

The key point here is that any form of external access, especially over a network, is a relatively expensive exercise in terms of performance. Caching can help, but this may only alleviate a small percentage of calls. Careful consideration should be employed to ensure that the best and most efficient form of communication is used in your given scenario.

Synchronous vs. asynchronous

Asynchronous operations are operations that run in parallel with each other. Developers often overlook the advantage of using asynchronous designs and features to provide better throughput in their applications, as it is somewhat natural to implement process flow in a procedural way, as shown in Figure 10.8.

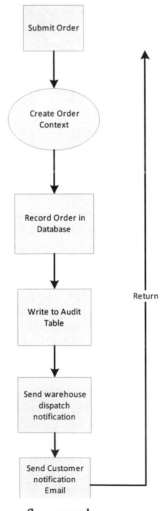

Figure 10.8: Synchronous process flow example.

However, a more efficient way might be to asynchronously perform the functions that don't require a response to the user or any initiating action. The same process could be designed asynchronously as shown in Figure 10.9.

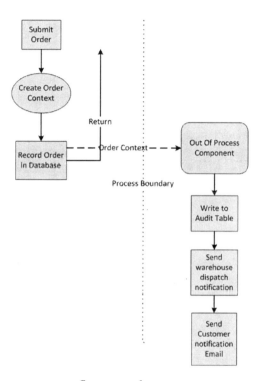

Figure 10.9: Asynchronous process flow example.

In this scenario, the Out Of Process component could be a service, a message queue, or any other component that executes in conjunction with the main process, but serves only to process certain requests. The main process can simply pass the necessary information to the external component and return to the caller (or initiating action) much more responsively; there is no need to wait for multiple processes to complete.

There are many ways to accomplish this. Microsoft Message Queue (MSMQ) is a great way to lodge custom messages for asynchronous processing. Applications can write to the queue, with an Out of Process service monitoring said queue and reading messages as they arrive.

SQL Server Broker also provides a similar set of features to those in MSMQ, but utilizes SQL Server as its backing store. MSMQ is arguably a simpler way to set up a message store for asynchronous processing, but the different supporting feature sets should be analyzed thoroughly to determine if the needs of your specific solution will be satisfied. Even a custom messaging solution using a technology such as WCF can be employed to provide asynchronous messaging.

Regardless of the technology chosen, the key point is to improve the responsiveness and throughput of the application by offloading tasks to the asynchronous process where possible. Some typical candidates for asynchronous operation include audit logging, sending emails, and report generation. The needs of the business and the application specifics will typically dictate what can and cannot be offloaded asynchronously.

Asynchronous web pages

ASP.NET 2.0 and later versions all support a feature called asynchronous pages. This feature allows an individual page to offload processing tasks to be performed asynchronously. The ASP.NET runtime then coordinates these tasks so that all tasks are completed when the page finally renders.

This is actually a little different from launching a separate thread from within your code and waiting for it to complete. ASP.NET provides a far more efficient mechanism for utilizing threads, and allows the request-processing thread to service other requests during the processing of the asynchronous tasks. This can mean better throughput for your web applications; some obvious candidates for an asynchronous task are pages that execute web service calls or database queries.

To implement this, asynchronous pages must first be enabled by including the Async attribute in a page, and setting it to true in the @Page directive as shown in the following snippet:

```
<%@ Page Async="true" ... %>
```

There are a number of ways in which asynchronous pages can be implemented, depending on how you intend to interact with the asynchronous tasks. The following simple example shows just one way. For this example, we'll emulate some long-running processes using the following code:

```
public class MySlowObject
{
    public string SlowMethod1()
    {
        int timeToSleep = 2000;
        System.Threading.Thread.Sleep(timeToSleep);
        return string.Format("Method1 slept for {0}
milliseconds", timeToSleep);
    }

    public string SlowMethod2()
    {
        int timeToSleep = 3500;
```

```
        System.Threading.Thread.Sleep(timeToSleep);
        return string.Format("Method2 slept for {0}
milliseconds", timeToSleep);
    }
}
```

To compare timings, we shall first implement a non-asynchronous page implementation to call the methods on the MySlowObject. The following code shows a simple implementation in the code behind a page.

```
public partial class _Default : System.Web.UI.Page
{
    Stopwatch _stopwatch = new Stopwatch();
    StringBuilder _msg = new StringBuilder();

    protected void Page_Load(object sender, EventArgs e)
    {
        _stopwatch.Start();
        this.PreRenderComplete += new EventHandler(_Default_
PreRenderComplete);

        MySlowObject obj = new MySlowObject();
        _msg.AppendFormat("<br />{0}", obj.SlowMethod1());
        _msg.AppendFormat("<br />{0}", obj.SlowMethod2());
    }

    void _Default_PreRenderComplete(object sender, EventArgs e)
    {
        _msg.AppendFormat("<br />Total time for page to render =
{0} milliseconds", _stopwatch.ElapsedMilliseconds);
        litMsg.Text = _msg.ToString();
    }
```

The preceding code fragment simply calls SlowMethod1 and SlowMethod2 synchronously, and displays the result by writing the results to a literal control. The output is shown in Figure 10.10.

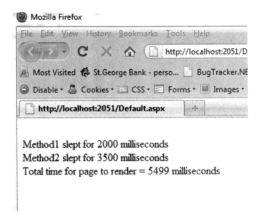

Figure 10.10: Synchronous page timing output.

The output shows that the total page time is approximately the addition of the time it took to execute the two methods. Now examine the following implementation which uses asynchronous tasks.

```
public partial class _Default : System.Web.UI.Page
{
    delegate string SlowThing();
    MySlowObject _slowObj = new MySlowObject();
    SlowThing _method1;
    SlowThing _method2;
    Stopwatch _stopwatch = new Stopwatch();
    StringBuilder _msg = new StringBuilder();


    protected void Page_Load(object sender, EventArgs e)
    {
        Page.RegisterAsyncTask(new PageAsyncTask(StartAsyncHandl
er1, EndAsyncHandler1, TimeoutHandler, null, true));
        Page.RegisterAsyncTask(new PageAsyncTask(StartAsyncHandl
er2, EndAsyncHandler2, TimeoutHandler, null, true));

        _stopwatch.Start();
        this.PreRenderComplete += new EventHandler(_Default_
PreRenderComplete);
    }

    void _Default_PreRenderComplete(object sender, EventArgs e)
    {
        _msg.AppendFormat("<br />Total time for page to render =
{0} milliseconds", _stopwatch.ElapsedMilliseconds);
        litMsg.Text = _msg.ToString();
```

```
    }

    IAsyncResult StartAsyncHandler1(object sender, EventArgs
e,AsyncCallback cb, object state)
    {
        _method1 = new SlowThing(_slowObj.SlowMethod1);
        return _method1.BeginInvoke(cb, state);
    }
    IAsyncResult StartAsyncHandler2(object sender, EventArgs e,
AsyncCallback cb, object state)
    {
        _method2 = new SlowThing(_slowObj.SlowMethod2);
        return _method2.BeginInvoke(cb, state);
    }

    void EndAsyncHandler1(IAsyncResult ar)
    {
        string result = _method1.EndInvoke(ar);
        _msg.Append("<br />" + result);
    }
    void EndAsyncHandler2(IAsyncResult ar)
    {
        string result = _method2.EndInvoke(ar);
        _msg.Append("<br />" + result);
    }

    void TimeoutHandler(IAsyncResult ar)
    {
    }
}
```

The preceding code registers two asynchronous tasks that execute one of the slow methods on the MySlowObject. The results are written to a string and output in the same way as the previous example. The output for this code is shown in Figure 10.11.

The timings shown in Figure 10.11 show a quicker execution, with the page render time taking only slightly longer than the slowest method, and the whole process being much quicker than the synchronous example.

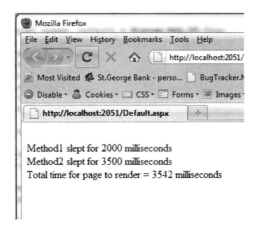

Figure 10.11: Asynchronous page timing output.

This is a simple demonstration, but it serves to emphasise that proper consideration should be given to asynchronous operations when designing systems and writing web pages. In particular, you need to ask what can be offloaded to run asynchronously and allow normal processing to continue. This certainly won't suit all situations, but the potential performance benefits of being able to utilize asynchronous functionality are great.

Web application specific

The next series of techniques are all only applicable in a web application scenario. We will be examining specific features of the ASP.NET runtime with regard to performance, and providing details on how to extract the best performance from those techniques. With the exception of data binding, all techniques can be applied to AAP.NET Webforms or ASP.NET MVC applications.

Data binding

Data binding in ASP.NET Webforms applications is a common practice to display lists or tables of information, and can also be used for simple element property manipulation for server-based controls. Data binding provides a maintainable and descriptive way of specifying how data can be presented in a page from a data source. This is often used to present a repeatable table of data such as a repeater control or GridView control. However, it does come at the cost of performance. In the majority of scenarios, this cost may be negligible, and worth the benefit of easy readability that data binding provides.

In many instances, implementations that abstract complexity to provide a generic and easy-to-use interface can often come at a cost to performance.

To illustrate this, the following example will show a simplistic comparison between using data binding, not using data binding, and a compromise that borrows a little benefit from both.

For this example, we'll use a common source of data that acts as a container with a list of items showing book authors, titles, and other information such as randomized display colors. The list of items will contain 2,000 separate line items of information. Note that, while displaying 2,000 line items on a single page is neither realistic nor practical, displaying 50 items on a page where there might be greater than 100 concurrent users is very realistic, and the net system performance effect would be even more pronounced. The implementation will be common across each web page, and is comprised of the following:

```csharp
public static class DataManager
{
    public static DataContainer GetData(string title)
    {
        var itemSelection = new DataItem[5];
        itemSelection[0] = new DataItem()  { AuthorName = "I.
Litterate", BookTitle = "Learning to read and right"};
        itemSelection[1] = new DataItem() { AuthorName = "Eta
Lottafood", BookTitle = "Handy recipes"};
        itemSelection[2] = new DataItem() { AuthorName = "Holin
Mipants", BookTitle = "Embarrasing moments"};
        itemSelection[3] = new DataItem() { AuthorName = "Mr D.
Hoffman", BookTitle = "The care and maintenance of chest hair"};
        itemSelection[4] = new DataItem() { AuthorName = "K.
Thefrog", BookTitle = "It aint easy being green"};

        var dc = new DataContainer();
        dc.Title = title;
        dc.Comments = string.Format("These are the comments for
the item titled '{0}'", title);
        Random rnd = new Random(DateTime.Now.Millisecond);

        dc.MajorVersion = rnd.Next(1, 9);
        dc.MinorVersion = rnd.Next(0, 20);
        dc.Revision = rnd.Next(0, 100);

        for (int i = 0; i < 2000; i++)
        {
            dc.Items.Add(itemSelection[rnd.Next(0, 4)]);
        }
```

```
        return dc;
    }
}
```

In order to surface this data in a web page, a typical data binding approach will be used. The following code example demonstrates the data binding implementation:

```
<form id="form1" runat="server">
<div>
    <div>
        <label>Title: </label>
        <label><%# BodyTitle %></label>
        <label>Version: </label>
        <span><%# Version %></span>
        <p><%# Comments %></p>
    </div>

    <asp:Repeater ID="rpt1" runat="server">
        <HeaderTemplate>
            <ul>
        </HeaderTemplate>

        <ItemTemplate>
            <li runat="server" style='<%# Eval("ItemColor") %>'>
                <span>Author:</span>
                <span><%# Eval("AuthorName") %></span>
                <span>Book:</span>
                <span><%# Eval("BookTitle") %></span>
            </li>
        </ItemTemplate>

        <FooterTemplate>
            </ul>
        </FooterTemplate>
    </asp:Repeater>
</div>
</form>
```

In the previous code snippet, an initial set of fields are databound to display the title, version and comments. Then a standard ASP.NET repeater control is used to iterate through the data item collection, display the **AuthorName** and **BookTitle** fields, as well as use data binding to set the color of the <li> element content. The supporting code-behind for this is also very simple:

```
public partial class _Default : System.Web.UI.Page
{
    private DataContainer _container = DataManager.GetData("Using
Databinding");

    protected override void OnPreRender(EventArgs e)
    {
        rpt1.DataSource = _container.Items;
        DataBind();

        base.OnPreRender(e);
    }


    public string BodyTitle { get { return _container.Title; } }
    public string Comments { get { return _container.Comments; }
}

    public string Version { get { return _container.VersionText;
} }
}
```

The previous code examples show HTML content which is very easy to understand and maintain, with very simple supporting code behind its implementation.

If we access the page a few times and then, using the trace.axd handler, view the detailed trace output that ASP.NET provides, we can see the timings, as shown in Figure 10.12.

Request Details

Request Details			
Session Id:	nktme1S5yli1bh5Smh2baSeo	Request Type:	GET
Time of Request:	21/10/2009 5:56:31 PM	Status Code:	200
Request Encoding:	Unicode (UTF-8)	Response Encoding:	Unicode (UTF-8)

Trace Information			
Category	Message	From First(s)	From Last(s)
aspx.page	Begin PreInit		
aspx.page	End PreInit	4.04281161726284E-05	0.000040
aspx.page	Begin Init	7.47041277106612E-05	0.000034
aspx.page	End Init	0.00011161675520635	0.000037
aspx.page	Begin InitComplete	0.00013974062423472	0.000028
aspx.page	End InitComplete	0.00016786456932309	0.000028
aspx.page	Begin PreLoad	0.00019467016809307	0.000027
aspx.page	End PreLoad	0.00022411238131984	0.000029
aspx.page	Begin Load	0.00025223629003482	0.000028
aspx.page	End Load	0.00028783060970872	0.000036
aspx.page	Begin LoadComplete	0.00031639395265691	0.000029
aspx.page	End LoadComplete	0.00034407842351439	0.000028
aspx.page	Begin PreRender	0.00037176289437187	0.000028
aspx.page	End PreRender	0.110061151920072	0.109689
aspx.page	Begin PreRenderComplete	0.11011256593737	0.000051
aspx.page	End PreRenderComplete	0.11013234055942	0.000020
aspx.page	Begin SaveState	0.399880649170081	0.289748
aspx.page	End SaveState	0.41029264682876	0.010412
aspx.page	Begin SaveStateComplete	0.41032780171239	0.000035
aspx.page	End SaveStateComplete	0.41034318197398	0.000015
aspx.page	Begin Render	0.41035724392743	0.000014
aspx.page	End Render	0.639366262912828	0.229009

Figure 10.12: Page event timings using databinding.

Figure 10.12 shows the two important times highlighted: the time taken to execute the PreRender event was 0.109689 seconds, and the total time for page execution was approximately 0.64 seconds. To have something to compare that against, let's take a very different approach to displaying exactly the same data in exactly the same way. In the next sample, the markup is comprised of the following:

```
<form id="form1" runat="server">
<div>
    <%= HtmlContent %>
</div>
</form>
```

As shown in the HTML fragment, there is no real markup at all apart from basic body, form and surrounding div elements. The <%= HtmlContent %> is simply performing a Response.Write of the HtmlContent property exposed in the code-behind, for which the implementation is:

```
public partial class ContentWrite : System.Web.UI.Page
{
    private DataContainer _container = DataManager.GetData("Using
literal content writing");

    public string HtmlContent
    {
        get { return GetContent(); }
    }

    private string GetContent()
    {
        StringBuilder content = new StringBuilder();
        content.AppendFormat("<div><label>Title: </
label><label>{0}</label>", _container.Title);
        content.AppendFormat("<label>Version: </
label><span>{0}</span>", _container.VersionText);
        content.AppendFormat("<p>{0}</p></div>", _container.
Comments);
        content.Append("<ul>");
        foreach (var item in _container.Items)
        {
            content.AppendFormat("<li style='{0}'>", item.
ItemColor);
            content.AppendFormat("<span>Author:</span><span>{0}</
span>", item.AuthorName);
            content.AppendFormat("<span>Book:</span><span>{0}</
span></li>", item.BookTitle);
        }
```

```
        content.Append("</ul>");
        return content.ToString();
    }
}
```

The previous code fragment shows a lot more work being done in the code-behind compared to the data binding example. In particular, the raw HTML response is being constructed as one big string and fed into the page for rendering. The page event timings for this example are shown in Figure 10.13.

Request Details

Request Details			
Session Id:	mshysb45ajmtfaiiqjvq2e45	**Request Type:**	GET
Time of Request:	21/10/2009 6:10:31 PM	**Status Code:**	200
Request Encoding:	Unicode (UTF-8)	**Response Encoding:**	Unicode (UTF-8)

Trace Information			
Category	**Message**	**From First(s)**	**From Last(s)**
aspx.page	Begin PreInit		
aspx.page	End PreInit	5.1853453352106E-05	0.000052
aspx.page	Begin Init	8.7008339 80652SE-05	0.000035
aspx.page	End Init	0.000121284348518485	0.000034
aspx.page	Begin InitComplete	0.00014852938330609	0.000027
aspx.page	End InitComplete	0.000176653290233446	0.000028
aspx.page	Begin PreLoad	0.00020389832504557	0.000027
aspx.page	End PreLoad	0.000231143359857693	0.000027
aspx.page	Begin Load	0.000258827830715173	0.000028
aspx.page	End Load	0.000288270045754081	0.000029
aspx.page	Begin LoadComplete	0.000315155080566205	0.000027
aspx.page	End LoadComplete	0.000343199551423685	0.000028
aspx.page	Begin PreRender	0.000370445862235808	0.000027
aspx.page	End PreRender	0.00040076567336543	0.000030
aspx.page	Begin PreRenderComplete	0.000440314917447545	0.000040
aspx.page	End PreRenderComplete	0.000468878260395739	0.000029
aspx.page	Begin SaveState	0.000794060933959793	0.000325
aspx.page	End SaveState	0.000932483288247195	0.000138
aspx.page	Begin SaveStateComplete	0.000968956480011812	0.000036
aspx.page	End SaveStateComplete	0.000997080386914649	0.000028
aspx.page	Begin Render	0.0010256437298284	0.000029
aspx.page	End Render	0.0213354988741649	0.020310

Figure 10.13: Page event timings using Response.Write of Content.

As with the data binding figure shown previously, the two important times are highlighted. The time taken to execute the PreRender event was 0.000030 seconds and the total time for page execution was approximately 0.02 seconds.

The direct writing of content yielded a performance thousands of times better than the data bound example, and the total page performance was approximately 30 times faster. While the times themselves are not large (not exceeding 1 second in any instance), the relative performance gain is easily seen.

Yet the writing of raw content to the output response is hardly a good way to write maintainable pages. In a complex page, where markup can be very intricate, this method can prove very difficult, in addition to providing difficulties to designers who may be creating the user interface. Furthermore, maintaining such code will prove arduous, time consuming and will make it easy for subtle rendering bugs to slip into your work.

It is, nonetheless, possible to achieve a compromise in terms of maintainability and performance, as is demonstrated by the following markup.

```
<form id="form1" runat="server">
<div>
    <div>
        <label>Title: </label>
        <label><%= BodyTitle %></label>
        <label>Version: </label>
        <span><%= Version %></span>
        <p><%= Comments %></p>
    </div>


            <ul>
<% foreach (var item in DataItems)
{ %>
                <li style="<%= item.ItemColor %>">
                    <span>Author:</span>
                    <span><%= item.AuthorName %></span>
                    <span>Book:</span>
                    <span><%= item.BookTitle %></span>
                </li>
<% } %>
            </ul>


</div>
</form>
```

The previous HTML fragment looks very similar to the data bound version, but no data binding is involved. Instead, the use of Reponse.Write is still maintained using the `<%= fieldname %>` expression syntax. In addition, some inline code has been introduced to iterate through the collection in much the same way an ASP.NET repeater control does but, because of the inline code, the Response.Write expression can still be used. The code-behind to support this markup is as follows:

```
public partial class MarkupAndResponseWrite : System.Web.UI.Page
{
    private DataContainer _container = DataManager.GetData("Using
markup and response writing");

    public string BodyTitle { get { return _container.Title; } }
    public string Comments { get { return _container.Comments; }
}
    public string Version { get { return _container.VersionText;
} }
    public List<DataItem> DataItems { get { return _container.
Items; } }
}
```

This shows a very simple code fragment behind the implementation, with no complex construction of markup. All markup has been left in the page, in a semantically correct manner (from a structural perspective), making maintenance relatively easy. The page event timings for this implementation are shown in Figure 10.14.

Request Details

Request Details			
Session Id:	pqpdgs55kfnziafquyqjji55	Request Type:	GET
Time of Request:	21/10/2009 6:22:46 PM	Status Code:	200
Request Encoding:	Unicode (UTF-8)	Response Encoding:	Unicode (UTF-8)

Trace Information			
Category	Message	From First(s)	From Last(s)
aspx.page	Begin PreInit		
aspx.page	End PreInit	4.83379649892514E-05	0.000048
aspx.page	Begin Init	8.26139765270842E-05	0.000034
aspx.page	End Init	0.000116889988064017	0.000034
aspx.page	Begin InitComplete	0.000144135022877041	0.000027
aspx.page	End InitComplete	0.000173137801870591	0.000029
aspx.page	Begin PreLoad	0.000200382836682715	0.000027
aspx.page	End PreLoad	0.000227627871494838	0.000027
aspx.page	Begin Load	0.000255312342352319	0.000028
aspx.page	End Load	0.000286512301572654	0.000031
aspx.page	Begin LoadComplete	0.000314196772430134	0.000028
aspx.page	End LoadComplete	0.000341881243287614	0.000028
aspx.page	Begin PreRender	0.000369126278099738	0.000027
aspx.page	End PreRender	0.000399007929184002	0.000030
aspx.page	Begin PreRenderComplete	0.0004284501442291	0.000029
aspx.page	End PreRenderComplete	0.000464044463896813	0.000036
aspx.page	Begin SaveState	0.000862173520990102	0.000398
aspx.page	End SaveState	0.00101202121245678	0.000150
aspx.page	Begin SaveStateComplete	0.00104981271235747	0.000038
aspx.page	End SaveStateComplete	0.00107959436244172	0.000030
aspx.page	Begin Render	0.00110869714243528	0.000029
aspx.page	End Render	0.020322159353572	0.019213

Figure 10.14: Page event timings using Reponse.Write and structural markup in the page.

The two important times are highlighted again: the time taken to execute the PreRender event was 0.000030 seconds and the total time for page execution was approximately 0.02 seconds. The timings are almost identical, and the overall page time is marginally faster.

These examples simply serve to demonstrate that data binding is a relatively expensive operation. Data binding utilizes reflection and generic mechanisms to make the construction of complex data in a web page easy, but at the cost of performance. Even if reflection is minimized via the use of strongly typed helper objects to replace the Eval("...") syntax, performance is still significantly lower compared to pages using Response.Write. This is a cost worth wearing for a majority of cases, as data binding is an elegant solution. However, if performance is critical, or perhaps a particular page is experiencing performance issues which utilize a lot of data binding expressions, then these alternative techniques I've mentioned may be useful.

Output caching

As discussed previously, caching data can provide a great performance boost, although the previous mention dealt more with caching data from a data store such as a SQL database. However, we can also utilize the ASP.NET runtime to cache the raw HTML output of our web controls. This means that the ASP.NET runtime will not invoke any processing or execution of logic while the cached content is still valid and has not expired. This technique can be used in both Webforms and ASP.NET MVC, and results in significant savings in processing time and CPU utilization.

When content is output cached, and a request comes in to be processed by ASP.NET, the framework first checks to see if the control or controller action has content that is output cached. If it does, then ASP.NET extracts the raw content, and bypasses the creation of the control or invoking of a controller action. If no matching output cached content is found, then request processing continues as normal. When a control or controller action has output caching enabled, ASP.NET will determine a unique key for the content, and add the content to the cache with the conditions specified in the output caching directive.

In a Webforms application, only user controls can participate in output caching via a simple control directive:

```
<%@ OutputCache Duration="60" VaryByParam="none" %>
```

This control directive states that the output of this user control will be cached for 60 minutes. That is, the raw HTML produced by this control when it was first invoked is cached by the ASP.NET runtime for 60 minutes. During that period, any time the contents of that control are requested, the raw HTML will be retrieved from the cache with no server-side processing performed at all. That is, no server-side logic of any sort (such as code-behind logic) is executed.

The equivalent technique in ASP.NET MVC would be applied at the controller level to a control action using the OutputCache attribute.

```
[OutputCache(VaryByParam = "none", Duration = 60)]
public ActionResult SomeAction()
{
    var data = _GetData();
    return View("MyView",data);
}
```

As with Webforms, no controller action is invoked if the output cached content is found. This is the reason why this technique is so efficient, as there is no server-side processing that occurs if the data in the cache can satisfy the request. The content is simply extracted from the cache and returned in the response.

While a good performance gain, this technique has potential negative side-effects where, if content is cached globally but is actually different for each user, then each individual user may view all the cached content, rather than the content specific to their context. For example, if a user's name was output cached for one hour and a different user accessed the site, then the original output-cached user name would always be presented to every different user for the next hour until the cache expired.

Typically, the type of content that lends itself well to output caching consists of items such as headers, footers, navigation elements, and other elements that are not dynamically generated on every request. However, output caching can be varied, based on a range of parameters within the incoming request, and can therefore be tailored as required.

A detailed examination of all the options available to tailor output cached content for both Webforms and ASP.NET MVC is far beyond the scope of this section. However, both Webforms and ASP.NET MVC can utilize other directives to ensure that cached content is only applicable under certain conditions. In addition to setting a duration for the cached content, the content can be uniquely cached based on the value of a control (VaryByControl attribute), the value of a URL query string, the value of a form post element (VaryByParam attribute), or even a custom implementation of your choosing (VaryByCustom). The VaryByParam attribute will cache content uniquely indentified by URL parameters (in the case of HTTP GET requests) and form post parameters (in the case of HTTP POST requests). For example, in ASP.NET Webforms:

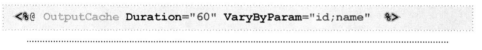

```
<%@ OutputCache Duration="60" VaryByParam="id;name" %>
```

> **Note**
>
> Webform controls require the presence of the VaryByParam attribute. If this is not required, the value should be set to none (VaryByParam="none").

And in ASP.NET MVC:

```
[OutputCache (Duration=60, VaryByParam="id;name")]
public ActionResult SomeAction()
{
    // ... some code
}
```

Both of the earlier statements will tell ASP.NET to cache the output of the control or action for a period of 60 minutes, based on the ID and name parameter of the query string (for HTTP GET) or the ID and name parameter of the form post collection (for HTTP POST).

Output caching is an extremely powerful mechanism to alleviate the amount of processing performed by an application but, like any cached content, it must be used with caution. We must ensure that cached content is presented only to the users to whom it is relevant, and careful consideration around how to vary the content, based on the available options, needs to be factored into any output caching strategy.

web.config

The web.config and machine.config configuration files are one of the easiest places to tinker to gain a performance boost. Too often, everything is focused on actual development, and the basic configuration elements can be overlooked. The following list highlights which configuration file and what configuration item to adjust, in order to gain maximum performance.

- File: web.config

    - **Section:** <system.web>

    - **Item Value:** <compilation debug="false">

    - **Details:**
      Setting this value to false will instruct ASP.NET to continually assemble and include debug information into the dynamically generated assemblies. This produces a leaner and better-optimized assembly suited for production scenarios. When a new project is created in Visual Studio, this value is set to false, but if any debugging has been performed, then Visual Studio prompts you to set this value to true.

- **File:** web.config

    - **Section:** <system.web>

    - **Item Value:** <trace enabled="false"/>

    - **Details:**
      This setting enables or disables the page tracing functionality of ASP.NET. Ensuring this is false means that ASP.NET will not generate and retain trace information for every request. This can result in a significant performance boost, especially in high volume sites.

- **File:** machine.config

    - **Section:** <system.web>

    - **Item Value:** <deployment retail="true">

- **Details:**
  This is one of the most important, but often overlooked, production level settings. It overrides all the previously mentioned settings and sets them to their appropriate production setting as described.

- **File:** web.config

  - **Section:** <httpHandlers>

- **Details:**
  This section is normally populated with some default handlers. Handlers are run on every request, so it is important that only the necessary handlers are present, in order to prevent excessive or unnecessary work being performed. This can often occur when a copy of a website is used to deliver only static content such as images, CSS files, etc. (This is often referred to as a CDN – Content Delivery Network, and will be discussed in a later chapter). In this case, static content does not normally require the same number of processing handlers as the normal ASP.NET website, so these elements can be removed to enhance throughout.

Conclusion

While each application is different, there are many common areas which can be addressed to help improve performance in most cases. This is especially true if a common underlying framework such as ASP.NET is used. Here, we've discussed many of these common aspects, taking a two-fold approach to the issue.

The first is to simply highlight the fact that particular areas can be places where performance may be an issue. With this knowledge, it is already much easier to address performance issues in the early stages of design and development, essentially preventing them before they occur.

The second is to provide actual examples of typical code which exhibits performance issues, and potential ways of resolving those problems. Obviously, the resolution of such issues will most likely be slightly different in each application, and this must be assessed for each specific set of circumstances.

In general, though, providing an abstraction over areas of complexity in order to simplify usage can often hide performance pitfalls. While these abstraction layers undoubtedly provide easier mechanisms for implementation and use, unmetered use can lead to performance problems, so their deployment must be carefully judged.

Chapter 11: Load Balancing

What is load balancing and how does it help?

Load balancing refers to an environment configuration that spreads the incoming requests between two or more servers. The load is effectively "balanced" between all the servers in the farm.

So, instead of a single server handling all the incoming traffic, there are now multiple servers, each sharing a part of the task of handling incoming traffic. This is typically the situation in web applications where multiple front-end web servers are used, but application servers that expose entry points such as web services will also benefit from load balancing.

The ability of an application to be spread across a farm of servers is referred to as its "scalability." This does not necessarily equate to a high performing application. Scalability simply refers to the ability to be distributed across a farm or cluster of servers to handle a greater load. This is often, but not always, tied to the stateful design of an application. An application can be quite inefficient or slow, yet still have good scalability.

Load balancing provides the ability to horizontally scale an application, as opposed to vertically scaling it. Vertical scaling refers to making more resources or computational power available to the application. This could involve adding more processors or more memory to the system, and is often referred to as "scaling up." Vertical scaling has limitations, though, in that you will eventually hit a limit to the amount of resources that can be added. A system can only support its maximum number of processors and addressable memory. Horizontally scaling an application involves adding more machines or servers to a "farm" of machines, to "scale out" the application.

Vertical scaling is beneficial, but it has limitations when dealing with serving network traffic such as HTTP or TCP traffic. Systems such as SQL Server can benefit greatly from vertical scaling due to the way that CPU and memory are utilized by the server. However, dealing with network traffic means having to efficiently manage I/O threads, I/O completion ports, request processing, and threads from the thread pool, to be able to serve all the incoming requests. Unless the hosted application is incredibly efficient, there comes a point where the sheer size of the load imposed on a system results in requests being queued or the CPU (whether singular or legion) being at maximum capacity. This aspect was discussed in Chapter 3 when we looked at performance test metrics, specifically, the ASP.NET performance counters dealing with request execution and pipeline instance counts.

Load balancing is really only applicable to server-based applications, such as web applications, services, and systems hosting web services. That is, systems serving multiple requests, typically across a network. The remainder of this chapter targets only these scenarios.

A word about threads

In general, a certain amount of threads are allocated to the system for processing work. These threads are spread across various tasks, such as I/O tasks, request processing and other functions. A pool of threads, or "thread pool," is used as a store house to which work can be allocated; this thread pool is a predetermined and finite resource, with a specific number of threads available per processor to prevent thread saturation (which would create a painful performance bottleneck). .NET uses an algorithm to determine the most appropriate number of worker threads, I/O threads, minimum waiting worker threads, and various other functions. The more processors available, the more threads can be utilized; too many threads per processor can actually decrease performance because of factors such as context switching between threads.

> *Note*
>
> *Thread processing in Windows is a complex topic, and is well beyond the scope of this book. The tuning of thread allocation and thresholds for .NET web applications can be altered in the* `machine.config` *file, within the* `<system.web><processModel>` *element. By default, this is set to* `<processModel autoConfig="true" />`*. It is recommended that this be left at its default, but manual configuration is possible by setting this element's attributes. It is not recommended that you do this without a thorough understanding of how thread processing and allocation works.*

While it is possible to increase the amount of processors in a system and, therefore, the number of threads available to process work, there is a degree of management and marshaling that must occur for all the threads to function efficiently. This means that simply adding a processor does not automatically equate to doubling the throughput and performance. Additionally, the more processors added to a system, the more complex the management and marshaling system must be, and this is why massively multi-processor systems are so expensive.

Introducing extra machines into a server farm offers a great way of sharing the load, and without the resource contention that exists on a single server. Additionally, extra servers, particularly virtual machines, also provide a more cost-effective way of distributing the load of a system.

Infrastructure considerations

The following diagram shows a simplistic load balanced scenario:

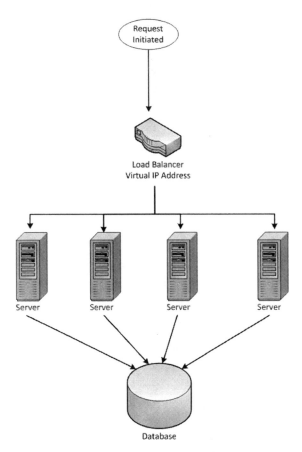

Figure 11.1: Simple load balancing example.

Like the multi-processor system discussed earlier, load balancing requires some degree of management and marshaling to direct traffic to the appropriate servers. Normally, a virtual IP address is created by the load balancing system and this is where all requests are directed. The load balancer intercepts these requests and redirects traffic to an appropriate server, which can potentially be any server in the farm.

The load balancer can be a software- or hardware-based system. Windows Server comes with a software solution known as Windows Load Balancing Service (WLBS). This can be used to create a virtual IP address and add or subtract servers to and from the farm. It is typically suited to smaller server farms in the range of 2–5 servers as, beyond this, the efficiency of the system decreases.

There are many hardware-based load balancers on the market which are generally much more efficient than software-based ones, but they are also much more expensive.

Hardware-based systems typically offer a variety of sophisticated options to determine how busy a server is, which is useful when deciding which server to send the next request to. By contrast, software-based systems utilize simpler means, such as using a basic round-robin system, or checking the number of connections per system. However, these systems don't take into account the actual load on the server, which can be dependent on the system specification and the type of requests being processed. Choosing a load balancing system requires consideration of all these options to ensure scaling-out is as effective as possible, but is also achievable within the given budget.

SSL/HTTPS

Many web applications today utilize Secure Socket Layer (SSL) over HTTP (the combination of which is more commonly called HTTPS) to provide secure communication of information over public networks. This must be considered in a load balanced environment, as the HTTPS protocol requires a connection back to the originating system where the SSL communication was initiated. This means that, once negotiation has completed (which itself involves multiple requests), the same party that established the communication must be used to transfer the secure, encrypted traffic.

As we have seen, load balancing can involve distributing incoming requests to different servers, which will cause problems when using SSL/HTTPS. To circumvent this, an SSL terminator can be used, which acts as the single point for SSL negotiation. An SSL terminator is a hardware device that is specifically designed to encrypt and decrypt SSL traffic. These devices are very efficient and can reduce computational load on the server itself. This device will also typically provide a virtual IP address, but will have additional functionality to efficiently process SSL traffic. Once this has been established, traffic is then passed, unencrypted, to the backend load balancer and servers. Obviously, the SSL terminator needs to exist within a secure environment so that unencrypted information does not flow via a public network. Diagram 11.2 illustrates this concept.

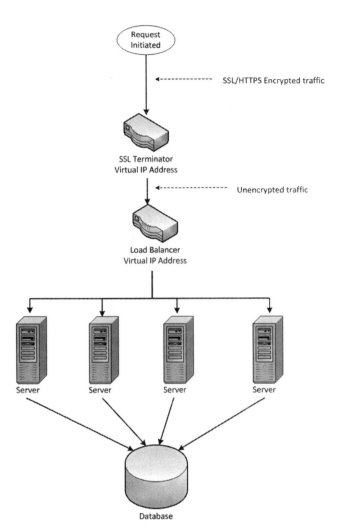

Figure 11.2: SSL terminator.

Most modern hardware load balancing devices now incorporate the SSL termination capability into the device itself and offer this as an integrated feature. This also has the benefit of offloading the encryption and decryption involved with SSL traffic onto the dedicated hardware device. As previously stated, encryption and decryption can be a computationally expensive exercise, and relieving the web server of this work means it can focus on processing application requests.

Application considerations

Theoretically, an application should not be concerned with infrastructure issues such as whether or not it will exist in a load balanced environment. However, reality is always different from theory, and system design needs to take this aspect of the application's environment into account.

HTTP is a stateless protocol, and web applications are stateless by nature, but a framework such as ASP.NET or Windows Communication Foundation (WCF) can make it seem as if the retention of an application state across requests happens automatically. By default, ASP.NET will retain its state in the server's memory, and whether or not this is occurring is identified in the web.config from the <sessionState> section as shown below:

```
<sessionState mode="InProc" ....
```

This means that whenever the ASP.NET session object is used to store objects or data, as shown in the following example, the corresponding object and data is stored in the server's memory.

```
Session["DataKey"] = MyDataObject;
```

If session storage is used in an application, then utilizing the server's memory is a fast way to do this. However, in the case of multiple servers in a web farm, a request can obviously go to any server to be processed. If the state is stored on one server, but the request is processed on a different server in the farm, then the state will clearly not be present in the memory of the server processing the request. At best, the application will appear inconsistent and, at worst, this may cause an error.

Fortunately, this is easily rectified by using a different session state mode. The mode attribute of the <sessionState> element described earlier can be set to either StateServer or SQLServer, and that should avoid this problem. Regardless of the session state mode, however, all objects that will be stored in session state must be marked with the [serializable] attribute. Objects that are not marked with this attribute will cause an exception at runtime when an attempt to store them in session is made. Primitive data types such as int and string do not require any special attributes.

StateServer allows states to be stored on an external machine and accessed via network calls to that machine. Alternatively, SQLServer allows states to be stored in a central SQL Server database. While solving the problem of consistent access of session state information in a web farm, both of these options affect performance. We considered the detrimental impact of network calls on performance earlier, and this must be taken into account when using StateServer mode. It's also worth noting that these options introduce a single point of failure within a distributed web farm; if the single state server fails unexpectedly, then all servers in the farm will no longer be able to store session information.

`SqlServer` session state mode is the most resilient, since SQL Server can be clustered for redundancy; however, it is also the slowest form of session state storage. In addition to a network call, SQL Server must also be enlisted to perform a database operation to store or retrieve the information.

It is easy to create a large set of session data, with larger amounts of data obviously taking longer to serialize or deserialize and send over the network. These aspects of using session state must be taken into account when designing a solution and determining how and where to store session information.

For applications or services that only need to cater for medium to low volumes of traffic, utilizing one of the modes of session storage provided by ASP.NET would not present a major performance issue (subject to performance goals and measuring impact, naturally).

For high-volume sites, setting the `<sessionState>` mode to `Off` is the recommended setting. Saving and managing state or contextual information across requests then becomes a function of the application itself, rather than the framework. This obviously takes extra work to implement, but also means that state information can be tightly controlled, and efficiently managed within the context of the application's requirements. Ideally, a combination of storage methods is the best approach, such as cookies for small items, and a database for all other data. Cookies are often used in web applications to store IDs, user roles, and other small items that enable the application to "rehydrate" the state of the request from the database when required. Cookies require no separate network access and simply accompany the browser request, but are limited in size (generally 4 Kb). Additionally, since cookies are stored by the browser on the client, they can present a security risk if not properly secured and encrypted. Fortunately, ASP.NET provides mechanisms to do this via the `System.Web.Security.FormsAuthentication` class using the `Encrypt` and `Decrypt` methods.

Many solution architects prefer to adopt an approach where session state is turned off for all applications. This is initially because of the performance and infrastructure considerations that have already been discussed, but also because it forces the architecture of the application (and its developers) to acknowledge the inherently stateless nature of the Web. Explicitly dealing with this aspect of web requests provides a greater degree of control over how the application operates, especially when it comes to performance tuning and optimization. When performing encryption and validation, a key value is typically used to generate the encrypted data, and then to decrypt that data again. In order to successfully decrypt data, the same key must obviously be used as when the data was encrypted. The `FormsAuthentication` methods described previously are no exception, and use an encryption key that is stored in the `machine.config` or `web.config` file on the system, within the `<system.web>` section. In addition, view-state encryption and validation (if used) also employ this same key.

By default, each application on the system uses an autogenerated key for this purpose. When an application starts, a new key is randomly generated by the ASP.NET runtime to use for encryption and decryption.

Also, by default, the configuration is not present in the `machine.config` file but defaults to the following:

```
<machineKey decryption="Auto" decryptionKey="AutoGenerate,
IsolateApps" validation="SHA1" validationKey="AutoGenerate,
IsolateApps"/>
```

The `AutoGenerate, IsolateApps` setting indicates that a new key should be randomly generated for each application. This means that, if multiple servers exist within a web farm, each application on each server will utilize a different key. If requests go to different servers in a typical load balanced scenario, then one server will not be able to decrypt data that was encrypted on a different server, and the application will throw an exception.

In order to prevent this, each server in the farm should be configured with a key value that is consistent across all the servers.

```
<machineKey decryption="Auto"
decryptionKey="12345678901234567890121234567890123456789001345678"
validation="SHA1"
validation Key="12345678901234567890123456789012345678901345678"
/>
```

The number of characters needed for a key value will depend on the encryption algorithm chosen, and the .NET configuration system will throw an exception if a key value of an incorrect size is used.

The `decryption` and `decryptionKey` configuration element pair is used for forms authentication, encryption and decryption, and for view-state encryption when validation is set to TripleDES (HTTP://TINYURL.COM/TRIPLEDES).

The `validation` and `validationKey` configuration element pair specifies the key used to validate encrypted data. `validationKey` is used when `enableViewStateMAC` is `True` in order to create a message authentication code (MAC) to ensure that the view state has not been tampered with. `validationKey` is also used to generate out-of-process, application-specific session IDs to ensure that session state variables are isolated between sessions.

Performance testing and load balancing

Load balancing introduces further variables into the performance testing equation, and poses some further questions.

- When executing performance tests, how do we take into account load balanced environments?

- Is it best to test against one server, or is it best to test in an actual load balanced environment against multiple servers?

Both of these questions need to be addressed together. Remember that, early in this book, we discussed what we are attempting to achieve as part of performance testing? Part of that answer was that we needed a well-defined set of metrics around how the application performs in a given situation, with the ability to predict application performance and infrastructure requirements. The primary driver for this was so that the business could be provided with accurate projections on what is required to support the current user base, as well as any peaks in usage and future growth.

Initially, isolating performance tests to a single server is essential to gathering specific metrics and benchmarks around how an application performs on a specific set of hardware. A single server provides the baseline, or core metric upon which we can base the application's performance at various load levels.

However, as already mentioned, this does not mean that introducing more servers in a load balanced environment results in a linear increase in the ability to handle more traffic. The ability of the load balancing solution to effectively and evenly distribute load across the servers will be critical to the percentage of extra capacity that introducing extra servers will provide. This will be influenced by factors such as the method of request distribution (basic round robin, number of connections, actual querying of the server to determine capacity, etc.), load balance device type (hardware or software) and features supported by the load balancer.

With this in mind, it is important to continue to performance test against one server, as well as measure the difference in capacity when introducing extra servers into a load balanced environment. This way, the "delta" (percentage increase) in load can be accurately recorded. The primary performance testing mechanism should always be a single server, as this has the least number of variables. This is especially important when attempting to optimize aspects of an application for performance.

Once the application has reached a relatively high level of maturity (with respect to the development cycle), then introducing performance testing in a load balanced environment and comparing against single server metrics is also important. It is at this point that problems with sessions and server affinity can appear, and testing in a distributed and load balanced environment is often the only place where these problems can be seen. Comprehensive and exhaustive testing processes are also required at this stage, as simple, manual, functional testing may not exercise the load balancer enough for it to distribute subsequent requests to different servers, which means session and server affinity issues will not be seen.

This also means that any metrics being recorded at the server level need to be recorded against all servers. Visual Studio Team Test can be configured to record performance data against any number of servers (discussed in a previous chapter). If PerfMon or other mechanisms are also used to record data at the server level, then the metric data that was being recorded on a single server needs to also be recorded on all servers in the farm.

Servers of different specifications in a farm

Just to add to all this potential complexity, it is not uncommon for servers in a farm to be of different physical specifications. It's not easy to predict the exact percentage change in performance or load capacity from one server to another if there are differences in CPU capacity, amount of memory, speed of memory, speed of the hard disk, etc. Introducing these servers into the farm for performance testing is important, particularly if the intended production environment also has these differences. When there are servers of varying specification in a farm, the method of request distribution provided by the load balancer is even more important. If requests are distributed evenly across the farm, but one server has less capacity than the others, then this server will more quickly reach a point where it is unable to field more requests, and potentially become the bottleneck.

To mitigate this, many load balancing systems provide a way of adding a weighting or bias to certain servers, so that some receive more or less traffic than others, as appropriate. Windows Load Balancing Service provides this feature, as does virtually every hardware-based solution on the market. The feature can require some practice and, perhaps, a little trial and error to get right in any given environment. The level of variance in the capacity of the servers, as well as how effective the system is at distributing the requests, will affect the weighting required, and existing performance test metrics will allow a close estimation as to the correct weightings.

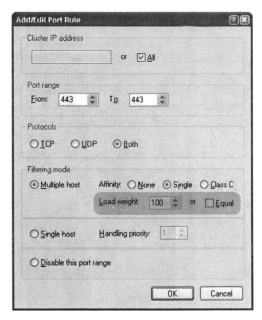

Figure 11.3: WLBS example weighting configuration dialog.

In many situations, the production environment will house a hardware-based load balancer, whereas the test environment may not have any load balancer, due to budgetary or other constraints. In this instance, the best course of action during testing is to use any available load balancing mechanism suitable for the environment. In the case of Windows Server-based systems, this will most likely be WLBS; it's a free and capable load balancing system. At the very least, it will provide a good indication of how an application can benefit in a load balanced environment. Given that hardware load balancers are typically better than their software counterparts, the performance gains seen when moving to the production environment would be even more pronounced.

Windows Azure

Windows Azure is a relatively new cloud-computing platform offered by Microsoft. It provides the "fabric" that allows an application to be hosted in the cloud, and be automatically scaled out according to the required load. It uses its own load balancing mechanism to distribute traffic to as many servers as have been provisioned, which is a significant change in perspective from the traditional hosting of applications.

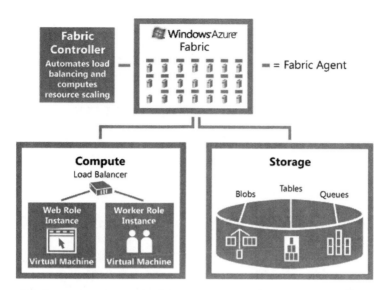

Figure 11.4: Windows Azure conceptual diagram.

In other words, Microsoft datacenters host virtual server instances which, in turn, host an application. When the virtual server instances reach capacity, the Windows Azure framework can automatically provision more instances as load dictates. Conversely, when load decreases, the number of provisioned servers can be reduced. This almost seems an ideal scenario; physical servers are removed from the equation and a significant cost factor can be reduced. It would also seem that the motivation for needing to know how well an application performs is greatly reduced, given that servers can be provisioned as needed, rather than estimated up front.

In reality, while the physical provisioning and capacity planning are significantly altered, there is still a monetary cost attached to provisioning virtual servers. Microsoft will charge according to the number of servers required, the traffic used, and a number of other variables that simply introduce a whole new landscape in capacity planning, rather than making the challenge magically go away.

In no way is the value of performance testing reduced; it is still just as important to be able to run your application as efficiently as possible in order to reduce costs. In addition, Windows Azure currently needs to impose certain restrictions to facilitate the ability to auto-provision servers. This may negate your ability (at least initially) to use the Azure platform and host your application in the cloud.

Windows Azure is a new platform that offers many advantages to traditional hosting, and it is certainly worth deeper investigation to determine whether it is appropriate for a given application, with a valid cost assessment being made. A detailed discussion is unfortunately beyond the remit of this book, but more information can be found at HTTP://WWW. MICROSOFT.COM/WINDOWSAZURE/.

Conclusion

Load balancing your application is a great way of giving it a higher capacity, and it does need to be considered in the design of the application itself.

In addition, performance testing against such an environment requires a knowledge of how load balancing works, and how best to measure its effects. This chapter has covered a number of important concepts.

- Traditional, single-server performance testing should always be performed and used as a core metric.

- The introduction of load balancing and measuring of effects.

- The comparison against the single-server metric to gauge the percentage difference provided by the introduction of extra servers.

- Ensuring the application has not made assumptions around state management and server affinity that will compromise its ability to scale out.

This approach will yield an accurate metric of the current capacity of the application in a given load balanced environment, as well as how well it can scale out when required, and by how much.

Where a farm of servers exists, particularly of varying specification and capacity, thorough and exhaustive testing is required to ensure the correct partitioning of load.

Finally, consideration must be given to new technologies related to cloud computing. This relatively new approach to dealing with scale, hosting, and provisioning can mean a lot of cost savings for businesses, but it also means that a new set of problems and issues is presented.

Chapter 12: Internet Information Server

Configuring Internet Information Server (IIS) correctly for your environment is a fundamental part of maximizing application performance and scalability. Assuming that the defaults will be good enough may be wishful thinking, and could lead to problems later on. A good understanding of IIS and its configuration will help you to decide the best setup for your application and environment, and that's what this chapter is all about.

But let's start with some background on IIS architecture, as this will make it easier to understand some of the more complicated configuration issues later on. If you are already familiar with this material, feel free to move on to the next section.

Background

A web server has two distinct functions: a listener that waits for HTTP requests from clients, and a request processor that receives requests from the listener, retrieves/builds content, and returns a response to the listener for dispatch back to the client.

To maximize the performance and scalability of IIS6, Microsoft decided to run the HTTP listener service as part of the operating system in "kernel mode." They also rewrote the request processor so that it allowed applications to have much better isolation, as well as adding different configurations and features allowing performance and reliability to be improved. The significant enhancements added to IIS6 and the subsequent release of IIS7 have placed IIS at the forefront of web server technology.

Kernel and user mode

Process threads running in kernel mode run at a higher priority, have direct access to hardware and system data, and are usually reserved for either operating system processes or device drivers. By contrast, user mode processes gain access to hardware and system data via either device drivers or specific application programming interfaces (APIs).

Running the HTTP listener (implemented as HTTP.sys) in kernel mode allows it to run at a high priority and gives it direct access to the network interface, vastly improving its performance. Consequently, IIS's responsiveness to HTTP requests has been maximized.

IIS6 and the application pool

IIS6 introduced the application pool or "app pool," which provides a conceptually simple model for isolating web applications from each other. One or more web applications can be added to an app pool, and each app pool runs within a separate process, meaning applications in different app pools can't cause each other to crash.

As well as isolation, app pools allow configuration for things like identity, .NET Framework version selection, health monitoring, and performance/reliability settings. A major part of maximizing the performance, scalability and reliability of your application is to configure your app pool correctly, and that's precisely what we'll cover later in this chapter.

Requests for each app pool are serviced by at least one executing process called the worker process. When a request is received for a specific URL, it's routed to the correct app pool and processed by that app pool's worker process.

An app pool can actually be configured to run with multiple worker processes, a concept known as a "Web garden." When an app pool is configured as a Web garden, requests received are routed in turn to one of the various worker processes in the garden.

Under the hood

As mentioned, to maximize the performance of IIS, the HTTP request listener (from IIS6 onwards) runs in kernel mode. Received requests are placed on application-pool-specific queues for processing by the user mode worker process(es).

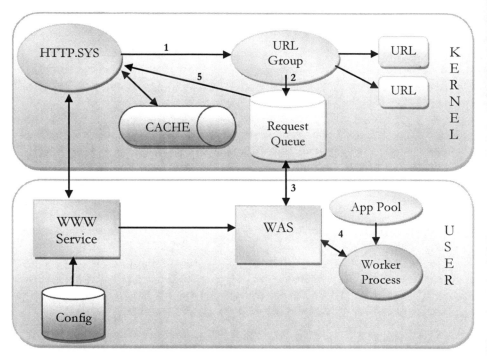

Figure 12.1: IIS7 processing model.

Figure 12.1 shows the general flow of request processing for IIS7, although conceptually it is almost identical to IIS6; in IIS6, WWW Service contains the functionality of Windows Process Activation Service (WAS). It might look a little chaotic, but don't worry, I'll explain it for you.

Request listening (HTTP.sys)

When a request is received by the HTTP listener (HTTP.sys), it is immediately routed to a specific kernel mode queue for subsequent processing by the user mode app pool worker process (following Arrows 1, 2, 3 and 4 in Figure 12.1). The request is routed to the correct queue based on the target URL because an app pool is configured to process one or more URLs. Queuing requests has the added benefit of releasing the HTTP listener thread to process another request.

When the response has been generated and is ready to be served, it is returned to HTTP.sys (Arrow 5) and then back to the client. HTTP.sys can also decide to cache the response, based on how it is configured; we will discuss that in greater detail later.

HTTP.sys actually maintains a kernel mode cache, which is significant because it is non-paged. This means it will always be kept in physical memory and not paged to disk, which would reduce performance. Request caching allows unchanged content to be served immediately from the memory cache, rather than recreated on each request via the user mode request processors; kernel mode caching of page content can give huge performance gains to a web application. We will talk more about caching and its configuration later on.

Request processing (user mode)

In IIS7, two services manage the configuration and activation of both the HTTP listener and the request processor. They are:

- WWW service

    - configures and updates HTTP.sys and WAS

    - maintains performance counters.

- Windows Process Activation Service

    - activates and alerts worker processes to process requests

    - manages running worker processes (recycling, performance limiting).

In IIS6 both pieces of functionality were combined into the WWW service, but they were split in IIS7 so that the request processing features of WAS could be provided to non-HTTP services such as Windows Communication Foundation services.

WWW service

The WWW service monitors the IIS configuration database (ApplicationHost.config) and is responsible for configuring and updating the HTTP.sys listener when changes occur. It also informs the WAS when an HTTP request is available for processing.

Windows Process Activation Service (WAS)

WAS has two main components: the configuration manager which monitors the IIS configuration database (ApplicationHost.config), and the process manager which starts, stops, configures, and recycles worker processes as needed.

WAS functions completely independently of the transport provider, and will work just as well with HTTP as with named pipes, message queuing, and so on. WAS also handles some key aspects of worker processes, so let's go through the main ones.

Process idle timeout

Worker processes for an application pool can be configured to timeout after a set number of minutes. When the timeout occurs, the process is stopped, which frees up unused resources.

Recycling

WAS can be configured, under certain circumstances, to stop one instance of a running worker process once it has finished its last request, and start another instance. This can alleviate problems caused by applications with known problems such as memory leaks, and a whole multitude of other issues. It buys you some time to investigate the cause of the problem, but is by no means a solution. An application pool can be configured to recycle worker processes:

• when allocated memory exceeds certain thresholds

• after a set number of requests

• every "x" minutes

• at specific times of day

• when a config change is made.

CPU limiting

This can be used to prevent a worker process utilizing too much CPU time. If a worker process exceeds certain thresholds over a set time period, WAS can be configured to either kill the process or write an entry to the event log.

Health monitoring

WAS can be configured to ping the worker process to ensure it is still alive. If a response isn't received within set thresholds, the process is assumed to be dead, and is terminated and restarted.

333

Rapid-fail protection

WAS can be configured to shut down an application pool if its worker process(es) crash within the configured thresholds (see the later section on rapid failure detection). If this occurs, the server would then give a "Server Unavailable" response, which would allow a load balanced setup to process the request via another server.

Worker process and the request pipeline

The worker process is where the actual work is done. Prior to IIS7, request processing required the following steps:

- request received

- authenticate request

- choose and execute handler for request:

    - static content

    - CGI

    - ISAPI application (ASP, ASPX, etc.)

- send response.

Implemented as a pipeline, the output of one step was handed as an input to the next. Modifying the pipeline involved writing a new ISAPI application, which was not an easy undertaking.

IIS7 has introduced a modular approach, in that a number of modules are provided for HTTP, security compression, content providers, diagnostics, and caching. Implemented either in native or managed code, they can be combined into the pipeline to give an extremely flexible and powerful processing model. ASP.NET is just one of the providers in the pipeline.

IIS7 can run request processing for an application pool in either Classic (IIS6 model) or the new, integrated (IIS7) model.

IIS common considerations

In this section we will go through some of the major configuration options available in IIS and ASP.NET and their impact on performance and scalability. It really is worth understanding the issues here, because just going with the defaults may not achieve what you need. Also, even if you aren't experiencing problems per se, understanding what the settings are doing can help you explain why IIS is causing your application to behave in a certain way.

Worker process recycling

Both IIS6 and IIS7 application pools can be configured to stop and start worker processes under certain sets of circumstances. This feature can be used to maximize the availability of an application, especially one which is known to have problems. Processes that are getting progressively slower or are starting to fail can be stopped and replaced with fresh versions.

Recycling is actually more intelligent than just a restart, because the old worker process is allowed to finish servicing its current requests. The new worker process is started in parallel and new requests are routed to it; only when the old process has completed its "in-flight" work load will it be killed. In IIS7, overlapped recycling can be disabled.

An important point to remember is that all "In process" states will be lost when a worker process is recycled, which includes both the session state and cache. If you have been using a process state up till now, it might be worth considering using a different state repository such as SQL Server or using the State Server service.

The recycling options below (from the **properties** menu of each app pool) are available in both IIS6 and 7.

Time based

Time-based recycling can occur every set number of minutes, or even at a specific time of day.

Minute frequency

You can configure an application pool to recycle worker process every "X" minutes and, by default, this is set to 1,740 minutes. If your application fails after a predictable length of time, then set the recycle minutes value to no more than 80% of the known failure time. Unchecking this option in IIS6 or setting the value to zero in IIS7 will switch the feature off.

335

This feature is frequently left switched to its default value of 1,740 minutes (just over a day) as a general health measure, even for applications with no known problems. That being said, this isn't the best way to achieve a consistently healthy application.

Time of day frequency

A better measure is to use the time-based scheduler, where the application pool can be scheduled to recycle at specific times of the day. This enables you to target times which are known to be problematic, or are times of low demand in which a general health recycle would have little impact.

Request count

Not surprisingly, this feature should be used when your application is failing after it has received a certain number of requests. It's not uncommon to hear reports of an application or service failing after a set number of calls, so this is just a quick fix solution. You won't be surprised to learn that the accepted practice is to set the recycle request count to be less than the failure request count!

Memory usage

An app pool can be recycled based on its memory profile, and you can use both its used and its virtual memory to determine when that takes place.

These features can be used as a defensive measure against applications that you suspect are leaking or over-allocating memory. The problem is that web applications often rely heavily on caching to maximize performance, and caching, to the untrained eye, can appear to be a leak. Recycling an application pool that was actually holding a lot of usefully cached material will obviously have an adverse effect on performance.

Understanding the issues involved here, and then carefully choosing the thresholds, is crucial.

Private bytes

This feature sets a limit to the amount of private unshared memory a worker process can allocate before being recycled. If an application is leaking memory, it will be most obvious from this performance counter, although it is by no means definitive.

In IIS6 the setting on the app pool recycling tab is called **Used Memory**, and is set in Mbytes. For II7, the setting is **Private bytes** and is in Kbytes.

The value you choose here is important because it will be directly affected by the way you store session state and utilize ASP.NET caching. If you set the value too low and make heavy use of caching, you may inadvertently cause process recycling and lose the performance gains made by data already cached.

ASP.NET 2.0 caching tries to avoid process recycling where possible by adopting a cache trimming policy, in which items are removed from the cache in an attempt to reduce private bytes when the threshold value is approached.

To give finer control, the actual cache trimming level can be set using the **privateBytesLimit** setting in the caching section of your application's web.config file.

```
<caching><cache privateBytesLimit=""/><caching>
```

The lower of either the **Private bytes** setting in IIS or **privateBytesLimit** in web.config is then the value used for cache trimming. If neither value is set by default, the following default limits are calculated:

User mode memory		
<=2 GByte	>2 GByte (32 Bit)	>2 GByte (64 Bit)
Lower than 60% physical RAM or 800MB	Lower than 60% physical RAM or 1800MB	Lower than 60% physical RAM or 1TB

You can also set the **percentagePhysicalMemoryUsedLimit** setting within the cache section of web.config to constrain how much memory can be used by the cache before trimming will take place. This value can be used to reduce the aggressiveness of the .NET garbage collector when it encounters low memory conditions. The garbage collector will run full garbage collections more frequently under low memory conditions, and this can be a major source of performance degradation.

My best advice is to test your application under load using the default values in IIS, and monitor the following performance counters:

- ASP.NET apps\cache API trims

  - cache items removed due to memory threshold reached

- Process\private bytes for w3pw.exe process

  - non-shared memory allocation for worker process

- ASP.NET\worker process restarts

  - Number of worker process restarts.

A combination of frequent cache trims and worker process restarts, together with evidence of private byte memory utilization drops will indicate a need for tuning.

Don't forget that, in addition to user mode caching, IIS6 and IIS7 offer kernel mode caching that will give significant performance gains. The main downsides at the moment are that it won't support Basic or Windows authentication, and can't cache using **VaryByQuerystring**.

Virtual bytes

Virtual bytes include the private and shared address space of a process, and also reserved memory. A worker process whose virtual memory profile continues to grow can indicate an application causing memory heap fragmentation, and unchecked heap fragmentation can cause premature **Out Of Memory** exceptions.

If you feel that you have a problem with virtual memory fragmentation, then initially set the recycle limit to around 70% of virtual memory and monitor the counter Process/Virtual Bytes of the w3wp.exe process under load. Reduce the recycle limit if virtual memory expansion for the process continues to be a problem.

Idle timeout

Another cause of worker process recycling is the idle timeout setting. This setting is designed to conserve processor and memory resources, and kills worker processes that haven't served requests for a set number of minutes. For an application that has built up cached data, this will obviously undo the performance gain the caching would have achieved. Careful consideration needs to be given to the use of this setting, and the default timeout of 20 minutes should be extended if the circumstances allow.

Dynamic idle

The idle timeout can be dynamically modified using the `dynamicIdleThreshold` setting in IIS7. The setting represents the percentage of physical RAM that will be used to trigger the idle timeout threshold to be reduced in stages.

The system monitors committed (not reserved) virtual memory to ensure that the value set in `dynamicIdleThreshold` is always greater than 100%, because we always have more virtual memory than physical. When committed virtual memory reaches 80% of the calculated `dynamicIdleThreshold` memory value, it will reduce the idle timeout by half.

Let's say the idle timeout is 20 minutes, the system has 4 GB of RAM, and the `dynamicIdleThreshold` is 150%; then the threshold memory value is 6 GB (4 x 150 / 100).

When committed virtual memory reaches 4.8 GB, (80% of 6 GB), idle timeout is reduced to 10 minutes (20 / 2). The following thresholds are used to reduce the timeout threshold:

Percentage of threshold	Idle timeout reduction
80%	0.5
85%	0.25
90%	0.125
95%	0.0625
100%	0.03125

Table 12.1: IIS worker process idle timeout thresholds.

By default, the setting is switched off (i.e. set to zero), although you can easily switch it on from the IIS PowerShell provider using the following script:

```
set-webconfigurationproperty /system.applicationHost/webLimits
-name dynamicIdleThreshold -value 130
```

Bitness (32- or 64-bit application pools)

Setting an application pool to run an application in 32-bit mode on a 64-bit operating system will often give a performance gain over the same application running in a 64-bit app pool. The reasons for this appear to be down to the extra overhead involved in 64-bit addressing and more efficient use of the processor cache.

If your application can live with a 4 GB address space and doesn't need 64-bit math, then this might be an option to try to squeeze a little bit more performance out of the server.

In IIS7, for an individual app pool, select **Advanced** settings and set **Enable 32-Bit Applications** to **true**. IIS6 requires a global change, in that the change applies to all app pools. Run the following script to enable 32-bit applications:

```
cscript %SYSTEMDRIVE%\inetpub\adminscripts\adsutil.vbs SET W3SVC/
AppPools/Enable32bitAppOnWin64 1
```

To ensure that the 32-bit DLLs are used by IIS for the ISAPI handler, we have to re-register ASP.NET. At a command prompt, simply type:

```
%SYSTEMROOT%\Microsoft.NET\Framework\v2.0.50727\aspnet_regiis.exe
-i
```

Also make sure the status of ASP.NET version 2.0.50727 (32-bit) in the web services extension, within IIS, is set to **allowed**.

339

Queue length

Queue length sets the limit on the number of requests that the HTTP request listener (HTTP.sys) can queue for an app pool. It is designed to avoid overloading a server with requests that an app pool is unable to handle. In the event of the limit being reached, a generic 503 error is returned.

By default the value is 4,000 but, if necessary, you could optimally tune this value under load for each app pool.

Pipeline mode

IIS7 introduced the integrated pipeline for app pools, bringing a modular, extensible approach to request processing. For backward compatibility, app pools can also run in classic pipeline mode, which gives compatibility with IIS6.

Integrated pipeline mode also introduced a significant optimization in app pool thread management but, to understand the optimization, we need to go through some background on how IIS6 thread pool management worked.

IIS6 thread pools

Each app pool maintains a pool of threads ready to service requests as they are received.

When a request is handed over to ASP.NET for processing, the CLR allocates a thread in the pool to it. To avoid a huge number of threads being created in times of peak demand, a limit is placed on the number of concurrently executing threads in the thread pool. The thresholds are controlled within machine.config as part of the **processModel**, and include maxWorkerThreads and maxIOThreads (both of which are per-logical-CPU settings).

If the thresholds are hit, then subsequent requests are placed in a request queue until other threads become available in the thread pool. This becomes a problem if web pages are carrying out I/O operations that involve Wait time such as, typically, database and web service calls. Requests waiting for I/O operations to return typically use very little CPU, but tie up threads in the thread pool. This can lead to web applications showing low throughput but also low CPU usage. You know you have this problem when the performance counter **ASP.NET Applications/Requests in Application Queue** is greater than zero.

Other than configuration change, the only way around the problem was to re-code the worst pages and services to use ASP.NET asynchronous page processing for the I/O intensive portions of their execution. This freed up worker threads to service incoming requests, and improved overall throughput.

IIS7 integrated mode optimizations

When running in integrated mode, application queues are no longer used, as the performance and memory impact of the CLR-based application queue used in IIS6 and IIS7 Classic Pipeline Mode is reputed to be poor. Instead, a global application pool queue has been implemented in native code, which is much faster and has less impact.

Instead of controlling the number of concurrently executing threads in the thread pool, the number of concurrently executing requests are managed globally across the applications in FIFO (first in, first out) order. The thresholds to control concurrent thread execution and queue length for this queue can be manually configured.

Prior to .NET Framework v3.5 SP1, you had to set a registry key DWORD MaxConcurrentRequestsPerCPU in :

```
HKEY_LOCAL_MACHINE\SOFTWARE\Microsoft\ASP.NET\2.0.50727.0
```

.NET Framework v3.5 SP1 release allows you to set this value much more easily in:

```
<system.web>
  <applicationPool maxConcurrentRequestsPerCPU="12"/>
</system.web>
```

CPU limiting

CPU limiting can be an invaluable tool, particularly if you have an application that periodically hits the processors hard for a sustained period, causing significant slowdown. This can often be due to a poorly-written or badly-behaving piece of functionality within an application.

In IIS6 you can set the maximum CPU usage as a percentage, as well as setting how frequently the number is refreshed.

IIS7 allows you to set the maximum CPU usage in an incredibly fine-grained $\frac{1}{1000}$th of a percent of CPU usage over a set period of time. If you want to trigger a CPU limiting action when a worker process used 75% of the CPU for 5 minutes, then set **Limit** to 75,000 (75 x 1,000) and **Limit Interval** to 5.

In both IIS6 and IIS7, you can set the action taken; to kill the worker process or take no action, and in the latter case an event will be written to the event log. A new worker process is started immediately after the old one is terminated.

CPU limiting shouldn't be used as a way to throttle CPU usage, as Microsoft Windows System Resource Manager is actually designed to do this. Instead, it is a safeguard system that can be used to protect system resources.

Processor affinity

Each app pool in IIS7 can have a hexadecimal processor affinity mask set. This simply represents a bit pattern (in hex or decimal) identifying which of 8 processors from 0 to 7 the worker processor can run on.

00000001 – indicates Processor 0; 10000001 – specifies Processors 0 and 7, and so on.

To make use of this functionality, you need to set both the Process Affinity mask and the Process Affinity Enabled flag to true.

If the app pool is set to run multiple worker processes (Web garden), then each one will run on the processors defined in the affinity mask.

Health monitoring

IIS can be configured to ping worker processes to detect ones that are no longer functioning. Processes can crash or become deadlocked, or they may not have a thread available to respond to the ping request, any of which is clearly a problem worth knowing about.

In IIS6 you can configure the ping to occur every "x" number of seconds, and in IIS7 you set the ping period in seconds, together with the maximum response Wait time before the process is shut down.

Rapid failure detection

IIS6 introduced rapid failure detection, which allows for graceful failover of a consistently crashing app pool worker process onto another load balanced server.

To achieve this, you configure the number of failures that must occur over a set time frame (measured in minutes). Once this threshold level has been reached, the kernel mode HTTP listener will return a HTTP 503 Service Unavailable (Out of Service) message. In a load balanced scenario (where the load balancer is HTTP aware), this will allow another server to service the request.

To configure this in IIS6, you go to the **Health** tab of the application pool properties and set both the **Failure count** and **Time** settings.

In IIS7, you set this up from the **Advanced Properties** of an application pool: set the **Rapid Failure Detection Enabled** property to **True** and the **Failure count** and **Failures Interval** values as appropriate.

You can also configure the type of response in the **Service Unavailable Response type** control. Setting it to **HTTPLevel** will return a HTTP 503, whereas **TCPLevel** will reset the connection. Depending on the load balancer used, either of the responses should allow the request to be redirected.

SSL server affinity and hardware acceleration

Processing Secure Socket Layer (SSL) requests can place additional load on systems, due to the extra overhead in dealing with the encryption/decryption involved. In fact, what appears to be a reasonably straightforward issue can quickly snowball into an issue requiring a fundamental rework of your system architecture.

How it works

When a client connects to a server over SSL (HTTPS), the following steps take place:

- Client begins a handshake protocol with the server by opening a connection to the server on port 443.

- Client sends a list of its supported encryption and hashing functions (cipher suites) to the server.

- Server replies to the client by indicating the strongest cipher it supports from the list.

- Server sends its digital certificate which includes its domain name, the certificate issuer and the public key the client can use for encryption.

- Client checks the validity of the certificate with issuer.

- Client generates a random number and encrypts it using the server's public key and asymmetric encryption then sends it to the server. This is called the premaster secret.

- Server decrypts the premaster secret using the private key of its digital certificate.

- Using the premaster secret key, both client and server create master secret strings and use them to generate session keys (large strings of data) which are used from then on for encrypting/decrypting all of the data passed between client and server.

- HTTP requests/responses are now encrypted and decrypted (using symmetric algorithms) by client and server using the session keys.

It's hardly surprising that the overhead of all of the handshake and subsequent data encryption is significant, and can seriously impact performance. As a result, optimizing the performance of HTTPS transactions is a key part of any high volume web strategy.

Load balancing and SSL

In IIS, SSL conversations occur at the HTTP.sys level, and SSL state information is cached to avoid having to go through the handshake protocol for every request made during a browser transaction. States held include the cipher suite used, the generated secrets, and the encryption keys, with a unique session ID identifying the browser session.

For this to work, the browser has to maintain contact with the same server so the encryption state can be reused. This will work for a single web server operation, but becomes a problem in a multi-server web farm with load balancing in place.

Although load balancers allow a group of web servers to appear to the outside world as one server, most load balancers allow you to configure them to direct each request from the same client session to the same server. This is called server affinity, but you will also hear it called "sticky sessions."

One way to solve the SSL problem would be to establish server affinity for port 443 (SSL) transactions. The major downside is that you would be kind of undermining the purpose of load balancing, in that you are forcing load to specific servers regardless of any other consideration. The load balancing equation gets skewed to an extent.

Another possible solution is to configure the load balancer (if capable) as an SSL Terminator. This involves installing your SSL digital certificate and allowing the load balancer to decrypt SSL transactions. The downside is, as you have probably guessed, that it adds additional (and significant) computation overhead to the load balancer.

Optimizing performance with SSL

Two main techniques are used to improve SSL performance: SSL acceleration and SSL offloading.

Both involve, to some degree, changing the location where SSL encryption and decryption is handled. However, the two methods naturally have their own benefits and potential pitfalls.

SSL acceleration

You can quickly improve performance of SSL processing using an SSL accelerator. This is a PCI or SCSI card containing an additional processor that carries out the SSL encryption, usually just the asymmetric variety (the symmetric encryption is still carried out by the main processors). These cards can significantly reduce the SSL processing overhead that would otherwise be incurred on the system CPUs.

SSL offloading

SSL offloading involves directing SSL traffic through an SSL processing device (either software or hardware based), where it is decrypted and then redirected to the web server(s) for processing in unencrypted form (Figure 12.2). The response is then encrypted by the proxy and sent back to the client.

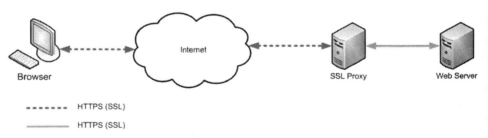

------- HTTPS (SSL)

━━━━━━━ HTTPS (SSL)

Figure 12.2: SSL offloading using an SSL proxy.

A big advantage is that the entire SSL overhead is completely removed from the web server. The HTTP request is decrypted and available for further analysis by other network analyzers, such as intrusion detection systems and load balancers.

SSL proxies effectively overcome the sticky session problem associated with load balancing SSL in Web farms (Figure 12.3). Because the request is pre-decrypted, load balancing can continue in the normal way, and each server in the farm is relieved of SSL processing responsibility.

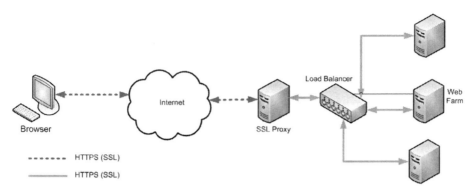

Figure 12.3: SSL proxy in a load balanced environment.

The major problems with SSL proxies are that you are introducing a single point of failure into your system, and that the link between the proxy and the web servers is unencrypted, which may not be acceptable to your specific requirements. The upsides of maximizing performance are, however, crystal clear.

HTTP compression

Compression can greatly improve a user's perception of server responsiveness, and is a greatly underused feature. Web pages mostly contain text data, with links to binary media such as images, video and Flash and, as such, are ideal candidates for compression (media files are already compressed).

Any browser that supports HTTP/1.1 will support compression so, today, browser coverage will be extremely high. Even if a browser doesn't support it, the exchange will simply occur without compression. As part of the HTTP request, the header includes an "Accept-Encoding" which lists the encoding schemes supported by the browser. If the browser supports one of them, then a compressed response can take place.

TCP effect

The main benefits of using compression are the increase in download speed and the reduction in bandwidth per request (and so less congestion on the pipe). Another benefit is the minimization of the TCP slow start effect.

TCP slow start is a TCP congestion control that adjusts the number and size of packets a new connection can initially send. The size of the data stream is subsequently increased but, with compression switched on, more of a web page will reach a client in a shortened space of time, which is particularly useful because more of the image/media links will be received in this window, and can therefore be requested sooner.

CPU effect

Like most things, benefits are counterbalanced with downsides and, for compression, the downside is the CPU overhead required to compress data on the server. Compression involves computationally intensive algorithms that require CPU time and that's going to hit server performance.

You first question when considering compression has to be, "Is the server bound by a CPU or bandwidth limit?" The answer to this will determine your compression setup.

If you do decide to go with compression, it is recommended that you run comparative load tests with compression switched on and off. If you can still hit your KPIs, then it's a win-win situation.

Static and dynamic content compression

IIS deals with static and dynamic content differently. Obviously static content doesn't change, so once its compressed, that's it. Dynamic content, such as the output from ASPX pages, changes frequently; consequently, compression will have to occur far more frequently, and so has much greater impact.

IIS 6

In IIS6, static and dynamic compression are on by default, and are managed by selecting the properties of the **Web Sites Folder** in **IIS Manager**, and then choosing the **Service** tab. The HTTP compression settings are shown in Figure 12.4. The **Compress application files** setting controls dynamic compression.

Figure 12.4: IIS6 compression settings.

Compression occurs after the first request for a static file, and the compressed data is stored in the temporary directory, as seen in Figure 12.4. The maximum size of files in the directory can be set, although this single setting will control all app pools. To gain more control over compression, you need to edit the **MetaBase** (or **MetaDataBase**) in: **C:\WINDOWS\ system32\inetsrv\MetaBase.xml.**

Specifically, you manage and control compression using instances of the <IIsCompressionScheme/> element. There will be one for the "Deflate" compression scheme, and one for "Gzip," and you can control which file extensions are compressed by which scheme, as well as whether dynamic and static compression will occur. There is also an attribute that controls the compression level called **HcDynamicCompressionLevel**. This defaults to zero, which is the lowest level of compression, but can be set as high as 10, giving maximum compression. It is worth doing some experimenting on your setup to get the right level of compression for your environment, with obvious extra CPU trade-off. Many users find that compression levels up to 9 are acceptable.

IIS7

IIS7 also allows you to control caching of static and dynamic content separately. On Windows Server 2008 you need to add both static and dynamic compression as web server roles. The compression configuration option will then become available on IIS server properties, and from here you can configure static and dynamic compression.

Static compression

Static compression caches data to disk, and the disk usage can be controlled on a per–app-pool basis, rather than globally (as in IIS6). You can also set a minimum file size to compress, as very small files can often end up larger when compressed. The optimum tends to be around 2,700 bytes, which is the default threshold.

Before compression will take place, the page in question has to reach the frequent hit threshold. It's set in ApplicationHost.config using the serverRuntime element:

```
<serverRuntime

   ...

   frequentHitThreshold="request count"
   frequentHitTimePeriod="time period in seconds"
/>
```

When a page has hit the set number of requests in frequentHitThreshold over the course of the time period in frequentHitTimePeriod, compression will occur.

Compression can be further controlled using settings within ApplicationHost.config, specifically within the <httpCompression> element. Deflate and Gzip compression schemes are configured separately, and you can define the response content types (mime types) that are applicable to each one. This differs from IIS6, which relied on file extensions.

To prevent compression adding to an already CPU-stressed server, two attributes can be set: staticCompressionEnableCpuUsage and staticCompressionDisableCpuUsage.

They turn compression on and off, depending on CPU utilization levels. staticCompressionEnableCpuUsage indicates the CPU level at which to enable static compression (the default is 5%), and staticCompressionDisableCpuUsage sets the CPU utilization percentage at which compression should be switched off again (the default is 100%).

When kernel mode caching is switched on and compression of static content is enabled, only the compressed version of the content will be cached, optimizing memory usage and speeding up page delivery.

Dynamic compression

Due to the constantly-changing nature of dynamic content, its compression product isn't cached to disk. Dynamic compression can also be controlled based on CPU utilization using the attributes dynamicCompressionEnableCpuUsage and dynamicCompressionDisableCpuUsage as with (and in a similar manner to) static content.

It's important to remember that compressing dynamic content will have the biggest CPU impact and won't benefit from caching, so you need to be sure your load tests prove that there is a definite benefit to be gained.

Static content

We've covered quite a lot of detail on static content, and how it can be both compressed and stored very effectively in a kernel mode cache, giving the most optimal performance possible. So let's now move away from compression and talk about the content itself.

IIS6 provides a feature that allows you to override handler selection, called "wildcard mapping." It's most often used for URL rewriting, allowing the .NET developer to write code to selectively map URL paths to whatever they want in their code. They achieve this by routing all requests through the ASP.NET handler.

It's easy enough to do; from **Web Site Properties** you go to the **Home** tab and select the **Configuration** button (see Figure 12.5).

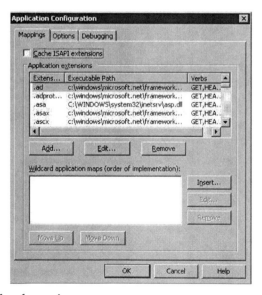

Figure 12.5: IIS6 wildcard mapping.

All you now have to do is choose **Insert**, and add the path to the **ASP.NET IASPI DLL**:

```
C:\WINDOWS\Microsoft.NET\Framework\v2.0.50727\aspnet_isapi.dll
```

The wildcard maps will appear in the configuration list in order of implementation.

The problem is that all content will be served by ASP.NET, including static content. ASP. NET has a basic HTTP handler, but it circumvents both the kernel mode static caching and the compression that would have otherwise taken place. In addition, the HTTP headers that would normally be applied are omitted.

The standard advice in this situation is, first of all, to be aware of these issues before making the decision to use wildcard mapping. If you decide to go ahead, do it with the knowledge of its impact and, even better, perform load tests to determine the extent of the impact.

Alternatively, IIS7 has a URL Rewrite Module that integrates into the pipeline, and has been designed to carry out rules-based URL rewriting without massively disrupting the rest of the process.

HTTP headers

Web pages contain links to static content that very rarely changes. Images are an excellent example of this, and downloading them fresh for every request to a web page would be crazy. That's obviously why browsers maintain a local cache of static files for reuse between requests. Overlooking local caching can lead to a browser performing unnecessary network round trips and server hits, consuming valuable bandwidth and CPU time.

Local caching is also why large organizations use proxy servers to manage Internet access for their employees. The proxy servers also maintain a cache to try to cut down on bandwidth usage for frequently accessed resources. Can you imagine the overhead of every employee in a large organization downloading the Google image every time? It might not seem like much, but these things can quickly mount up.

Used correctly, the cache has the potential to maximize both server performance and bandwidth usage and, thus, the positive user experience.

Freshness and validation

Caching content locally is only part of the story because, whenever a page reloads or is revisited, the browser needs to know if each of the references it has cached has changed on the server.

In the absence of any "freshness" information, the browser sends a validation **GET** request to the server containing the ETag (unique file identifier) and the Last-Modified date of the file. If the file hasn't changed on the server, it replies with a HTTP 304 "Not Changed" message. This is great because it avoids downloading a new copy of files each time a page is loaded, but it still involves a server round trip. Ideally, we have to have a way to give each of our resources a "Best Before" date, and that's kind of what content expiration is all about.

Content expiration

Content expiration allows you to say, "This resource won't expire for a really long time," which is handy for an image that will never change. Equally, you can say, "This expires immediately," which is useful for something more volatile, like the output of a pseudo-real-time .ASPX page.

The information used in content expiration is placed in the HTTP response header for every piece of content retrieved from the server.

The excerpt below illustrates an HTTP header for a JavaScript file. Notice the Cache-Control, Expires and ETag entries. Expires sets an absolute date when the content should expire, and works for both HTTP/1.0 and 1.1 compliant browsers. The Cache-Control header is compliant with browsers from HTTP/1.1 onwards, and allows you to set a maximum age of a resource in seconds.

```
HTTP/1.1 200 OK
Server: Microsoft-IIS/6.0
X-Powered-By: ASP.NET
Cache-Control: max-age=604800
Expires: Fri, 29 Nov 2009 11:01:59 GMT
Date: Fri, 22 Nov 2009 11:01:59 GMT
Content-Type: application/x-javascript
Last-Modified: Fri, 12 May 2006 18:54:28 GMT
ETag: "70c1d1a4a775d41:df3"
Content-Length: 287
```

The Cache-Control header allows you to take more control over how browser and proxy caches behave by allowing you pass various directives. The table below lists some of the most important ones.

max-age (seconds)	the maximum time from the time of the request that the resource will be considered fresh
s-max-age (seconds)	same as max-age, but applies to proxy server
Private	indicates that the resource should only be cached by browsers and not proxy servers
Public	resource can be cached by a proxy server

no-cache	insists that the cache manager submits a validation request to the server every time before a cached copy is used; this is often used to enforce validation and freshness on a resource
no-store	instruction to never cache the resource
must-revalidate	instructs browser to rigidly apply freshness and validation rules
proxy-revalidate	instructs proxy server to rigidly apply freshness and validation rules

Controlling content expiration in IIS

Once you understand the importance and power of content expiration, the good news is that to control it in IIS is really easy. You can control content expiration globally (websites), at site level, at folder level, and at file level.

To choose the appropriate level in IIS6, select the **Properties** of the site, folder or file, and choose the HTTP Headers tab. You can **Enable Content Expiration** and then set **Expire immediately** (set Cache-Control: no-cache), **Expire after** (x days, hours, minutes) (set Cache-Control: max-age), or **Expire on** a specific date (sets the Expires header).

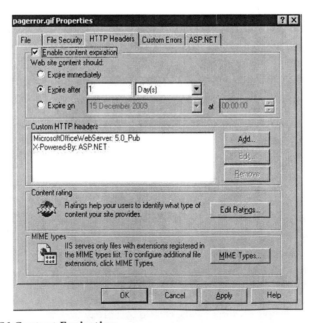

Figure 12.6: IIS6 Content Expiration.

353

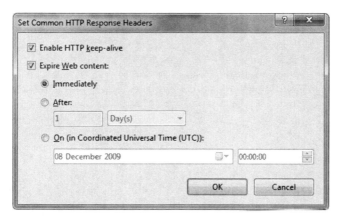

Figure 12.7: Content Expiration in IIS7.

For IIS7 you can set exactly the same content expiration details for each level by choosing the server, site, folder or file, and then selecting **HTTP Response Headers** from the **Features** window. Bring up the context menu by right-clicking on the item you want to manage, and select the **Set Common Headers** menu option. The dialogue shown in Figure 12.7. will be displayed.

Tools

There are a couple of Firefox add-ons that can really help when investigating caching. YSlow is a great all-round tool for identifying a multitude of possible reasons why your site might be slow. Caching is just one of them!

Live HTTP Headers will display the actual headers sent and received as part of the HTTP conversation you start in Firefox. Looking for the HTTP 304 of static files is a good starting point.

Caching tip

Media files such as images, Flash, video and sound are your biggest bandwidth consumers, so a good caching tip is to place really long expirations on these files, and then change their filenames and file references when you need to update them. Even better, make file references dynamic and based on version numbers.

Reverse proxy

A reverse proxy server helps reduce the load on busy web servers by caching static content on their behalf and serving it directly to client browsers. They sit directly between the web server(s) and the clients, and forward requests for all dynamic content and any static content which has not yet been cached (see Figure 12.8).

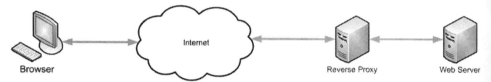

Browser   Internet   Reverse Proxy   Web Server

Figure 12.8: Reverse proxy overview.

To the client they appear as the primary web server, but they're configured to direct traffic to one of multiple actual web servers and return the response after obeying any caching directives. Subsequent requests can then be served directly from the proxy cache, if valid.

Reverse proxy servers relieve the web server of the responsibility for static content caching and greatly increase the performance of web servers in serving dynamic content. This is, quite simply, because, more of the web servers' CPU time can be spent serving dynamic content.

Strategically placed reverse proxies are used to maximize network infrastructures by placing cached content as close to content consumers as possible. Putting a reverse proxy in place will also help overcome the problems caused by wildcard mapping, as discussed earlier in the section on static content.

IIS6 considerations

IIS6 doesn't have reverse proxy facilities and so, if you want the performance gain, a third-party solution is required. Providers include the Open Source **Squid** product running on an Apache server.

IIS7 considerations

IIS7 has introduced an extension called Application Request Routing which can be configured as a reverse proxy and load balancer. For more information and to download it go to www.iis. net/expand/ApplicationRequestRouting.

With the availability of these powerful features in IIS7, using reverse proxy to maximize the performance of your IIS web server implementation is now achievable.

Content Delivery Networks

Downloading static content accounts for the majority of the initial download time for a web page. Because of network latency, the closer your static content is to your user, the faster it will download; so it makes sense that, if possible, you want to point your users' pages to static content that is as close to them as possible.

There are a number of ways to do this. You could do it manually, by hosting the content on servers on multiple continents, detecting geo-location by IP address and dynamically assigning static URLs at runtime. If you're a developer, you are probably already thinking about a cool data model and design pattern. That's great if you're starting from scratch, but what do you do with an existing infrastructure? The simple answer is Content Delivery Networks, or CDNs.

CDNs allow you to publish your static content files to their servers, to eventually become replicated across a network of servers around the world. Each content file is assigned a unique URL, and you place these URLs in your web pages. When a browser requests one of your pages, it will make its request for the page's static content to the CDN. The CDN will determine which is the best server to deliver the content and transfer will begin. Your servers are now free to focus on processing and delivering just the dynamic content.

CDN service providers

For a fee, you can use one of the many CDN service providers to host your static content and streaming media. They have large numbers of content servers geographically spread throughout the Internet, as close to the edge networks (i.e. the ones users are directly connected to) as possible. They also implement optimized links between servers in order to minimize transfer times and avoid the normal Internet network performance limitations.

When a given piece of content is requested from a client browser, the CDN performs request routing, determines the best server to deliver the content from, and reroutes the request to that server. This may be the closest one to the client, or it may simply be the one with the best current performance.

CDNs place content closer to your users, which means they will be able to download the largest parts of your web pages faster. This also means your servers don't have to use valuable CPU and bandwidth serving static content or carrying out compression and caching.

A great example of a CDN provider is Amazon Simple Storage Service (Amazon S3) at HTTP://AWS.AMAZON.COM/S3/. You need to sign up for the service and download one of the many S3 clients that you can use to manage your file transfers, file permission, and content expiration.

Others include:

- Akamai Technologies (WWW.AKAMAI.COM)

- BitGravity (WWW.BITGRAVITY.COM)

- CD Networks (WWW.US.CDNETWORKS.COM).

Plus many others. It's worth doing the math because the costs of using a CDN are very competitive and could be a better deal than the bandwidth deal you have already.

CDN and IIS7 Application Request Routing

IIS7 plus the Application Request Routing (ARR) extension can be configured to act as a miniature CDN service, in that it can be configured to route requests rather than just cache them. You can configure ARR to route requests to specific static content servers, based on predefined rules.

Your application would then hold links to content on the CDN server, which would reroute to the appropriate content server based on the configured rules.

Browser limitations

HTTP 1.1 specifications limit the number of concurrent requests a browser can make per domain to just two (the limit for HTTP 1.0 was four). Depending on the browser, this is usually configurable in the registry, but we should always assume that most users will have the default settings in place. When a page is loading, assuming these limits are in place, then resources located on the same domain will have to share the connection pool limit, and wait until a free connection is available before they can be downloaded.

Placing static content on CDN networks gets around some of this problem, particularly if you distribute media, scripts, and style sheets separately. The browser will be able to download static content from multiple domains on multiple concurrent connections, dramatically improving the user experience.

Script CDNs

Microsoft provides a CDN to serve the standard AJAX JavaScript libraries including:

- ASP.NET Ajax library

- JQuery library

- ASP.NET MVC library.

For the embeddable script links and more detail, go to WWW.ASP.NET/AJAXLIBRARY/CDN.ASHX.

The script links will be resolved to servers located as close as possible to the requesting browser, and will maximize browser connection limits. Google also operates a free CDN script library for many widely-used Open Source JavaScript libraries including the jQuery JavaScript library. For more information, go to HTTP://CODE.GOOGLE.COM/APIS/AJAXLIBS/.

Summary

IIS has many features that you can now use to improve the performance and reliability of your applications. I hope this chapter acts as a call to action for you to think about such issues as:

- optimal IIS configuration

- content compression

- server caching and using reverse proxies

- using Content Delivery Networks

- content expiration and local/proxy caching

- SSL optimization.

But remember, fundamentally there is no substitute to proving your optimization with a complete set of load test results!

Chapter 13: HTTP Optimization

So, you've profiled your server code on each layer, it's as efficient as you can make it, and the database layer has every .NET positive optimization possible. Sadly that's still only part of the story because, to recap some material from Chapter 6, server processing time is only one of three possible bottlenecks in a client exchange. The other two are network transfer time and client processing time.

With all the focus on optimizing server performance it is often a surprise to many that, according to Yahoo's Exceptional Performance team, as much as 80% of web response time occurs within the browser itself (Theurer T, 2006).

When you analyze a page's load profile, the page load itself is usually pretty fast, and the rest of the time is spent downloading and processing referenced static files such as images, JavaScript and CSS. Obviously this is a bit of a generalization, so you need to determine what the page load profiles are for *your* critical web pages.

This chapter is all about analyzing and optimizing the web page load profile so that it transfers as quickly as possible, and can be parsed and processed on the client in the most optimal way. Not surprisingly, to do that we need tools and some guidance on how to use them.

Tools

The first piece of good news is that there are a lot of freely available tools out there to help you debug and optimize client processing and network transfer time. The other piece of good news is that we're going to cover the great ones here. Let's start with the first one you absolutely have to have, and that's Firebug.

Firebug

Firebug is a Firefox browser add-on that allows you to debug HTML/CSS, giving a deep, navigable analysis of all aspects of a page and its architecture. You can install it within Firefox (V3.x) from the **Tools > Add-ons** menu. In the search box at the top of the **Get Add-ons** tab, just type in *Firebug*.

It's an invaluable web page deconstruction tool, used for debugging and investigating structural issues with HTML, CSS, JavaScript and images. One of its lesser known but, for our purposes, extremely powerful features is its Net Analysis capability.

Net Analysis

Net Analysis, when enabled (click the **Net** tab, then **Enable**), will analyze all of the HTTP traffic originating from an initial browser URL request. The initial page request and all subsequent images, JavaScript and CSS requests will be timed, giving all the statistics we need to identify where the time is being spent for a page request (client, network, or server). That sounds pretty useful, don't you think?

Figure 13.1 shows a sample Firebug Net Analysis, and you can see each request with its HTTP status, domain, size, and a histogram detailing the above timings. Hovering over a bar on the histogram will display the detailed statistics, (shown in the table below) and a color key chart.

DNS lookup	time spent resolving the URL against the DNS
Connection	time taken to establish a TCP connection
Queuing	time spent waiting for a connection to become available due to connection limit
Waiting for response	time spent waiting for a response from the server. This can be approximated as "Server Processing Time"
Receiving data	time taken to transfer data from server to client
DomContentLoaded event	elapsed time from the start of loading the resource that the **DomContentLoadedEvent** fired for the main page; **DomContentLoadedEvent** fires after content has loaded but ignores image loading
Load event	elapsed time from the start of loading the resource that the page **Load** event fired for the main page; **Load** event fires after all content and images have loaded

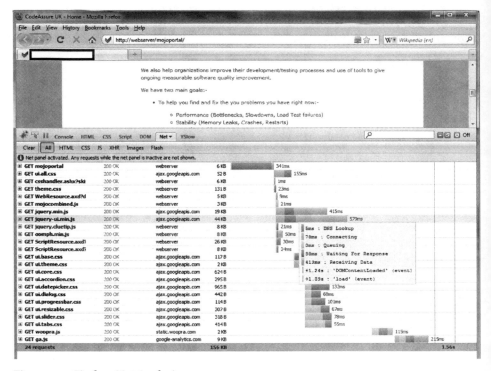

Figure 13.1: Firebug Net Analysis.

The key statistics to look at are:

- Waiting for Response

    - relates to server processing time

- Receiving Data

    - network transfer time

- Queuing

    - Time spent queuing due to browser connection shortage per domain

- **DomContentLoaded** (event) – for the main page

    - Indicates when the **DomContentLoaded** event fires for the page, which is after the scripts and CSS have loaded but excluding image loading time (some images will have loaded in parallel)

361

- **Load** (event) – for the main page

    - Indicates when the Page Load event fires, which is when all scripts, CSS, and images have loaded.

From these statistics you can determine where the bottleneck is; is it the server, or is the network transfer slow for this connection?

DomContentLoaded and **Load** event times are important because they allow you to assess the overall impact of image loading over pure content loading. To do this, you need to offset the other stats (DNS Lookup, Connecting, Queuing, Waiting for Response, Receiving Data) in order to get a meaningful metric.

The outcome from this process is a general assessment of relative performance statistics for a web request, which you can use to gauge where your optimization efforts should be focused. I say "general" because, at the time of writing, Firebug version 1.4.5 is reported to have some accuracy issues that will be fixed in the upcoming 1.5 release.

Cached or Uncached

It's a good idea to run these tests first with a clear browser cache (pressing Shift + Reload in Firefox will reload the page and clear the cache), and then with a loaded one. Obviously the results will differ quite a bit.

The weight you give each result set depends on the general profile of your web application. If it's a "sticky" site, in that the same users tend to return frequently, then obviously the cached result set is the one to focus your efforts on. Watch out for lots of HTTP 304 status codes for image files on the cached run, as they may indicate possible candidates for long content expiration settings on the server (see Chapter 12 on HTTP headers). For one-shot sites, you need to optimize for an empty cache (which we'll cover a little later).

JavaScript profiler

Firebug also has a JavaScript profiler built into it, and I'll describe that later in the "Javascript considerations" section of this chapter.

Fiddler

Just as Firebug is able to analyze a Firefox HTTP request profile, Fiddler is a tool you can use to debug HTTP (or TCP/IP) interactions. It hooks into the Winlnet TCP/IP stack used by Internet Explorer and Microsoft Office products, gives a far more detailed view of network traffic than Firebug Net Analysis, and can also be used for debugging purposes. You can get a copy at HTTP://WWW.FIDDLERTOOL.COM, and there is actually a great instructional video on the site, so I won't spend a lot of time going through features in detail.

Basically, you can inspect HTTP traffic generated from a HTTP request. Fiddler will display a list of all of the requests subsequently launched, and each one can be inspected (see Figure 13.2).

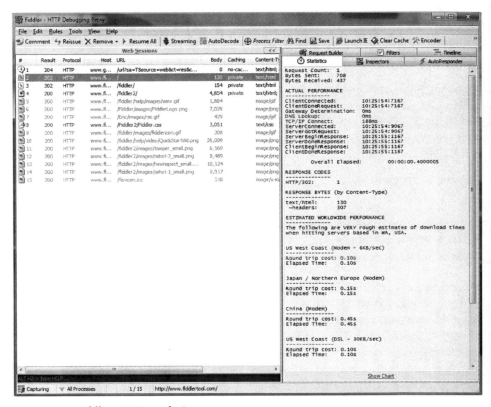

Figure 13.2: Fiddler HTTP analysis.

You can select individual or multiple HTTP requests from the list on the left-hand side, and view a detailed analysis of the selected items using the tabbed interface on the right side. The available tabs are described below.

Statistics

This tab gives general statistics about the request(s), including bytes sent and received, and wall-clock timing information. An estimate of the worldwide performance is also given which, by Fiddler's creator's own admission, is very rough.

Inspectors

The **Inspectors** tab allows you to take a more detailed look at a request. You can inspect the headers of the request/response in detail, and view both in text, Hex, raw, and XML views.

The response analysis can be configured to transform the response back into a readable view if it is compressed. There are also additional options to view as image or web page, and look at both privacy and caching information.

Request Builder

This allows you to generate and send a request manually without the need for a browser. Useful when debugging.

Timeline

The timeline view is most useful when multiple requests are selected, displaying when each request started relative to each one.

Filters

This tab allows you to filter out request traffic which you're not interested in. You can also set flags and breakpoints. Fiddler also has a customizable script, written in JavaScript, that you can modify to add more complex filtering.

AutoResponder

This tab will allow you to record specific responses and use them to reply to given requests, allowing you to limit yourself to local content or replay specific test scenarios.

YSlow

YSlow is another free-to-download Firefox add-on, created by Yahoo's Exceptional Performance team. It's underpinned by a large amount of research and is an excellent starting point for HTTP optimization.

As with Firebug, you can install YSlow from within Firefox from the **Tools > Add-ons** menu. Just type *YSlow* into the search box, and then install the add-on once Firefox has found it for you. After restarting Firefox, you will see a YSlow icon in the bottom right-hand corner of the status bar, although it is also available as a tab within Firebug.

YSlow will analyze the HTTP traffic behind any URL you submit, and give you an A–F rating based on one of three predefined performance rule-sets, as well as on rule-sets you can define for yourself around known performance issues. It doesn't make a judgment on the way the site is constructed, it just assesses how efficiently it achieves what it is actually doing, and suggests improvements (see Figure 13.3).

Grade tab

Figure 13.3 shows the YSlow **Grade** tab results, giving the page's overall result and a breakdown by grade for each rule. The results can be filtered by selecting issues relating to either content, cookies, CSS, images, JavaScript, or server(s).

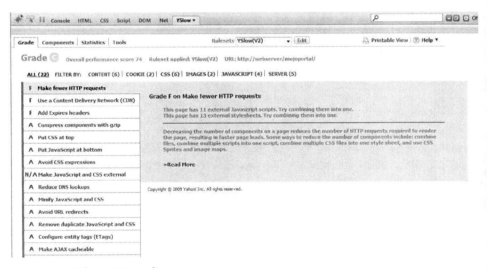

Figure 13.3: YSlow URL grading.

The great thing about this tool is that it gives detailed explanations for each of the rules, and allows you to create and edit your own rule-sets which contain only the subset of rules that are critical to your environment. You can see some of the included rules on the left-hand side of Figure 13.3.

Because this is such an important tool for HTTP optimization, let's go through the main rules (all of which covered in more detail later in the chapter).

Make fewer HTTP requests

Every HTTP request consumes CPU cycles on the server and incurs whatever network latency cost exists between the client and server. Reducing application chattiness is a fundamental optimization you make to any system.

Web applications are no different, and if you think about the number of additional resources required to build a page (CSS, images, Flash, JavaScript), each requiring a separate HTTP request, it's no wonder web pages are usually very chatty.

Yahoo's Exceptional Performance team has determined that 80% of end-user response time is taken up by the client browser, most of which is in downloading content and processing script. If this holds true for your website, then reducing the number of HTTP requests will significantly improve overall response time.

The simplest way to reduce chattiness is to combine content files. This applies equally to text files and images.

- Multiple JavaScript files can be combined.

- CSS files can be combined into one file.

- Images can also be combined.

- Images used for toolbars and banners can be combined into an image map to make one image file, with specific regions assigned to appropriate URLs.

- CSS Sprites use multiple background images combined into one file. The portion of the desired image can be referenced using the **background-position** CSS keyword.

This optimization will improve the response time for new visitors to your site because they will have an empty cache, and the greatest need for an optimal download experience.

Use a Content Delivery Network (CDN)

This material was covered in more detail in the last chapter but, just to recap, a CDN is a third-party hosting service that will host your static content on an optimized Content Delivery Network. Typically, providers host content servers close to the edge servers which the majority of Internet users connect to, meaning your content will never be more than a couple of hops from most worldwide users.

Removing the responsibility for static content delivery from your servers to a third party will free up your servers to generate dynamic content. It will also reduce the memory and processor overhead involved with compression and caching of static content.

If your site is suffering from latency problems inherent with a worldwide user base, then this is a great first step before re-architecting your solution.

Add expiry headers

This is a recap of what we covered in the Chapter 12 section on content expiration in IIS. Adding a far future expiry date to static files that you only modify rarely will allow them to be cached by client browsers for longer periods. If your site is "sticky," then this will significantly reduce the amount of static file serving that your servers have to do, as your true static files will be served from the browser cache.

Properly configured file content expiration will even avoid the classic HTTP 304 request. This occurs when a static file is found in the browser cache but the browser isn't sure how "fresh" the file is. To find out, it sends a request to the server with the file's unique identifier (ETag) and its Last-Modified date. If the file hasn't changed on the server, it responds with an HTTP 304 Not Modified message. This saves re-downloading the same image, but still constitutes an HTTP round trip.

You will get the biggest gains in this area from images and other media files. The main downside is that cached objects are difficult to update. The answer to that is not to try, but to just change the name of the static files and their references, using a simple versioning mechanism.

Use compression on the server

Compression of text-based content reduces its size, and consequently its download time, by up to 70%. There is a slight penalty incurred by the need to decompress the content at the client end, but the benefit outweighs it. Put simply, compression delivers more of the content faster, allowing the referenced resources to begin downloading more quickly.

Most browsers are capable of handling Gzip/Deflate compression, so it pays to ensure the web server is configured to allow compression. See Chapter 12 for more details.

Put scripts at the bottom

When a browser begins downloading a script file, it won't start any other downloads until complete. Because of this, the recommendation is to place script references at the end of web pages, wherever possible. We will discuss JavaScript issues in more detail in the "Javascript considerations" section.

Don't embed JavaScript and CSS

Always put your JavaScript libraries and CSS definitions in separate files so they will be downloaded and cached for future use. This will reduce the size of the actual rendered page for every user request.

Compress JavaScript and CSS

To make it easy to read, JavaScript and CSS contain a lot of white space and comments. Reducing the size of these files by reducing any unnecessary content will reduce download time. Popular tools include JSMin, YUI Compressor and Packer. See the "Javascript considerations" section later in this chapter for more details.

Eliminate 404 Not Found

If a resource isn't found, the web server will return an HTTP 404 Not Found message. This can often go unnoticed on a website, and either means the page isn't displaying as intended or the resource is no longer in use. If the resource isn't in use, then it's a waste of an HTTP request and will hit performance, and so it should be removed (see the "HTTP 404 responses" section towards the end of the chapter).

Minimize image sizes

Make sure the images you are using are as small as they can be, because smaller files obviously download faster (see the "Image optimization" section later on).

If you are reducing the size of an image by scaling it from its actual size in HTML or CSS, then the image is bigger than it needs to be.

Reduce cookie size

Storing large amounts of state information in cookies will increase the payload of every request, hitting performance.

Minimize DOM access

Querying and navigating the browser Document Object Mode (DOM) in script has a significant overhead and should be avoided where possible (and it usually is).

Reduce the number of DOM elements

Pages with large, complex element structures take time to parse and render. Simpler DOM trees with as few elements as possible are more efficient.

Components tab

The **Components** tab gives a detailed breakdown of every content type retrieved by the request, including documents, JavaScript, CSS, and images. The breakdown includes sizes, response times, URL, and ETag (see Figure 13.4).

Figure 13.4: YSlow's Component tab.

Using this tab, you can determine the total weight of the page and assess where the majority of the page weight (usually images) is concentrated.

Statistics tab

This tab gives a graphical representation of page weight, based on both a new user with an empty cache, and a recent user with a primed cache.

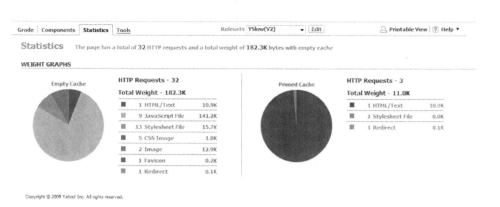

Figure 13.5: YSlow's Statistics tab.

Tools tab

This tab lists a number of built-in tools that you can run against the resources in the current page. They include:

JSLint	runs JSLint, JavaScript's Code Quality tool, against all JavaScript referenced by the page, displaying the results in a separate tab
All JS	displays all JavaScript in the document
All JS Beautified	displays an easy-to-read format of all JavaScript in the document
All JS Minified	displays a minified version of all JavaScript in the document
All CSS	displays all CSS
All Smush.it™	runs Yahoo's Smush.it image optimization tool against all of the page's images; it will then indicate how much each image can be optimized, and you can download them in a zip file
Printable View	displays a printable report of the results for this YSlow analysis

YSlow is a fantastic tool and you can use the recommendations it makes to effect real improvements in every page.

Internet Explorer Dev toolbar

The last tool to mention is Internet Explorer's Dev toolbar.It's a kind of Firebug equivalent but for IE, with the added benefit of a script debugger and profiler. Once you get used to it, it's a really great tool to use , and you can download it from HTTP://TINYURL.COM/ DEVTOOLBAR. Dev toolbar helps you do the things described below.

HTML and CSS debugging

Dev toolbar lets you analyze and control a loaded page using a separate UI. You can inspect a page's HTML tree or CSS hierarchy, and switch off or change the style in place, and the changes are then updated in the browser. This is great, because it helps you understand where your styling/layout issues are, with instant feedback.

Figure 13.6: Dev toolbar, HTML view.

Script debugging

This is a full-featured code debugger, allowing you to set breakpoints, step through code, inspect local variables, view the call stack and set up variable watches. This is pretty powerful stuff and really useful if you have a script problem.

Profiling

The toolbar also has a code profiler, which is described in more detail in a later section.

JavaScript considerations

Depending on the demographic profile of your website, a large proportion of your users may be new visitors with empty caches. We already know that downloading static content contributes up to 80% of the load time for a page (Theurer T, 2006), so anything you can do to reduce static file sizes and download latency effects will speed up the overall load time of a page.

JavaScript always adds to initial page weight and will impact browser performance to some extent. How big these problems are depends on the amount of JavaScript involved, and the amount of processing carried out.

The increasing use of AJAX to create more responsive and richer user experiences has created a surge in the amount of JavaScript now written for, and executed on, web pages. That being said, there are many examples of brilliantly targeted AJAX features that just make life easier for the user. They can also reduce load on servers, because they allow for partial page updating and retrieve comparatively tiny fragments of data, compared to executing an entire page request.

We will discuss AJAX issues later on but, for now, let's just agree that JavaScript use is increasing within pages, so now we'll look at the steps you can take to reduce the impact of your scripts on the HTTP and processing overhead of your web pages.

Use compression

Looking back to Chapter 12, static text files make ideal compression targets, so it makes sense to configure your script files for compression. Browsers that support HTTP/1.1, and most out there today do, can benefit from compression rates of 60–70% on text files, which is clearly significant. Smaller files download much faster, and faster downloads are going to reduce the total time taken to render the page. Chapter 12 has a lot more detail on the topic of static compression within IIS6 and 7.

Minify scripts

"Minifying" your JavaScript is another essential step in reducing download durations. This is worth doing even if you are allowing compression, simply because there is less to compress and decompress, and ultimately the compressed file sizes will be smaller.

A number of tools are available to minify JavaScript using techniques including white space and comment removal, as well as code obfuscation to reduce variable name lengths. The most popular tools for minification include:

- JSMin

    - HTTP://WWW.CROCKFORD.COM/JAVASCRIPT/JSMIN.HTML

- Dojo compressor

    - HTTP://O.DOJOTOOLKIT.ORG/DOCS/SHRINKSAFE

- YUI compressor

    - HTTP://DEVELOPER.YAHOO.COM/YUI/COMPRESSOR/

- Packer

    - HTTP://DEAN.EDWARDS.NAME/DOWNLOAD/#PACKER

- Google Closure Compiler

    - HTTP://CLOSURE-COMPILER.GOOGLECODE.COM/FILES/COMPILER-LATEST.ZIP

Ideally you would incorporate minification into your build/release procedure prior to testing.

Adopt a caching policy

If you adopt the policy that, once a file is published, it can't be changed, it's then much easier to take advantage of far-future content expiry. This means you can set a content expiry date on things like script files, which will enable browsers and proxy servers to cache them indefinitely. That's good because it reduces the number of requests for the file from your servers, and allows the client to retrieve the files from instantly available sources. Chapter 12 discusses how you can set content expiration on files.

Place JavaScript files at the end of pages

Browsers treat script references in web pages differently from other content. With other content, a browser will try to parallel download as many content files as possible (within the constraints of the TCP connection limit per domain). That's not the case with a script reference because, once a script download has started, no subsequent downloads will begin until it has completed. That will cause a considerable download bottleneck unless your script references are placed at the end of the web page.

If you think about it, script can contain code that modifies the page output flow such as:

```
document.write('hello world');
```

You can add a DEFER attribute to the script tag that indicates there aren't any document. write statements and allows for deferred loading, but it doesn't work well or even cross-browser, so the advice is, place script at the end, if you can.

Reduce the number of scripts

There is a tendency to separate scripts out into separate files based on their functionality type. This is great for debugging and development purposes, but it increases the number of HTTP request that have to be made.

Every additional HTTP request incurs latency costs and TCP slow start issues (see Chapter 12), and may cause request queuing due to HTTP/1.1 domain connection limit restrictions. These restrictions are now largely browser-dependent, but they can limit a browser from making more than two concurrent connections per domain.

Where possible, combine your JavaScript files to avoid making multiple HTTP requests for separate script files.

Use a Content Delivery Network (again)

So now your JavaScript is as small, compressed, and high performing as possible, and hopefully it exists in just a few separate files to cut down on HTTP requests. The last thing you can do to improve download speeds, and so page load time, is to locate your files on a Content Delivery Network.

A CDN will host data and media on their servers for a charge, although there are free ones available. The great thing about them is that they place large numbers of content servers in geographically spread out locations throughout the Internet, close to the edge networks (i.e. the ones users are directly connected to). When each piece of content is requested from a client browser, the CDN performs "Request Routing," determining the best server to deliver the content from, and rerouting the request to that server. This may be the closest one to the requesting client, or just the one with the best current performance.

You could opt to use a CDN for all of your static content or, as a starting point, you could use the free AJAX CDNs described below.

Common JavaScript CDNs

As mentioned in the CDN section in the previous chapter, Microsoft and Google both operate CDNs for some of the most widely used JavaScript libraries currently in circulation. For more information and embeddable script links, go to:

*   HTTP://WWW.ASP.NET/AJAXLIBRARY/CDN.ASHX

*   HTTP://CODE.GOOGLE.COM/APIS/AJAXLIBS/.

JavaScript performance analysis

JavaScript processing may itself contribute significantly to page responsiveness (or a lack thereof). If a page is slow to display because a complex JavaScript call tree is taking a long time to complete, we need to know about it. With the increasing use of AJAX within web pages, it makes sense to try and identify bottlenecks in script.

What to look for

Isolating performance issues in JavaScript requires the same techniques we discussed in Chapter 7, in that you are looking for functions or function call trees that are taking a significant portion of the processing time. As in .NET, function call trees are the sequence of calls that occur when one function calls another, and so on.

But we also need to compare JavaScript processing time with overall page processing time because if, for example, a JavaScript function is taking up 50% of the overall page load time, we may have a problem. We certainly have a situation that needs looking at.

I guess it comes back to one of the main reasons for performance analysis, and that's to identify problem code that you wouldn't otherwise realize was a problem. The most innocuous, seemingly-benign sets of functionality can actually hide a major performance problem. Performance analysis just makes you look at your implementations again and asks you to validate that "it has to do that and there's no way around it."

Profilers

All of the main browsers have a JavaScript profiler available, and it's worth noting that how the JavaScript performs will, to some extent, depend on which browser it executes in. Here are some of the main JavaScript profilers available.

Firebug's JavaScript profiler

Firebug has a basic JavaScript profiler that will identify slow functions and call trees (see Figure 13.7). You access it using the **Profile** button on Firebug's **Console** menu.

Function	Calls	Percent	Own Time	Time	Avg	Min	Max	File
init()	46	5.8%	1.634ms	1.663ms	0.036ms	0.006ms	0.129ms	jquery.min.js (line 13)
t	11	4.84%	1.363ms	1.813ms	0.165ms	0.09ms	0.27ms	ga.js (line 5)
T()	57	4.41%	1.241ms	1.322ms	0.023ms	0.007ms	0.095ms	ga.js (line 2)
add()	13	4.21%	1.186ms	1.186ms	0.091ms	0.006ms	0.226ms	jquery-ui.min.js (line 11)
createCallback()	3	4.04%	1.139ms	1.139ms	0.38ms	0.148ms	0.805ms	ScriptRe...fa014b569 (line 6)
createCallback()	10	3.62%	1.02ms	1.02ms	0.102ms	0ms	0.488ms	ScriptRe...fa014b569 (line 6)
WebForm_InitCallback	1	3.43%	0.967ms	1.421ms	1.421ms	1.421ms	1.421ms	WebResou...060000000 (line 222)
createCallback()	2	3.14%	0.884ms	9.633ms	4.817ms	4.563ms	5.07ms	ScriptRe...fa014b569 (line 6)
F()	1	3.1%	0.873ms	1.046ms	1.046ms	1.046ms	1.046ms	jquery.min.js (line 20)

Figure 13.7: Firebug's JavaScript Profiler.

When you load a page, the profiling results will be displayed as in Figure 13.7. The profiling techniques you can use are the same as the ones outlined in Chapter 7, but the key stats to look for are those in the following table.

Own Time	finds the slowest function – time spent in function, excluding time spent in calls to other JavaScript functions
Time	finds the slowest call tree – time spent in function, including time spent in calls to other JavaScript functions
Calls	helps find the most frequently called function – high call counts sometimes indicate a problem and need to be validated

Google SpeedTracer

Another great tool for investigating the client experience is Google's SpeedTracer. It's an extension to their Chrome browser, and allows you to analyze the performance of a web page from both a UI processing and a resource contention perpective.

A page may be slow because the UI is taking a long time to load and paint itself (sluggishness) and/or because its resources are taking forever to download (network issues). SpeedTrace helps you identify where the bottlenecks are and is a great new tool to add to your belt.

Both sluggishness and network issues are tracked on separate performance graphs and both issue types can be explored using tabs for each.

Sluggishness is all about the speed of the browser UI operations, and although it tells you most about how Chrome itself deals with your page, it should give key insights into how your page will behave in general.

The **Network** tab gives similar data to that in Firebug with Net Analysis. The really nice thing about SpeedTracer is that this data is overlaid against the sluggishness data, giving more of a unified view. From here, you can view when resources downloaded and how long they took.

Figure 13.8 shows a set of results from a SpeedTrace analysis. Notice the two graphs at the top; you can select a portion of the graphs to just focus on the events that took place during that time.

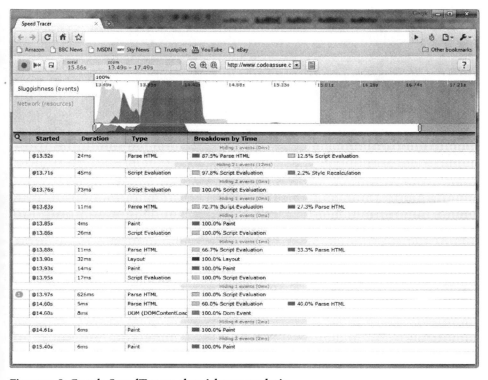

Figure 13.8: Google SpeedTracer, sluggishness analysis.

This analysis is looking for parsing, script evaluation, painting, layout, and DOM processing issues that could be causing bottlenecks.

Key issues are flagged on the left side of each item, with info markers which can be expanded by clicking on them, giving additional detail. In the above case, a script evaluation took 626ms, which exceeds Google's recommended processing threshold of 100ms per event.

IE Dev toolbar profiler

Internet Explorer 8 Dev toolbar's profiler will analyze the performance of all the script functions called by the browser and display them for analysis. You can look at the performance of individual functions and function call trees.

Chapter 7 details how to carry out performance profiling but, to summarize, we basically want to find if there is a function or call tree causing a performance bottleneck.

To do this you need to:

- Start the profiler by pressing the **Start Profiling** button in Dev toolbar

- Run your test against your page in the browser

- Press **Stop Profiling**

The profile results will be displayed in function view (see Figure 13.9), and you can also choose to display the results by call tree.

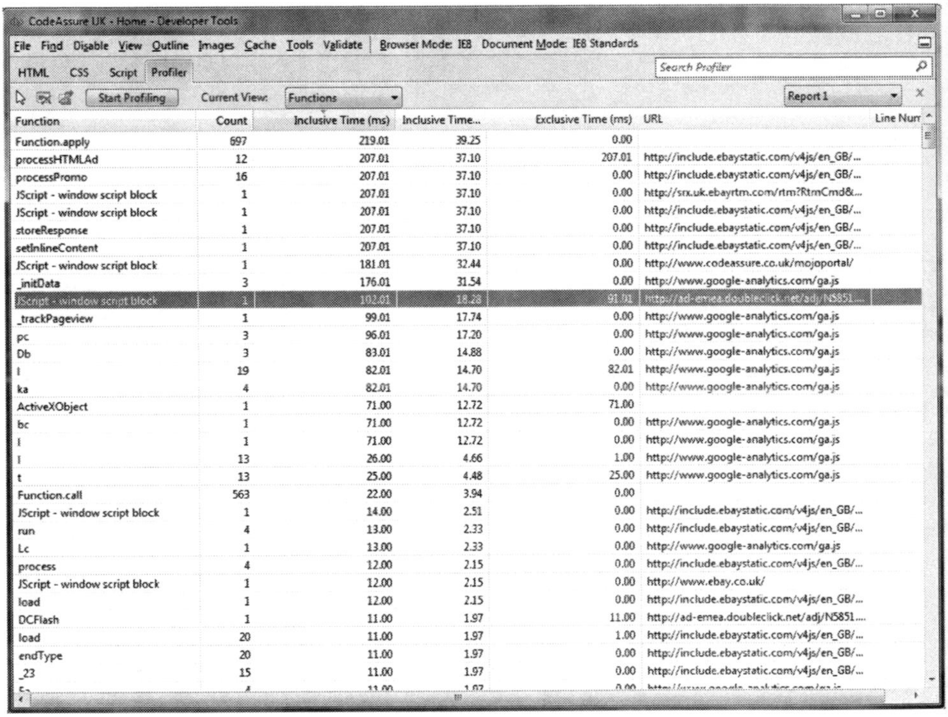

Figure 13.9: Dev toolbar, performance profiling results in function view.

You should sort the function list by descending **Exclusive Time**, as this will quickly reveal the slowest functions where the function itself is responsible for the time (this excludes calls the function itself makes to other script functions). If the function duration is significant, then it may need debugging to understand where it can be optimized.

Sorting the list by descending **Inclusive Time** gives the function that begins the slowest call tree. Inclusive time includes time spent in calls to child script functions.

A better way to analyze the call tree is by just using the **Call Tree** view. This gives a hierarchical view of the call tree, which can be navigated through to find any bottleneck functions within the call tree.

Microfocus DevPartner Studio Professional 9.0

Described in Chapter 7, this (non-free) tool suite also profiles JavaScript running within Internet Explorer. It gives performance results down to the code-line level, allowing you to identify the slowest line within the slowest function. The graphical call graph explorer can also be used to investigate call tree bottlenecks and critical path analysis.

This profiler can present actual time and an accurate figure for CPU time by deducting the effect of the performance measurement. As such, it is an extremely accurate profiler.

Microsoft Visual Studio 2010

Again, as described in Chapter 7, Visual Studio 2010 can also profile JavaScript as an option within its **Instrumentation** settings.

CSS optimization

CSS optimization involves encapsulating your site style into a compact format containing as much inheritance and reuse as possible. Ideally, you need to think about the design of both the HTML and CSS from the beginning of the development process.

A well-designed CSS style definition will allow you to quickly change the look and feel of the entire site, which really is the whole point of CSS. Usually, this also means the CSS has few repeated definitions because, if a style is easy to change, it's unlikely that there are lots of places where the same thing has to be modified. Repeated definitions are inefficient because they make the CSS larger than it needs to be which, in turn, requires more bandwidth and extra client processing.

So, ideally we need the CSS to be concise with few repeated style definitions. While I could write an entire book on designing and writing optimal CSS, here are my top six recommendations:

* encapsulate your style definitions into external CSS file(s)

* design your CSS styles and reuse where possible

- keep each CSS style definition as concise as possible

- use CSS instead of JavaScript if possible

- use CSS Sprites to improve HTTP performance

- remove white space and comments before publishing.

Externalize your style definitions

Too many web pages have hard-coded CSS instructions attached directly to HTML elements in repeated sequences as seen in Code Example 13.1, a technique known as "CSS inlining."

```
<div id="Content">
<table>
<tr>
<td style="font-family:Arial;font-size:12px">12.99</td>
<td style="font-family:Arial;font-size:12px">25.99</td>
<td style="font-family:Arial;font-size:12px">19.99</td>
</tr>
</table>
</div>
```

Code Example 13.1: CSS optimization – using inline CSS styles.

HTML that contains inline CSS style is much larger than it needs to be and, unless the page is static, it won't benefit much from browser caching.

One of the key benefits of CSS is that complex style declarations can be placed in an external file and reused across multiple web pages. The added benefit is that, once the CSS file is downloaded, it will be cached by the browser and reused.

At the risk of teaching you to suck eggs, the HTML in Code Example 13.1 could be replaced by putting the following definition into a separate **.css** file:

```
.Price {font-family:Arial;font-size:12px }
```

... and, although still inefficient, the HTML changes to:

```
<td class="Price">12.99</td>
```

Design your CSS for reuse

HTML is a hierarchical language, and CSS styles are inherited by descendant elements unless they are overridden or restricted. We can use this to reduce the number of definitions we have to make.

Inheritance

We *could* control inheritance from the entire page downwards, but it makes more sense to split the page into logical areas, and use CSS identifiers to control style inheritance. A page may have the following logical areas:

- header

- menu

- content

- footer.

The basic style for each region can then be defined:

```
#Content {font-family:arial; font-size:10px}
```

And now the table definition from Code Example 13.1 becomes:

```
<div id="Content">
<table>
<tr>
<td>12.99</td>
<td>25.99</td>
<td>19.99</td>
</tr>
</table>
</div>
```

The **<div>** container has been given the ID "Content," which allows all containing elements to inherit the style defined by #Content above.

The only problem is that, in Code Example 13.1, the font size required was 12px not 10px. Luckily, this is easily fixed, as the CSS definition can be modified to include an override for specific elements, in this case <td> as shown below.

```
#Content {font-family:arial; font-size:10px}
#Content td { font-size:12px }
```

Intelligent and careful use of CSS identifiers and inheritance will result in much smaller HTML pages and more compact CSS files. Site style is so much easier to control as well!

Combine and reuse definitions

You can reuse and combine existing styles, which avoids redefining style definitions. Code Example 13.2 illustrates two class definitions that are both used to define the style for a <span> tag in.

```
.title {font-size:14px;font-weight:bold}
.logo {color:blue}


...


<span class="title logo">About Us</span>
```

Code Example 13.2: CSS optimization, combining styles.

You can also combine definitions that have the same style settings to reduce repetition. So, the definition:

```
.ContentText {font-family:verdana;font-size:11px;}
.HeaderText  {font-family:verdana;font-size:11px }
```

then becomes:

```
.ContentText,HeaderText{font-family:verdana;font-size:11px;}
```

Keep your CSS concise

As well as maximizing inheritance and reuse, it's also a good idea to keep the CSS style definitions as concise as possible. Here are a few tips on how to achieve that.

CSS abbreviations

CSS has many abbreviations that you can use and, although I can't list them all here, I can illustrate the point.

Defining a font can be easily abbreviated from:

```
.Title {font-family:Arial;font-size:12px; font-weight:bold }
```

to:

```
.Title {font: bold 12px arial }
```

Other CSS abbreviations include ones for border, margin background, list style, padding, and outline.

Use CSS default values and replication

It seems obvious, but don't define CSS properties for default values. For example font-weight defaults to normal unless it has been overridden. Also bear in mind that CSS will replicate a value across multiple related properties. Here, for example, all four sides of the border will be set to 2px:

```
.Box {border: 2px solid}
```

... whereas in this example the borders at top/bottom will be 2px and at left/right will be 4px:

```
.Box {border: 2px 4px solid}
```

Eliminate unnecessary characters

These are some additional simple suggestions for reducing file size:

- reduce the length of your Class and ID names; obviously there is a fine balance between readability and length but the shorter the better

- don't type 0px or 0em, as zero is zero in any measurement

- abbreviate hexadecimal values for colors etc., so #11aa00 becomes #1a0.

Use CSS instead of JavaScript if possible

Before resorting to writing JavaScript to achieve a specific HTML behavior, it's always a good idea to ensure there isn't a way of achieving the same effect in CSS alone. If in doubt, Google it!

CSS effects are far more efficient and take less browser processing than the equivalent JavaScript. A classic example is the button/menu rollover effect, such as when the user positions the mouse pointer over a button and it becomes highlighted. This kind of effect is often achieved using JavaScript, looking something like:

```
<a href="/Profile.aspx" name="profile" class="effectButton"
                onMouseOver="rollover()"
                        onMouseOut="rollout()">View Profile</a>
```

The `rollout()` and `rollover()` JavaScript functions would dynamically set style properties to achieve the rollover effect, for example changing the background color from silver to blue.

A much simpler mechanism simply uses CSS to define a "hover" behavior on the anchor tag:

```
a.effectButton:hover {background-color:blue; color:white}
```

Even more complex effects can be achieved using images and preferably CSS Sprites (see later).

Avoid CSS expressions

Internet Explorer versions 5, 6, and 7 allow you to include CSS expressions which dynamically set CSS properties at runtime. To achieve this, you include the `expression(..)` function in your CSS style definition, which will return a value based on the evaluated code within the expression.

CSS expressions are no longer supported in IE 8 Standard mode, and they should be avoided anyway because of their performance overhead.

Use CSS Sprites to improve HTTP performance

A CSS Sprite is a single image that actually contains multiple images placed next to each other. With the clever use of CSS it is possible to display just the portion of the image you want to use, and so benefit from only having to make a single HTTP request to download the image file. Don't forget that the fewer HTTP requests the browser makes, the faster the user experience will be.

In the example of the button rollovers earlier, using separate images for the hover effect will cause an image download to occur when the first rollover takes place, and maybe generate a slight delay. Not ideal.

Here is an example of using a CSS sprite:

```
a {background-image:url('Buttons.gif')}

a.Ok {background-position:0px 0px}
a:hover.Ok{background-position:0px -72px}
a.GoHome {background-position:0px -143px;}
a:hover.GoHome {background-position:0px -215px;}

...


<a class="Ok" href="/profile.aspx"/>
<a class="GoHome" href="/default.aspx"/>
```

The image sprite is loaded for the anchor tag, but only a portion of it is displayed using the background-position property for each of the CSS classes and hover state. Note the negative positioning to move the correct image into view when the images are positioned left to right.

Remove white space and comments before publishing

To aid readability, CSS files usually contain a lot of white space which includes multiple spaces, tabs, carriage returns, etc. Comments and commented-out styles are usually quite common as well. All of this information is pretty much redundant, and can be removed without any impact.

The benefit is that the CSS files become smaller, and smaller is better. Making your static files, including CSS, as small as possible will improve a user's first visit response time, and first impressions count.

There are a number of tools available which you can use to remove white space and compress the CSS. Probably the most widely used is Yahoo's YUI Compressor. For more information, go to: HTTP://DEVELOPER.YAHOO.COM/YUI/COMPRESSOR.

HTTP efficiency

I will keep this bit really simple. Don't make the browser perform pointless network round trips.

If you use FireBug or Fiddler on many popular websites, you will see requests that failed because content wasn't found (HTTP 404 status) or where a redirect instruction was issued (HTTP 301/302). In both cases, the browser request and latency time incurred are pointless and wasted.

HTTP 404 responses

When a browser gets an HTTP 404 response it means the requested content wasn't found on the server. The browser has wasted a connection and Wait time for a resource that didn't exist. The amount of Wait time depends on the network latency, and the server queuing/ processing time.

This could mean one of two things; either the web page no longer needs the file reference, or it does need it, and so probably isn't behaving as intended. If it's the first, then you can make a quick HTTP optimization, and if it's the latter, you can fix a broken page. Either way it's a win.

The problem can arise from simple server file mismanagement and complex multi-browser handling. Often pages reference different CSS, scripts and images based on browser type and, without testing the page against all browsers, inadvertent file errors can be missed, leading to the 404.

Always test your pages with a network analyzer using multiple browsers and look for 404 errors.

HTTP 301/302 redirect responses

A server redirect response tells the browser to navigate to a different URL. It's the telephone equivalent of being put on hold, only to then be told to dial a different number instead. The original request is a waste of a connection and causes unnecessary Wait time. There are ways to avoid this on the server, such as ASP.NET's `Server.Transfer` for example.

When you analyze the request profile of your page with Fiddler or Firebug, have a look for 301/302 responses and validate if they are necessary.

Image optimization

I can't state this strongly enough: make sure your images are only as large as they need to be. Images will account for the largest proportion of the overall page weight and will have the biggest impact on a first-time user's experience.

You need to make sure the images you are using are the correct resolution for the area you will be displaying, and use the best compression format (gif, jpeg or png). There is no point using a 1920 x 1024 image to be displayed in a 400 x 213 area.

All the main graphics editing packages allow you to control image resolution and file formats. Lowering resolution and changing the compression will reduce the size of the image and thus download time / bandwidth usage.

Yahoo's Developer network has a tool called Smush.it that you can use to analyze your page images. It will suggest any image optimizations and will actually create a zipped version of the optimized images that you can download and use. You can access the tool via YSlow within Firefox.

Page weight

So far, we've looked at the references to static files and how optimization, minification, and compression can reduce their weight on the wire, and so reduce bandwidth usage whilst increasing user response times.

It's now time to look at the actual web pages themselves and how they can have their weight reduced.

Look at any website, using Fiddler or Firebug's Net Analysis, and you will see the dynamic web pages are re-requested every time, whereas the static files are served from cache or request a file modified status from the server. As mentioned earlier, YSlow will also give a breakdown of the request weight for a site, comparing empty and primed browser caches.

Page weight reduction is one of the most important HTTP optimizations you can make, because any reduction will benefit new visitors with an empty cache, *and* returning visitors.

Let's now go through some things you can do to reduce your page weights in ASP.NET applications.

Reducing ViewState overhead

ViewState was devised as a mechanism to maintain the state of server controls between page postbacks. It allowed the ASP.NET programming model to become analogous with the event-based WinForms model with which so many developers were already familiar. This made web application development much simpler and far easier than classic ASP development.

ViewState is stored as a BASE64 encoded string held in a hidden field within ASPX pages. It stores any programmatic state changes to controls, allowing these changes to persist across postbacks. Every time a page posts back to the server, the ViewState goes along for the ride, there and back again.

You know what I'm going to say now, don't you? ViewState strings can be quite large, and large strings increase page weight, and that's not what we want when trying to optimize client response time.

So, the best advice is to only use ViewState when you absolutely need to, because you can switch it off whenever you like.

Switching off ViewState

ViewState can be switched off at the server control level by setting on each control:

```
EnableViewState="false"
```

You can also switch it off at the page level using:

```
<%@Page EnableViewState="false" %>
```

Or, for the whole site in the web.config using:

```
<configuration>
    <system.web>
        <pages enableViewState="true" />
    </system.web>
</configuration>
```

Alternatively, if you just want to be more concise with your ViewStates, ASP.NET 4.0 has an enhancement that allows controls within a PlaceHolder to inherit a ViewState setting. Using the ViewStateMode property on the PlaceHolder, all child controls will inherit the ViewState setting (see below).

```
<asp:PlaceHolder ID="p1" runat="server"
                        ViewStateMode="Disabled">

   <asp:Label ID="label1" runat="server" Text="Test1" />
   <asp:Label ID="label2" runat="server" Text="Test2" />

</asp:PlaceHolder>
```

ViewState and ControlState

ASP.NET 2.0 changed the way ViewState worked, mainly because switching it off often caused the basic operational behavior of more complex controls to fail. A way was needed to separate state changes which were necessary to maintain the UI aspects of a control from the actual contents of the control.

To achieve this, page state was split into two parts: ControlState for storing control behavioral state, and ViewState for a control's UI content. Crucially, ControlState couldn't be disabled, whereas ViewState could.

Now control writers could develop controls that maintained behavioral state (in ControlState) without the fear that a developer might come along later and switch off the state control mechanism.

For example, a DataGrid would hold paging information in ControlState, but the data content could be stored in ViewState, or it could be switched off and the data grid regenerated for every postback.

The point is that, from ASP.NET 2.0 onwards, you can switch off ViewState on controls without fundamentally affecting their basic behavior, as long as you repopulate the contents of the control for each request.

ViewState optimization

ViewState will dramatically increase the size of a page and a page's impact on server processing. In combination with data binding, ViewState strings can become very large and can easily exceed 85 Kbytes, which is the threshold for allocation onto the Large Object Heap, with all of the problems that come with it (see Chapter 8).

The best advice is to switch off ViewState unless you need to use it. It can be quite a tricky judgment to make. If ViewState will reduce load on the database server or, maybe, reduce server cache impact, and those are already problem areas, then you could probably justify it after conducting comparative stress tests.

Control ID page bloat

When you place controls within item templates for grids and repeaters, etc., the size of the ID generated in the HTML can be huge, and this can add significantly to page weight. Here, the generated ID for a label generated within a repeater control is 43 characters long!

```
<span id="ct100_ContentPlaceHolder1_Rep1_Ctl01_Label1">
Hello
</span>
```

Prior to ASP.NET 4.0, the only way to overcome this problem was to override the ClientId property of an inherited version of each control to be used, and instead return a hash of the result (Code Example 13.3):

```
public override string ClientID
{
    get
    {
        return base.ClientID.GetHashCode().ToString()   ;
    }
}
```

Code Example 13.3: Overriding ClientId to reduce ID bloat.

ASP.NET 4.0 provides greater control of IDs using the **ClientIDMode** property on databound controls. Using Predictable Mode, the IDs assigned to the databound control itself and the template controls are used to create a unique name. The shorter you make these IDs the better.

HTML white space

Another simple observation, but it makes sense to remove white space from your ASPX pages. The challenge is to maintain readability whilst minimizing the page weight added by white space. One way to achieve it would be to place server side comments around the white space in the page, which wouldn't then be rendered to the client. For example, the following code:

```
<html><%--
    --%><body><%--
            --%><p>Some Stuff</p><%--
                    --%><span>More Stuff</span><%--
                    --%><div> Some Div content </div><%--
        --%></body><%--
    --%></html>
```

391

...would be rendered to the client as:

```
<html><body><p>Some Stuff</p><span>More Stuff</span><div> Some
Div content </div></body></html>
```

Layouts using tables

Using tables to create your page layout creates significantly more markup than if you used CSS layout; typically, as much as 25–50% more (Zeldman J, 2010). The other downside to table usage is that it results in a much larger and more complex tag hierarchy for the browser Document Object Model parser to process.

Avoid this practice, and remove it from legacy code where possible as part of a page weight optimization process.

AJAX considerations

AJAX (Asynchronous JavaScript) has made a huge impact on website design and on the overall user experience. It enables developers to write user interfaces that communicate directly with data sources without users having to resubmit pages. Done well, the results are fantastic, with rich, almost instantly responsive UIs giving a really positive user experience.

Although AJAX interfaces can be written from scratch, it's far more common for developers to use libraries such as ASP.NET's AJAX library or jQuery. These libraries provide lots of additional functionality and rich user interface elements, allowing developers to easily build dynamic and interactive UIs.

There is actually nothing complex about AJAX. Underlying it is a simple JavaScript accessible object called XMLHTTP that can be used to send HTTP requests to specific URLs and receive the responses. The response can either be in text or XML format, and can be executed synchronously or asynchronously. All that the AJAX libraries do is wrap the use of this object and, to some extent, the manipulation of the browser DOM.

Proper use of AJAX can reduce the overall HTTP payload of an application UI sequence, because full page requests to achieve basic functionality can be avoided.

Problems with AJAX

AJAX is great when it is targeted well and is achieving something of real benefit to the user experience. Google's search suggestions functionality is a brilliant example of well-targeted AJAX. The trouble is that there can be a tendency to apply AJAX to anything and everything possible, regardless of whether it's actually helpful to the user. The result can be pages that create large numbers of asynchronous HTTP requests for no real user benefit.

You really do need to be sure the AJAX load for a page is as light as you think it is, which is why you should always analyze your AJAX pages using some of the tools we discussed earlier (including Fiddler and Firebug's Net Analysis). Look at the response times and payload sizes, and ensure they are acceptable.

Browser concurrent connections

Depending on your browser type and version, there is a restriction on the number of concurrent connections that can be made to individual domains; the HTTP 1.1 specification actually limits the number to two per domain. This is usually configurable in the registry, depending on the browser, but that is of no use, because very few of our users will have changed the defaults (fortunately, Internet Explorer 8 now defaults to six for non-dial-up connections).

The result is that you could be firing off asynchronous AJAX requests which are actually queuing whilst waiting for other AJAX requests to finish. Suddenly, what you thought was an efficient asynchronous model actually has significant blocking.

You can easily spot the blocking behavior within the Firebug Net Analysis by looking for the queuing time for the AJAX calls.

Network latency and performance

Multiple calls across the network to fetch data are inefficient and, depending on the location of client and server, will suffer from latency effects every time. If it's possible to retrieve more data in one call, then do that, even if it means caching it internally.

That brings me to another point – AJAX libraries aren't currently great at caching (or, at any rate, caching when you actually want it!), so any manual data-caching you can do locally will help performance, because you can avoid re-requesting data with low volatility.

AJAX data formats

The two most common AJAX return data formats are XML and JSON, and the format you choose will affect AJAX response times.

XML

XML is a rich and powerful markup language that can describe complex hierarchical data structures. The great thing about XML is that it can be processed easily using an XML Document Object Model parser with its own navigation syntax and query language (XPath). Code Example 13.4 is a simple example of an XML structure describing a book list.

```
<books>
    <book isbn="12345">
        <title>XML 101</title>
        <price>32.99</price>
        <authors>
            <author name="Fred"/>
        <authors/>
    </book>
</books>
```

Code Example 13.4: Example XML data structure

The trouble is, for the sake of 21 characters of information, I have used 99 markup characters.

XML is both human readable and machine readable, which is great for sharing data with others but not so good when trying to maximize HTTP performance. The same data could have been represented in a simpler format, such as:

```
12345,XML 101,32.99,Fred
```

There is also a performance overhead to processing XML using an XML parser, which gets worse depending on the size and hierarchical complexity of the XML structure.

JSON

JavaScript Object Notation (JSON), a common alternative to XML, is a lightweight data format that is easily processed within JavaScript. Code Example 13.5 is an example of a book represented in a JSON string.

394

```
{
    "isbn": "12345",
    "title": "XML 101",
    "price": "32.99",
    "authors": [
        { "name": "Fred" }
    ]
}
```

Code Example 13.5: JSON data definition.

A JSON string can be parsed to an object in JavaScript using either the **eval** function or **JSON.Parse** (FireFox 3.5 or IE 8).

```
var data=eval(" (" + jsonData + ")");
alert(data.isbn);
```

Code Example 13.6: Parsing a JSON data string.

Code Example 13.6 shows some JavaScript parsing a JSON data string containing the book data defined in Code Example 13.5. Once parsed, the isbn data value can simply be accessed as an object property within code.

JSON is both a lighter-weight and easier to process data interchange format than XML, and it will make your AJAX operations faster and more efficient than they would otherwise be.

Windows Communication Foundation 3.5 (WCF)

With a simple configuration change, WCF 3.5 now natively supports returning JSON instead of SOAP XML envelopes from web service calls. In your contract definition, you need to specify ResponseFormat=WebMessageFormat.Json, as seen in Code Example 13.7.

```
[WebInvoke(Method="POST",ResponseFormat=WebMessageFormat.Json)]
    [OperationContract]
    string TestMethod();
}
public class ServiceTest : Service
{
    public string TestMethod()
    {
        return "Test";
    }
}
```

Code Example 13.7: WCF contract definition.

Then, in the **web.config**, you specify the binding to be `webHttpBinding` and enable
WebScript in the behavior section (see Code Example 13.8).

```xml
<system.serviceModel>
  <services>
    <service name=" ServiceTest ">
      <endpoint
          address=""
          binding="webHttpBinding"
          contract="Service"
          behaviorConfiguration="WCFServiceAspNetAjaxBehavior"/>
    </service>
  </services>
  <behaviors>
    <endpointBehaviors>
      <behavior
          name="WCFServiceAspNetAjaxBehavior">
        <enableWebScript />
      </behavior>
    </endpointBehaviors>
  </behaviors>
</system.serviceModel>
```

Code Example 13.8: WCF Web.Config JSON Configuration.

ASP.NET AJAX

The ASP.NET AJAX UpdatePanel is a great way to add AJAX functionality to a web page, but
it has some major problems that you need to be aware of. UpdatePanels post back almost
as much data to the server as a standard postback, and that includes the ViewState. Also, on
postback, the page goes through pretty much its complete life cycle, including firing **Init,
Page_Load, PreRender** and **Unload** events. Even the page's control event handlers fire.

You can reduce some of the problem by setting the **EnablePartialRendering** attribute on the
ScriptManager to `true`, and **UpdateMode** on the UpdatePanel to `conditional`, as seen in
Code Example 13.9:

```
<asp:ScriptManager ID="ScriptManager1" runat="server"
                   EnablePartialRendering="true"  />
<asp:UpdatePanel ID="UpdatePanel2" runat="server"
                 UpdateMode="Conditional">
```

Code Example 13.9: UpdatePanel setting the UpdateMode.

Setting the **UpdateMode** to `conditional` will only return data for the panel if a postback was caused within that panel. However, full ViewState information from all the other panels will still be transferred.

The thing to remember is that UpdatePanels make it easy for you to eliminate page flicker and give the appearance of an AJAX-enabled site, but it doesn't give you the efficiency benefits of AJAX enablement itself. For that, you need to write some code!

You can still use the functionality provided by the ASP.NET AJAX ScriptManager, with its web service reference interface and script reference (see HTTP://WWW.ASP.NET/AJAX for more details).

jQuery

I can't talk about AJAX without mentioning jQuery in a little more detail, because it's probably the most popular AJAX library in use today. It is really lightweight yet powerful, combining both asynchronous data transfer (XML and JSON) with animation functions. Its other great feature is that it is unbelievably concise.

To use jQuery you need to include a script reference. Code Example 13.10 is a minified version hosted on the Microsoft Script CDN.

```
<script
src="http://ajax.microsoft.com/ajax/jquery/jquery-1.4.2.min.js"
type="text/javascript"/>
```

Code Example 13.10: jQuery script reference.

Just to illustrate how compact and easy to use the library is, here is an example (Code Example 13.11) of some jQuery AJAX that retrieves data from a **GetBooks.aspx** URL. It passes some data in the query string and passes the returned result to an anonymous JavaScript function that is just displaying it in an alert box.

If it's AJAX you need, then direct use of jQuery is a very lightweight and powerful tool.

```
$.ajax(
{
  type: "GET",
  url: "GetBooks.aspx",
  data: "genre=fiction",
  success: function(dataIn){ alert(dataIn);}
}
);
```

Code Example 13.11: jQuery AJAX example.

Summary

You can potentially make huge improvements to page load times and thus to every user's experience of your web application. I hope that, as you've been reading through the chapter, you have been downloading and trying the tools mentioned, and gaining real insight into where you can improve your web applications.

It always amazes me how many of the world's websites, when you analyze them, have major performance flaws that could *easily* be fixed. Why not have a go? Use YSlow and Firebug to see the problems. It will make you feel better about the issues you've found in your own pages!

If you think about it, all I've really been saying through the whole chapter is:

- Make all of your static files as small as possible on the wire.

- Reduce your page sizes and compress whatever you can.

- Optimize your JavaScript and CSS and use HTTP efficiently.

The tools are there; you don't have to pay a fortune to use them, and it's not going to take you huge amounts of time!

A call to action

- Analyze your site with YSlow.

- Use Firebug's Net Analysis to discover your page processing profile.

- Look at content expiration and compression.

- Profile your JavaScript-rich pages first.

- Compress your images as much as possible.

- Use CSS Sprites.

- Look for 404 errors.

- Remove white space and comments.

Sit back, and enjoy the feeling that you've just made your web application as fast as humanly possible.

Index

Symbols

A

B

C

K

Kernel mode 329
kernel mode cache 332, 338

Key stakeholders. *See* **Stakeholders**

L

Large Object Heap (LOH). *See* **Memory profiling**

Last-Modified date 367

Line-level analysis 160

LINQ (.NET Language Integrated Query) 27

LINQ to SQL 284

Live HTTP Headers 354

Load balancing 315–327. *See also* **Windows Load Balancing Service (WLBS)**
and performance testing 323–325
different server specifications 324
infrastructure 317–319
scalability 315

Load testing 22
bottlenecks 189–190
choosing a profiler 193
competing resources 191
information from 188–189
key metrics 194–197
types of profiler 192–193

logman (tool) 150–155

Long reference chains 237

Loosely-coupled implementation 269

M

Machine.config 313–314

MaxConcurrentRequestsPerCPU 341

Memory 315
memory leak detection 182
memory usage 44, 276

Memory profiling 225–264, 234–239
finalizable objects 231–235
garbage collection (GC) 162, 227
Large Object Heap 231
LOH fragmentation 183
managed heaps 225–234
memory issues 235–239
inefficient allocation 235–237
memory fragmentation 238
memory leaks 237
Small Object Heap (SOH) 226–227
tools used 239–264
ANTS Memory Profiler 5 240
CLR Profiler 259
DevPartner Studio Professional 9 252
Visual Studio 2008/2010 247

Metrics 23, 43–73
basic metrics 43–50
CPU utilization 50
detailed metrics 62–70
database 68
general 63
web / ASP.NET specific 66
memory utilization 51–53
response time 53–54
using the information 70–72
web application basic metrics 46–50

Microsoft Message Queue (MSMQ) 298

.NET and
SQL Server Tools
from Red Gate Software

SQL Server Execution Plans
Grant Fritchey

Execution plans show you what's going on behind the scenes in SQL Server and provide you with a wealth of information on how your queries are being executed. Grant provides a clear route through the subject, from the basics of capturing plans, through their interpretation, and then right on to how to use them to understand how you might optimize your SQL queries, improve your indexing strategy, and so on. All this rich information makes the execution plan a fairly important tool in the tool belt of pretty much anyone who writes TSQL
to access data in a SQL Server database.

ISBN: 978-1-906434-02-1
Published: June 2008

The Art of XSD
Jacob Sebastian

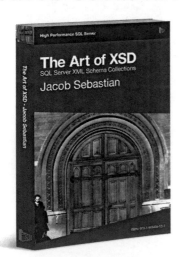

This book will help you learn and use
XML Schema collections in SQL Server.
Prior knowledge of XSD is not required to start with this book, although any experience with XSD will make your learning process easier. A lot of applications exchange information in XML format, and this book will take you from the basics of XML schemas and walk
you through everything you need to know, with examples and labs, in order to build powerful XML schemas in SQL Server.

ISBN: 978-1-906434-17-5
Published: April 2009

Don't Just Roll The Dice
Neil Davidson

How do you price your software? Is it art, science or magic?

How much attention should you pay to your competitors?

This short handbook will provide you with the theory, practical advice and case studies you need to stop yourself from reaching for the dice.

ISBN: 978-1-906434-38-0
Published: October 2009

Defensive Database Programming
Alex Kuznetsov

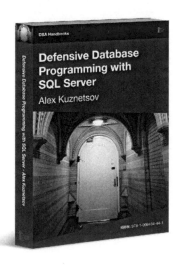

he goal of Defensive Programming is to produce resilient code that responds gracefully to the unexpected. To the SQL Server programmer, this means T-SQL code that behaves consistently and predictably in cases of unexpected usage, doesn't break under concurrent loads, and survives predictable changes to database schemas and settings. Inside this book, you will find dozens of practical, defensive programming techniques that will improve the quality of your T-SQL code and increase its resilience and robustness.

ISBN: 978-1-906434-45-8
Coming Soon

Breinigsville, PA USA
15 October 2010
247431BV00002B/2/P